ON THE WINGS OF
GRACE
ALONE

THE TESTIMONIES OF THIRTY CONVERTED
ROMAN CATHOLICS

ON THE WINGS OF
GRACE ALONE

THE TESTIMONIES OF THIRTY CONVERTED
ROMAN CATHOLICS

Edited by
Richard M. Bennett and Glenn R. Diehl

SOLID GROUND CHRISTIAN BOOKS
Birmingham, Alabama USA

Solid Ground Christian Books
PO Box 660132
Vestavia Hills AL 35266
205-443-0311
mike.sgcb@gmail.com
www.solid-ground-books.com

On the Wings of Grace Alone
The Testimonies of Thirty Converted Roman Catholics
Richard M. Bennett and Glenn R. Diehl

Cover design by Borgo Publishing
Contact them at borgogirl@bellsouth.net

ISBN: 978-159925-34-9-7

Contents

Preface

THE THIRTY AUTHORS OF THIS BOOK COME FROM VARIOUS ETHNIC BACK-grounds and different countries. Some of us have now ventured into the closing years of our lives while others still have many ventures to go. You will read testimonies from former nuns, laypersons, and more insight into my own life as a priest. We all have a different story to tell, but there is a common thread in all our stories.

It has often been quoted that all roads lead to Rome. For those of us who contributed to the writing of this book, that was true. However, the road to Rome was a road that led us away from Jesus Christ. It was a road that led to a lack of peace with God and finally would have led us all to eternal damnation. We discovered that the Roman Catholic Church was teaching things that were completely opposite to what our Bibles taught. There are many deviations of doctrine within the Roman Church, but the one that ensnared us that are represented here is the same one that has ensnared each and every Catholic for centuries. You will read of this deviation. You will also read of the spiritual hunger that we had even while deeply engaged in the Catholic religion. Priests and nuns alike, we who were busy in doing the Church's work found our lives empty and unsatisfied. Laypeople, too, were left hungry for more than mere tradition and rituals. The redundancy of the deadness and repetitious prayers offered no real meaning. We found ourselves asking serious questions about the Eucharist and the Church's priesthood. The system of belief behind these shared experiences is revealed in many of our testimonies. The basis of truth and the Gospel are quite compromised in Catholicism—to the point of being damaging to one's soul.

This book tells of thirty people who have found peace with God, freedom from the bondage of sin, and deliverance from the wrath of God. Our desire is that all who read this book will find true salvation in Jesus Christ and will experience the same joy we have found. As we publish this book, all the authors are alive. Some of us have given our email address where you may contact us.

Before you are through reading this book, it is our sincerest prayer that it will help many more find their way "On the Wings of Grace alone."

—*Richard Bennett and Glenn Diehl*

PETER SLOMSKI

From Polish Catholicism to Trusting Christ Alone

"AS A ROMAN CATHOLIC I HAVE ALWAYS BEEN A CHRISTIAN AND WHEN I die God will judge me by the good I have done in my life." That is what I had believed from a child, until a school friend challenged me to rethink my belief and see what the Bible actually said.

Polish Catholic Foundations

From the moment I was born, the influence of the Roman Catholic religion was present. I was born, with my twin brother, on 29th June 1970, in Halifax, England. That date was not insignificant, for it was Saint Peter and Paul's Day in the Roman Catholic calendar. It was therefore natural for my mother to name my brother and me, "Paul" and "Peter," after these "Roman Catholic saints." As Polish Catholics, "saints" and their "names-days" featured prominently in my parents' lives. It was the lives of Roman Catholic saints, which would have an impact on my understanding of what it meant to be a Christian.

My parents had left their native Poland in the 1960s to come to England for a new and better life. Poland was still under the dark shadow of communism and the British Isles offered opportunity and hope. They settled in the northern English town of Halifax, where with many other Eastern European immigrants, my father found work in the local mills. My mother, a trained midwife, eventually found work in the hospital where I would be born. My parents were typical Polish Catholics. They did not particularly question their faith, but followed it like a faithful animal its master—obediently but without understanding. Catholicism had always been the warp and woof of the Polish nation. It is said that to be Polish is to be Catholic; Catholicism ran through a Pole like the blood in his veins. Of course, not every single Pole was Catholic, but the vast majority was. It was that which historically set apart Poles from their eastern neighbors on the map of Europe. As one writer has said, speaking of the times when my parents were born and growing up in Poland, "The Roman Catholic Church has no more faithful followers in the world than are to be found in Poland. Here is no sophisticated modernity, but a simple solid faith expressed freely in every form of human life."

Ignorance and Darkness

And so my childhood was very Polish and very Catholic with its language, food, customs, and religion. My brother and I were baptized into the Catholic Church as infants. As was the tradition, Paul and I had people who were set aside as our godparents; these were people, who along with our parents, would have the task of ensuring we were brought up in the Catholic faith. That rite of baptism was meant to wash me from my (original) sin. I, being a baby, was entirely ignorant of this and ignorant of what the truth was; I needed a work of *God's grace* in my inner being to spiritually awaken me, and not a work of a priest's hands pouring water over me. I needed to consciously turn from my sin to the Savior. I needed a personal faith in Jesus, and not a faith that my parents or godparents had on my behalf. The apostle Peter said, *"Repent, and be baptized every one of you in the name of Jesus Christ for the remission of sins."* (ACTS 2:38) A conscious repentance and faith in Jesus must come first. I needed an inward working by God's Spirit to give me a sense of my sin against God, and a faith in the Savior Jesus. I, however, was yet an infant unable to believe and very far from the Savior.

Every Sunday my parents took my brother, older sister, and myself to Polish Mass. Very little of it ever made any sense to me. I would sit in the pew and watch and listen, as the priest would go through all the formalities and ceremonies. I do not ever remember the priest encouraging anyone to read the Bible. The Bible itself was a "closed book" to me. Here was this "tome" with all its pages—what did it all mean? If only I had been told what the Bible says of itself: *"How sweet are thy words unto my taste! Yea, sweeter than honey to my mouth"* (PSALM 119:103) and *"The entrance of thy words giveth light; it giveth understanding unto the simple."* (PSALM 119:130) But all was darkness when it came to understanding; such things were only for the priest to know, and not for us who were "simple."

Praying for the Dead

In those early years of growing up in the Catholic Church I accepted what I was told, believing that my prayers, participating in the church sacraments such as attending confession, going to Mass, and being a good person would earn me the right to get to heaven. Of course, even after doing all these things, I could never be sure of heaven. And so, I was taught that there was a place called purgatory, where all the sins that I had not made amends for would be dealt with—here would be the place where I would have to suffer for a time. One childhood memory was of my brother and I snuggling up in my grandmother's bed in the morning and she would teach us what to pray. One of those prayers was for the dead.

People in the church would constantly give the priest money to say a Mass for their loved ones in purgatory. If that was done, then their relatives' time would not be so long, and they would sooner be in heaven. Oh, how that pain and misunderstanding could have been alleviated for so many people, if only they knew what God had said in His Word. The Bible has nothing to say about purgatory, but everything to say about a Savior who endured all the suffering necessary for the sin of all who belong to Him.

There are those wonderful, consoling words we find in the Bible: *"Every priest standeth daily ministering and offering oftentimes the same sacrifices, which can never take away sins: But this man, after he had offered one sacrifice for sins for ever, sat down on the right hand of God."* (HEBREWS 10:11, 12) The priest and the Mass can do nothing for the dead, but for those who believe, Christ has suffered all the punishment necessary: hell itself—*"one sacrifice for sins for ever."* But I still had not truly recognized who Christ was and what He had accomplished on the cross.

Called by God?

At the age of about seven, my brother and I had what would be called our "First Communion." This was supposed to be a very important event, confirming what our faith was to mean to us. At the time, I did not understand its significance, but I must have sensed its importance, because my brother and I had to get dressed in white suits, which had been specially made for us, and then attend a ceremony at the church, where the priest blessed us. There was something else that was significant on that occasion. I recall having a special meal at our home, when friends came to visit. The guest of honor was our Polish priest, Father Tadeusz Gaik. He was a gentle man and had suffered imprisonment during the Second World War under the Nazis in Auschwitz and Dachau concentration camps. (An acquaintance of Father Gaik whilst in Poland was Karol Wojtyła, who would in time become known as Pope John Paul II.) I, therefore, respected Father Gaik, and as was instilled in us, the priest was above all other men. It was what he brought that day that would shape my thinking for the next few years of my life. As the guests gathered around, he presented a container with various folded-up pieces of paper. On each paper was written a career in life. The one that I picked out had written on it "KSIĄDZ"—it was

First Communion (I am on the right with Father Gaik in the centre).

the Polish word for "PRIEST." There was no question: God had spoken. From then on, I was resolute on becoming a priest for God.

Saints and Missionaries

Growing up in a Polish Catholic home, my parents involved my sister, brother, and me not only in Mass on Sundays but also our lives as children were active, attending and participating in Polish Catholic festivals, processions, gatherings, and events. As a young Catholic, I took an interest in the "Catholic saints" and remember coming across a book telling of their miraculous and sacrificial lives. One story, told by a teacher in the Catholic school I attended, had a great impression on me. He spoke of a particular man who wore a heavy chain around his waist, which would wear away his flesh. The point was, that in suffering in this way, he was making amends for his sin. But in glorifying this act of suffering, this denied the "perfect" suffering that Christ suffered, once and for all, for His people on the cross. Such stories of "saints" fortified me in my thinking to live and suffer for God, but in this zeal for the Catholic religion I did not realize how blasphemous it was to claim that my suffering could atone for my sin.

I did not realize that by trying to earn my salvation by "good works," I was stealing away Christ's glory and seeking to be a "co-savior." I did not understand that God does not share His glory or His work of salvation with another: *"I, even I am LORD, and beside me there is no Savior."* (ISAIAH 43:11)

Inspired by the saints, and with an apparent calling from God, I had set my vision on becoming a priest for God. I particularly became attracted to a Catholic missionary movement known as the Verona Fathers, primarily through contact with one of their priests. I began to collect literature about them and, in particular, became fascinated with Daniel Comboni, the missionary priest to Africa who founded the Verona Fathers. His life and sacrifice gripped me, and by the age of ten I was all set to attend the Verona Fathers' boarding school. At this school I could learn more about my "faith," about becoming a priest, and even perhaps a missionary. To me the life of a priest was a life pleasing to God, and I was very excited. But "providence" had other plans for me. After some thought, my mother did not want to let me go out of her sight, and I ended up staying at home and attending a local school. Perhaps, if I had gone, things may have turned out very differently.

Fallen Men and False Mediators

I continued being active in the church. From a young age to the age of eighteen, my brother and I were altar boys, ministering to the priest as he performed the Mass. This also meant attending to the priest on other occasions, such as Friday Mass and masses in other towns. Being so much closer to the priest, I began to see that this was a mere man, with faults. Following Father Gaik's death, we had a younger, more confident (and more rotund) priest who was very different. Over time, the mask of religion began to fall away and reveal a man not devoted to God, but to himself. He lived in luxury and had little about him to attract a young Catholic wanting to serve God. My brother and I would also sing Polish hymns before the congregation. I recall another priest, who trained us in our singing, as likeable but quite worldly in his habits. Some of the priests did appear sincere, and one, in particular, lived a very ascetic and humble life. But all these men ultimately kept me from God.

These "men of God" stood between God and me, not as mediators, but barriers. They never encouraged me to read the Bible; they never emphasized to me the enormity of my sin; they never explained the finished

As altar boys singing a Polish hymn (I am pictured on the left).

sacrifice of Christ on the cross; above all, they never urged me to look to Jesus as the all-sufficient Savior. Instead, they emphasized their own position, the position of the Church and its sacraments, saints, and Mary above or equal to Christ. Yet, I did not understand that the only way to God, the only way to obtain peace with God, was through the Lord Jesus Christ. It was through Him with no add-ons. The Bible is very clear: *"For there is one God, and one mediator between God and men, the man Christ Jesus."* (1 TIMOTHY 2:5) These "men of God" were blind, leading me, their blind follower. I had met, known, and respected so many of them, and yet none had led me to the One True Mediator.

A Challenge from a Friend

Throughout my teens, I continued to attend the local Polish Catholic church in Halifax, but my interest in the priesthood began to fade. I began to grow discontented with the church, and within myself I began to ask questions. A school friend, who claimed to be a true Christian, challenged me as to whether the Catholic Church was teaching according to the Bible, and whether I was living according to the Bible. I normally retorted with the usual claims of a Catholic: that the Catholic religion was the oldest church in the world with Peter as the first pope. This I said in pride and ignorance, knowing only the version of history that the Church had taught me. I had not been brave enough, or bothered enough, to check what the reality was. I had never examined history's testimony regarding the Catholic Church and the Christian faith. Most important of all, I had not considered the Bible's testimony, and in particular, what it said regarding Christ.

I continued having the verbal sparring with my friend, but as time passed by, my whole belief system began to crumble. By the time I finished secondary school, at eighteen years of age, I was in doubt about whether there really was a God at all. At that point I left the Catholic Church, disillusioned and confused. I had not left earlier out of loyalty to my mother. I began to attend a Protestant church with my Christian school friend, and over the next year or so sought to learn what the truth was. Little by little I began to believe again there really was a God, and at this point thought I had become a Christian. But it was not until a couple years had passed that I saw something still very much amiss in my life.

Ignorant of the Gospel

At the age of twenty, I had returned to my second year of university with some confidence that I had a real belief in God. I involved myself in the university Christian Union and for a time was happy. But as I got to know, in particular, a few of the Christians there, I began to realize they had something in them that I did not have. Perhaps it was just a few words they shared about what they had found in the Bible, or perhaps it was the way they prayed—I knew I was missing something. More and more I began to see that I did not understand what it was to be a Christian. I recall one Christian Union meeting where the guest speaker threw out a question for us all to consider: "What is the gospel?" I was sitting next to a girl who had apparently just become a Christian. We sat there and looked at each other, but neither of us had much to say. Perhaps she was young in her faith and understanding, but deep down I knew that for me something was not quite right. I now know that the gospel is the very heart of the Christian faith. The word "gospel" means "good news;" it is good news that Christ came to suffer the punishment that sinners deserve and thus save them completely. The apostle Paul proudly proclaimed, *"I declare unto you the gospel...By which also ye are saved...that Christ died for our sins."* (1 CORINTHIANS 15:1-3) Sitting there in that meeting, I knew this in my head, but not knowing it personally in my heart, how could I ever grasp that this was "good news"?

What is the Truth?

Things seemed to come to a head in the summer of 1991. I had volunteered to go to Poland for two weeks with a student Christian organization to tell people about Christianity. As my parents came from Poland, and I could speak Polish, I saw this as an ideal opportunity to share my "faith in God" with my "fellow Poles." Perhaps I was no longer a Catholic, but I still had that "missionary" spirit. As I went out with other students onto the streets and the beach in the Polish coastal town, I would tell people that they needed to give their lives wholeheartedly to Christ—it was not enough for them to simply go to church and say their prayers; their whole lives should be different. Those things that I said were true, but I still had not grasped that my "good life" was not good enough to get me to heaven. As it is written of the Jews in the Bible, I had *a zeal of God, but not according to knowledge. For they being ignorant of God's righteousness, and going about to establish their own righteousness, have not submitted themselves unto the righteousness of God."* (ROMANS 10:2) I needed the righteousness Christ to save me, and not my own "righteousness."

Inside, however, God was working; I realized something was wrong. I became conscious that what I was telling people was not the entire message. I lacked conviction that this was "the truth" that could give them a new life in Christ. In fact, I was conscious that I did not appear to have that new life. And so, whenever I had the opportunity, I listened to these Christians sharing the Gospel, the Good News of Jesus, straining to understand "the truth." When I was asked to give my testimony to the people on the promenade, I was troubled. As I began to share what I believed was my faith, I faltered.

I returned to England with a heavy heart. I began to talk to Christian friends and read books, searching for an answer. One friend pointedly asked me, "Why do you believe?" I tried to give him various reasons, but his response to this was: "I believe it because it is the Truth." I knew then and there that I could not say that. Could not Islam or Buddhism or any other religion also have the answer? Could they not be the "truth?" What is it that sets apart the Truth?

Light Breaking Through the Darkness

And so I carried on asking, reading, and searching. Outwardly, everything seemed fine to my acquaintances. I was enjoying my studies and friendships at university, but inwardly I was in darkness wondering what the truth to life was. It was the winter of 1991, with a few weeks still remaining of my study before the Christmas break, when everything changed. I was in my room sitting at my desk listening to an audiotape. What I was listening to was taken from the Bible (1 CORINTHIANS, CHAPTER 1) concerning Jesus Christ and how it appeared foolish to people that He needed to die on the cross. Here are some of the words I heard:

"We in our foolishness thought we were wise,
He played the fool and He opened our eyes.
We in our weakness believed we were strong,
He became helpless to show we were wrong."
—MICHAEL CARD, *GOD'S OWN FOOL*

In that moment it was as if the light came and dispelled my darkness. For the first time in my heart, I grasped why Jesus Christ had to die on the cross. I saw that I was not good enough or strong enough to save myself and get into heaven. It took Jesus, the perfect Son of God, to die on the cross—carrying my sin and guilt. Only He could fully take the punishment for what I had done wrong and so cleanse me from all my sins.

For years, I had been trying to earn my way into heaven. I wanted God to accept me because of the good things I had done. The years in the Catholic Church had instilled in me that good works save. Above all, my sinful human pride had convinced me that I could do something to earn heaven. Now I realized this was foolishness; the Bible tells us very clearly, *"There is none righteous...there is none that doeth good, no, not one."* (ROMANS 3:10, 12) We are all helpless to save ourselves—we need an all-powerful Savior. Every other religion and belief system tells us in some way it depends on us, whether it is through good deeds, keeping all the commandments, carrying out rites and sacraments, working together, thinking hard enough, or making the right decisions. This is what the Catholic Church teaches, and it is no different from all the other religions of the world. But, the Bible tells us it is not you or I, but God alone in Christ that can save. *"For by grace are ye saved through faith, and that not of yourselves: it is the gift of God: Not of works, lest any man should boast."* (EPHESIANS 2:8, 9) In that moment, I knew Christ as my Savior. I trusted Christ alone to save me.

Rejoicing in the Saviour

I rejoice that my salvation is all of Christ and does not depend on me. Following my salvation in Christ, in April 1992, I was baptized out of obedience to my Savior, and in identification with what He had already done for and in me. He had washed me of my sins, and in Him I had been buried with my old life of sinfulness and raised again to a new life. That is what baptism symbolizes—God's inner work in a sinner. And it is because of what God has done for me in Christ that, in thankfulness and love,

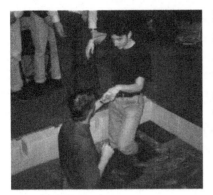

Baptism in April 1992

I now seek to please Him, in obeying His Word—the Bible. Now, being a new creation in Christ by the work of the Holy Spirit, I strive to do good—not to earn heaven, but because heaven is already mine because of Christ and what He accomplished for me.

"Come to the Saviour"

Those are the words with which I would like to end. I would urge you, dear reader, to "Come to the Savior." It may be that you are a Catholic. It may be that you are relying on Jesus Christ plus your good works. Or, it may be that you are not a Catholic by name, but "by practice"—you are relying on your good deeds and your own efforts to be right with God and enter heaven. Perhaps, even you do not have a strong belief in God, but you are "hedging your bets" by relying on the "good things" that you have done in your life. I would say strongly but lovingly to you: "Do not be deceived!" The Bible speaks clearly to us, that not only have we "all sinned," but we have all *"come short of the glory of God."* (Romans 3:23) And, there is nothing we can do to make up that distance between God and ourselves. It is no good saying, "I will do my best and God will take care of the rest." The Bible solemnly tells us: *"For whosoever shall keep the whole law, and yet offend in one point, he is guilty of all."* (James 2:10)

I had been so long deceived in the Catholic Church. Even when I left the Church, that deception remained in my heart, and I believed I could do something to earn my salvation. But all that we can "do" is "believe" on the One who has done all that was needed for salvation. Jesus Himself said: *"This is the work of God, that ye believe on him whom he hath sent."* (John 6:29) I am overwhelmed that God had mercy on me, and opened up my heart to see my insufficiency and Christ's perfect sufficiency. Even now He is calling with the Gospel—the good news that there is a Savior. Will you acknowledge your

sin and your inability to save yourself? Will you turn to the Savior now? Christ died on the cross, but three days later He rose triumphantly from the dead and sits enthroned in heaven. He hears when we call to Him. Will you "fall to your knees" and call to Him? He has accomplished all that was needed to save a sinner like you. I urge you that you turn from anything and anyone as a means of salvation, and trust only in Christ. The Bible has this wonderful promise: *"Whosoever shall call upon the name of the Lord shall be saved."* (ROMANS 10:13) It is not the priest, not the pope, not the saints, not even Mary, but only on the Lord Jesus Christ we are to call. With all my heart I say this: "Come to the only true Savior, Jesus Christ."

I end with two Bible verses that are precious to me; *"For God commendeth his love toward us, in that while we were yet sinners, Christ died for us."* (ROMANS 5:8) *"Christ the power of God, and the wisdom of God."* (1 CORINTHIANS 1:24B)

—PETER SLOMSKI

Please feel free to write to me at:
ul. Babimojska 8/12
60-161 Poznan. POLAND
Or email at: peterslomski@gmail.com

Bernard R. Hertel

Treadmills, Bondage, Tombstones, and Grace

As a child, I tried desperately to be good, yet constantly failed. I was born in Milwaukee, Wisconsin in 1944 to a "good" Catholic family. Along with my older brother and sister, I went to Catholic grade school, high school, and college. I liked all the priests and nuns who taught us in our home parish, St. Nicholas. Although I considered it a privilege to be chosen to serve Mass, I knew my overt and covert sins put me under God's wrath. Each night after dinner, we said the rosary. My mother, sister, brother, and I took turns washing and drying dishes while Dad and the others took turn leading and answering the Hail Marys. My friends later told me that they always knew not to come over too soon after supper, or they would be corralled into joining in on the rosary.

Treadmill Living

I kept trying harder to be good, failing again and again, while making confessions to the priest so that I would not go to hell. Staying out of the fire of hell was a strong motivation. Yet, my sin nature triumphed. I felt as though I was on a treadmill—commit those favorite sins, feel guilty, rush to  ST. NICHOLAS GRADUATION 1959 find a priest, confess, and feel safe—only to fall again. I was in bondage to my sin nature and to a sacramental system that demanded I be dependent upon the priest and a hope-for-salvation.

It was true of me when the apostle John said, *"Ye are of your father the devil, and the lusts of your father ye will do. He was a murderer from the beginning, and abode not in the truth, because there is no truth in him. When he speaketh a lie, he speaketh of his own: for he is a liar, and the father of it."* (JOHN 8: 44) The apostle Paul described my situation, *"And you hath he quickened, who were dead in trespasses and sins. Wherein in time past ye walked according to the course of this world, according to the prince of the power of the air, the spirit that now worketh in the children of disobedience: Among whom also we all had our conversation in times past in the lusts of our flesh, fulfilling the desires of the flesh and of the mind; and were by nature the children of wrath, even as others."* (EPHESIANS 2:1-3)

Divergent Drive

During high school, we commonly had career days. One constant presentation was by priests, brothers, or nuns suggesting that maybe "you too" have a calling from God to that higher spirituality of the religious life. I doubted that I was good enough to get in; yet, I felt a desire to do something to get into God's good graces. After all, I had a lot to make up for all my sin. Maybe, if I became a priest, He would look upon me with favor and keep me out of hell. The summer after freshman year of high school, we visited a novitiate in Arlington Heights, Illinois. The priest who was in charge of vocations wrote to me for about a year, he also sent me fliers and newsletters. I decided to visit the novitiate with my family that summer, on a vacation that took us through the Chicago area. I was disheartened that the building and location looked nothing like the pictures. I returned to Messmer High School, the Catholic school I had been attending. In the next two years, I experienced two conflicting forces within me: an increasing attraction to the high school girls that were in my classes, as adolescence emerged into manhood, and an apposing allure and gravitation to a priestly, celibate vocation. I had trouble reconciling these two divergent drives.

Seminary Life

Meanwhile, our parish had increasing numbers of young men going to St Francis Seminary on the south side of Milwaukee. By the summer of my junior year of high school, I decided that I had to find out if I had a vocation. The pastor at our parish, Monsignor Stehling, suggested the

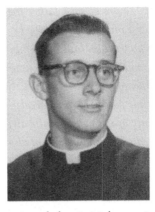

way to find out was to attend seminary. So, at the beginning of my senior year, I switched from Messmer High School to De Sales Prep Seminary.

I bonded with the forty other guys in my class as we lived, ate, and roomed together. It was the closest familiarity I had experienced up until that point in my life; perhaps it was similar to the bonding or camaraderie often described in the military at war, when men need to depend upon one another. I greatly enjoyed that initial experience.

However, I still struggled with sin, continuing on the treadmill of trespasses, feeling guilty, finding a priest, confessing, and hoping again. I got creative, trying different confessors. Maybe I would find one more lenient, more understanding, more accepting of my sin. In the end, I was still a lost sinner, trying harder, yet unable to stop sinning. I was still on the treadmill and in bondage.

I remember envisioning myself living to a ripe old age, trying very hard to be good, always turning over a new leaf, but just at the last minute of my life doing some stupid sin and losing it all, ending up in hell. The anxiety frustrated me.

Also, it was during my third and fourth year in the seminary that Vatican II was being implemented. Eating meat on Fridays was no longer a mortal sin, whereas only a few weeks earlier people supposedly went to hell—for all eternity—for eating meat on Fridays. This change disturbed me and raised some doubts. The liberal culture of the 1960's also caused me to doubt my ability to live a celibate life. So, after four years, I left the seminary in 1966.

Married with Children

During the following twenty-three years, I met my wife Mary, a former nun, and we raised three daughters, Laura, Sarah, and Allison. We were good Catholics: going to Mass each week, attending the sacraments, getting our children baptized and confirmed, distributing communion at Mass, teaching catechism, et cetera. We trusted "the one true church" implicitly.

In 1988, we were teaching a confirmation class to thirteen sophomores. We, along with the students, were given a Catholic Bible by one couple in our Catholic church. We began reading it. I particularly liked the words in red, the indication that Jesus is the one speaking. The words seemed to speak to my deep inner needs, and Jesus Christ seemed so compassionate and loving.

At this same time, our local public school was attempting to introduce sex education into the curriculum. About three hundred parents, many who were Christians, were working against this. Through this group, we were introduced to Christian radio. I liked the conservative perspective. We went to our local priest to ask the church to help us fight against this curriculum. Instead of helping us, they came out endorsing it, and they even suggested they would help teach the sex education teachers. A red flag went up in our consciences; we were confused. So, we tried the following:

- Moving to a more conservative Catholic parish.
- Reading more Bible.
- Listening to the conservative Christian radio.
- Finding a Catholic dogma book and comparing it with Scripture.

A Life Changing Message

I remember first hearing the clear gospel message while driving on a business trip to Burlington, Iowa. As I drove, I was surfing for a Christian station while listening to the radio. Some preacher gave the message: "We are all sinners, deserving of hell—not able to make it to heaven on our own." I knew I was a sinner; I could relate to that. *"For all have sinned, and come short of the glory of God."* (ROMANS 3:23) *"As it is written, 'There is none righteous, no, not one: There is none that understandeth, there is none that seeketh after God. They are all gone out of the way, they are together become unprofitable; there is none that doeth good, no, not one.'"* (ROMANS 3:10-12) *"But we are all as an unclean thing, and all our righteousnesses are as filthy rags; and we all do fade as a leaf; and our iniquities, like the wind, have taken us away."* (ISAIAH 64:6)

The preacher was talking about me. He said that Christ had died for our sins. I had heard that before—but now I heard that he had died for "my" sins. *"For when we were yet without strength, in due time Christ died for the ungodly. For scarcely for a righteous man will one die: yet peradventure for a good man some would even dare to die. But God commendeth his love toward us, in that, while we were yet sinners, Christ died for us."* (ROMANS 5:6-8) The message continued: He was buried and rose again according to the Scriptures. Whosoever believes on Him shall have eternal life. That was simple. It was so simple that I did not feel inclined to believe it. My whole background predisposed me to expect "to do something." I expected a *quid pro quo*; i.e., I do something in order to get something. I had a merit mentality that presumed I could gain God's favor with enough good works. My religious background predisposed me to reject a free gift.

Yet, after turning this over in my mind for a number of days, I realized it had to be true. By God's grace, I repented of the merit mentality, believed in Jesus Christ, and received from Him the gift of salvation. I knew that from my track record of sin and failure, if it were left up to me to attain or maintain my salvation, I would fail. I only needed to believe on the finished work of Christ on Calvary to be saved. Many verses confirmed this simple truth:

- For God so loved the world, that he gave his only begotten Son, that whosoever believeth in him should not perish, but have everlasting life...He that believeth on the Son hath everlasting life: and he that believeth not the Son shall not see life; but the wrath of God abideth on him. (JOHN 3:16, 36)
- But these are written, that ye might believe that Jesus is the Christ, the Son of God; and that believing ye might have life through his name. (JOHN 20:31)
- And brought them out, and said, "Sirs, what must I do to be saved?" And they said, "Believe the Lord Jesus Christ, and thou shalt be saved, and thy house." (ACTS 16:30, 31)
- Therefore being justified by faith, we have peace with God through our Lord Jesus Christ: (ROMANS 5:1)
- Knowing that a man is not justified by the works of the law, but by the faith of Jesus Christ, even we have believed in Jesus Christ, that we might be justified by the faith of Christ, and not by the works of the law: for by the works of the law shall no flesh be justified. (GALATIANS 2:16)
- But the Scripture hath concluded all under sin, that the promise by faith of Jesus Christ might be given to them that believe. (GALATIANS 3:22)
- That being justified by his grace, we should be made heirs according to the hope of eternal life. (TITUS 3:7)

- But without faith it is impossible to please him: for he that cometh to God must believe that he is, and that he is a rewarder of them that diligently seek him. (HEBREWS 11:6)

Truth Clarified

As I kept reading Scripture, I found more and more error that the "one true church" espoused. I studied Roman Catholicism and the Bible. What I discovered in Roman Catholicism was death instead of life. Here are some of the tombstones:

1. It became clear that you could not have two final authorities: Scripture and *tradition*. Rome ultimately holds tradition above Scripture. *"All scripture is inspired by God, and profitable for teaching, for reproof, for correction, for training in righteousness: so that the man of God may be adequate, equipped for every good work."* (2 TIMOTHY 3:16, 17)
2. Rome holds to a doctrine of Purgatory. *"And as it is appointed unto men once to die, but after this the judgment: So Christ was once offered to bear the sins of many; and unto them that look for him shall he appear the second time without sin unto salvation."* (HEBREWS 9:27, 28) *"We are confident, I say, and willing rather to be absent from the body, and to be present with the Lord."* (2 CORINTHIANS 5:8) These Biblical concepts negate purgatory.
3. Rome holds that Mary was sinless from birth, yet the Scripture has recorded her own words voicing the need of a savior. And, as the Bible makes clear, only sinners need to be saved. *"And Mary said, 'My soul doth magnify the Lord, And my spirit hath rejoiced in God my Savior.'"* (LUKE 1:46, 47)
4. Rome encourages the use of the Rosary. *"But when ye pray, use not vain repetitions, as the heathen do: for they think that they shall be heard for their much speaking."* (MATTHEW 6:7)
5. Rome encourages prayers to Mary because they say she is the mediatrix to God. *"For there is one God, and one mediator between God and men, the man Christ Jesus."* (1 TIMOTHY 2:5) *"Jesus saith unto him, I am the way, the truth, and the life: no man cometh unto the Father, but by me."* (JOHN 14:6)
6. Roman Catholicism calls the Mass a propitiatory, unbloody re-sacrificing of Christ on Calvary. *"And almost all things are by the*

law purged with blood; and without shedding of blood is no remission." (HEBREWS 9:22) "But this man, after he had offered one sacrifice for sins forever, sat down on the right hand of God; From henceforth expecting till his enemies be made his footstool. For by one offering he hath perfected forever them that are sanctified." (HEBREWS 10:12-14)

7. Rome presumes a sacerdotal approach to God—saying we need to use the sacraments and the priestly system to approach God. *"Seeing then that we have a great high priest, that is passed into the heavens, Jesus the Son of God, let us hold fast our profession. For we have not a high priest which cannot be touched with the feeling of our infirmities; but was in all points tempted like as we are, yet without sin. Let us therefore come boldly unto the throne of grace, that we may obtain mercy, and find grace to help in time of need."* (HEBREWS 4:14–16) Christ has given us direct access to God: *"And, behold, the veil of the temple was rent in twain from the top to the bottom; and the earth did quake, and the rocks rent."* (MATTHEW 27:51)

In Catholicism we called the priest Father and Reverend. *"And call no man your father upon the earth: for one is your Father, which is in heaven."* (MATTHEW 23:9) *"He sent redemption unto his people: he hath commanded his covenant forever: holy and reverend is his name."* (PSALMS 111:9) Another Bible text states that we are the priests—*"Ye also, as lively stones, are built up a spiritual house, an holy priesthood, to offer up spiritual sacrifices, acceptable to God by Jesus Christ."* (1PETER 2:5)

Roman Catholicism says that you sin the sin of presumption to think that you are saved without merit, but the Bible says you can know that you have eternal life. *"My sheep hear my voice, and I know them, and they follow me: And I give unto them eternal life; and they shall never perish, neither shall any man pluck them out of my hand. My Father, which gave them me, is greater than all; and no man is able to pluck them out of my Father's hand. I and my Father are one."* (JOHN 10:27-30) *"Verily, verily, I say unto you, He that heareth my word, and believeth on him that sent me, hath everlasting life, and shall not come into condemnation; but is passed from death unto life."* (JOHN 5:24) *"And this is the record, that God hath given to us eternal life, and this life is in his Son. He that hath the Son hath life: and he that hath not the Son of God hath not life. These things have I written* unto you that believe on the name of the Son of God; that ye may know that ye have eternal life, and that ye may believe on the name of the Son of God." (1JOHN 5:11-13)

Sharing the Message

I hope that no one gets the impression that I am against Catholic people. I love the Catholics I know and realize that most are very sincere in their beliefs, very sincere. Sincerity will not save, however. I love these people but object to a system that masks the truth and garbles the gospel. The truth of the gospel will set people free—free from the penalty of sin—free from a dead works approach to salvation on the installment basis. My hope and prayer is that all my Catholic relatives, friends, and acquaintances, will come to a saving knowledge of Jesus Christ.

When I realized that the Roman Catholic Church had deceived me, I was exceedingly angry. How could they tell me all those years they were "the one true church" and that they were the only pathway to heaven? In John's gospel, we read, *"Jesus saith unto him, I am the way, the truth, and the life: no man cometh unto the Father, but by me."* (JOHN 14:6)

I attempted to tell all my relatives what I had learned—how Christ had died for my sins—and that belief on Christ alone is what saves. It is my earnest desire that they know and understand the truth. Some have believed. All, however, are now more fully accountable before God after having been exposed to the truth.

Since I have believed on Jesus Christ alone for my salvation, I have eternal security. I know I am going to heaven when I die. I no longer need to be anxious, but rather can rest upon the finished work of Christ.

- *And I give unto them eternal life; and they shall never perish, neither shall any man pluck them out of my hand.* (JOHN 10:28)
- *All that the Father giveth me shall come to me; and him that cometh to me I will in no wise cast out.* (JOHN 6:37)
- *To an inheritance incorruptible, and undefiled, and that fadeth not away, reserved in heaven for you, Who are kept by the power of God through faith unto salvation ready to be revealed in the last time.* (1PETER 1:4, 5)
- *Wherefore he is able also to save them to the uttermost that come unto God by him, seeing he ever liveth to make intercession for them.* (HEBREWS 7:25)
- *For I am persuaded, that neither death, nor life, nor angels, nor principal-*

ities, nor powers, nor things present, nor things to come, Nor height, nor depth, nor any other creature, shall be able to separate us from the love of God, which is in Christ Jesus our Lord. (ROMANS 8:38, 39)

Trusting what the Bible says gives me a great sense of security.

Ongoing Battle

I still fall into sin. Being a born-again Christian does not negate the "old sin nature." Besides being indwelt by the Holy Spirit, the old sin nature still resides within and is at war against the Holy Spirit. However, Christ died for all my sins: past, present, and future. When He died, of course, all my sins were future, for I had not yet been born. Sin is no longer the issue. I am no longer anxious about my destiny. In fact, I learned that man sins because he is a sinner, rather than becoming a sinner because he sins. Think about that. Do we see ourselves as good, only occasionally sinning, or as a sinner who occasionally does something righteous? But, the Bible calls our righteousness filthy rags, in other words, abominable. In actuality, our goodness is mere self-righteousness, which is condemned by God. The Bible says we all are sinners: *"The heart is deceitful above all things, and desperately wicked: who can know it?"* (JEREMIAH 17:9) *"And GOD saw that the wickedness of man was great in the earth, and that every imagination of the thoughts of his heart was only evil continually."* (GENESIS 6:5) Sinners need a savior; we cannot save ourselves. Jesus Christ did it for us. Jesus is the Savior.

Walk of Faith

Most recently, I have been learning more about how to walk in the Spirit. *"For by grace are ye saved through faith; and that not of yourselves: it is the gift of God: Not of works, lest any man should boast. For we are his workmanship, created in Christ Jesus unto good works, which God hath before ordained that we should walk in them."* (EPHESIANS 2:8-10)

Believers still have an old sin nature, so I am still tempted and still do sin. However, it is liberating to reckon and count on the truth that the power of sin no longer enslaves me. Because of what Christ did on Calvary, and because the Holy Spirit indwells me, I do not have to sin. I can now choose to follow the leading of the Holy Spirit. I try to read and study Scripture consistently. As I read the Word and gain God's viewpoint, by the new nature, I will respond against the old sin nature by following the Holy Spirit's desires for my life. My day-by-day goal is to walk in the Holy Spirit, i.e., to abide in Christ.

- *Abide in me, and I in you. As the branch cannot bear fruit of itself unless it abides in the vine; so neither can you unless you abide in Me.* (JOHN 15:4)
- *It was for freedom that Christ set us free; therefore keep standing firm and do not be subject again to a yoke of slavery.* (GALATIANS 5:1)
- *...contend earnestly for the faith which was once for all handed down to the saints.* (JUDE 3)
- *For sin shall not be master over you, for you are not under law, but under grace.* (ROMANS 6:14)
- *Even so consider yourselves to be dead to sin, but alive to God in Jesus Christ.* (ROMANS 6:11)
- *That in reference to your former manner of life, you lay aside the old self, which is being corrupted in accordance with the lusts of deceit, and that you be renewed in the spirit of your mind, and put on the new self, which in the likeness of God has been created in righteousness and holiness of the truth.* (EPHESIANS 4:22-24)
- *See then do not be foolish, but understand what the will of the Lord is. And do not get drunk with wine, for that is dissipation, but be filled with the Spirit.* (EPHESIANS 5:17-19)

Yielding myself to the Holy Spirit is the goal. I know that as I abide in the Holy Spirit, Christ will use me as a willing instrument and spiritual fruit will occur. None of this can be credited to me, because I died, and now Christ lives in me. *"How shall we, that are dead to sin, live any longer therein? Know ye not, that so many of us as were baptized into Jesus Christ were baptized into his death? Therefore we are buried with him by baptism into death: that like as Christ was raised up from the dead by the glory of the Father, even so we also should walk in newness of life."* (ROMANS 6:2B-4) Bernie Hertel must diminish and Jesus Christ must be magnified. To Him be the glory. *"I beseech you therefore, brethren, by the mercies of God, that ye present your bodies a living sacrifice, holy, acceptable unto God, which is your reasonable service. And be not conformed to this world: but be ye transformed by the renewing of your mind, that ye may prove what is that good, and acceptable, and perfect, will of God."* (ROMANS 12:1, 2)

Jesus Christ is the author and finisher of my faith. The Holy Spirit will conform me to the image of Jesus Christ over time—through trials, through fellowship with believers, and through knowledge of His Word. I wait with expectation and excitement to see how God will continue to work in my life.

If you have tried to be religious: doing good, keeping the Ten Commandments, doing the sacraments, following church rules, et cetera, in order to win God's approval, then may I invite you to repent (change your mind). Change your mind about how sinful man becomes saved. *"Now to him that worketh is the reward not reckoned of grace, but of debt. But to him that worketh not, but believeth on him that justifieth the ungodly, his faith is counted for righteousness."* (ROMANS 4:4, 5)

I invite you to repent of any "merit mentality"—attempted good works to earn God's favor and approbation. Change your mind about how salvation is attained. Give up the quid pro quo, the need-to-work-to-get idea, and accept GRACE, the truth that salvation is a gift. Salvation is free and yours for the acceptance of Jesus Christ. The work was done on Calvary. It is finished! *"To him give all the prophets witness, that through his name whosoever believeth in him shall receive remission of sins."* (ACTS 10:43) *"And the Spirit and the bride say, Come. And let him that heareth say, Come. And let him that is athirst come. And whosoever will, let him take the water of life freely."* (REVELATION 22:17)

An Invitation

If you are a Catholic, we love you and want you to know the truth. Do not trust what any sinful man says. God's inspired Word, the Bible, is TRUTH. *"Sanctify them through thy truth: thy word is truth."* (JOHN 17:17) It is trustworthy. Read Scripture! Begin by reading the Gospel of John. Read the epistles to the Romans and to the Galatians. Check what Scripture says against what any church or man says. The Holy Spirit will help you. "If any of you lack wisdom, let him ask of God, that giveth to all men liberally, and upbraideth not; and it shall be given him." (JAMES 1:5) Pray for wisdom, so that God's Holy Spirit will lead you to the truth.

If you have Catholic relatives or friends, pray for them; share with them the gospel of grace: how Christ died for sins according to the Scriptures, was buried, and rose again. Boldly challenge them to trust Christ alone as their Savior. Remember to allow the Spirit of God to move their hearts.

He convicts them of their sin and moves them toward Christ as Savior. You may give them this testimony or, better yet, share your own.

Some of you know that I am an insurance agent. One of my habits is reading local death notices to see if any former clients have died. It is amazing what people put down on paper to summarize what thirty, fifty or even eighty or more years represent. Whether I live a short while or quite a while the following is true:

Here I am, Bernard R. Hertel, husband of Mary, father of Laura, Sarah, Allison, and grandfather of Katherine and David. I was born a sinner on December 16, 1944, into a Catholic family, and I lived by man's religion for 44 years. I tried repeatedly to do what was right, but I continually failed. I offended God and my fellow man in thought, word, deed, by omission and commission. I deserve eternal hell. Yes, I deserve hell—eternally. Yet, God in His infinite mercy extended His love to me while I was yet unrighteous, showing me how God's only begotten Son, Jesus Christ, came to die for my sins, was buried according to the Scriptures, and rose again to prove that my sins were propitiated and fully paid for by Jesus Christ. Scripture says that whosoever believes on the **Lord Jesus Christ** shall be saved. I believed God that this Scripture is true and faithful, and that faith was counted unto me for righteousness. My sin was imputed (charged) to Jesus Christ. Jesus Christ's righteousness was imputed to me. **God did it all! God gets all the glory! Jesus Christ is to be magnified! Amen.**

—BERNIE HERTEL

If you have any questions or comments please email me at: brhertel@wi.rr.com

ALEXANDER LENNOX

Snake Poisoned, Then More Than Revived

I FIRST HEARD THE GOSPEL IN 1968 WHEN I WORKED AT THE KING GEORGE the 5th Docks in Glasgow as a stevedore. One day, a young man by the name Tommy Lavery came to work in my gang, Tommy, being a blood-washed, born-again believer in Jesus Christ, lost no time proclaiming Jesus Christ as the Saviour. The Jesus that Tommy spoke of captivated me; no one had ever told me that he could save me from my sin, in fact, the term "saved" was not even in my vocabulary. The Jesus that he preached was not the Jesus that I was familiar with. The Jesus that I knew was a rather sad character whose one-dimensional picture appeared in storybooks. Sad to say, two years were to pass, before—by the Grace of God—I would surrender my life at the feet of Jesus and cry out for mercy and grace. My year of jubilee came on February 1970, at the age of 29, when Jesus delivered me from my bondage and set me free.

1940

I was born into a Roman Catholic family and a superstitious one at that. On my father's side, I had a staunch Roman Catholic grandmother, and my grandfather was a Scottish protestant and a member of the Orange Lodge. Theirs was a strange union, but strangely enough, they apparently were in love. Grandmother obviously was the dominant one, because my father and his brother attended a Catholic school. I can well remember my little Irish grandmother dressed in her Queen Victoria garb smoking her broken clay pipe. It

would hang on the side of her mouth pressed against her jaw; hence, it got the name, "Jaw Warmer."

My grandmother's house was a poor house, if indeed it could be called a house. Every room was a shrine to some saint or angel. There were wooden floorboards, life-size statues; but then again they would have appeared life size to a small child like me. There were barrels of holy water in all the rooms, while vases with flowers adorned the same. Sketches and photos of popes, right up to Pope Pius the 12th, lined the walls throughout the house. My grandmother influenced me more than did my grandfather. I knew nothing of his religion.

My Lithuanian grandmother, unlike my Irish one, would send her children to the Famous Glasgow Tent Hall where my mother and her sister would hear the Gospel at the Sunday school meeting. The poor children of Glasgow were fed body and soul at these meetings and at the end of the meetings; they would take home a big jug of soup and bread rolls for their parents. When the parish priest objected to my mother attending the Tent Hall, my grandmother replied, "If they are good enough to feed our bodies, then they are good enough to feed our souls." She then chased the priest from her home. My mother didn't know it then, but the seed of truth had been planted in her heart, and in 1976, I would have the privilege of watering that seed that had lain there dormant since 1924. I would see it blossom into full salvation. My mother, Ellen Lennox, born in 1914, went home to Glory in 1976.

One Sows and Another Reaps

The policy of Rome in the 1940's was to keep ordinary Roman Catholics in ignorance, and this was done by not allowing them to make an independent study of the Bible for themselves. As a child, I was not encouraged, or allowed to read a Bible or even own one. I remember, as a child, I asked the priest, "Father, why am I not allowed to read the Bible for myself?" His reply was confusing, especially to my little child like mind. "It's a blue book son, there's far too much begetting in it," he said. Even at that tender age, I knew what the term blue book meant. I did not realize it then, but as a little boy I was spiritually blind, being led by spiritually blind leaders whose minds had been darkened by the prince of this world. The Bible says, *"Let them alone: they be blind leaders of the blind. And if the blind lead the blind they shall both fall into the ditch."* (MATTHEW 15:4) Nevertheless, unknown to me at the time, God was working in my life, because I was allowed to read a little book based on the Bible which was called, "The Bible History", and it was in this book that I was to read the story of Adam and Eve. Little did I realize at the time, but I was to discover something called the origin of sin. Adam and Eve had sinned, and because they had sinned, we were all sinners and all on our way to Hell. But no one bothered to tell me that there was a way of escape, and because I was not told, I was to live in fear of Hell right up until 1968, when the Gospel was proclaimed in my ears. Truly it was the power of God as Bible says; *"the gospel of Christ is the power of God unto salvation to every one that believeth."* (ROMANS 1:16) That power I experienced as I was, "justified freely by his grace through the redemption that is in Christ Jesus." (ROMANS 3:24) Faith was to know the joy of sins forgiven. *"So then faith cometh my hearing, and hearing by the word of God."* (ROMANS 10:17)

When God saved me, I did not come out of Rome. God took Rome out of me. God is in the business of taking religion out of those whom He saves. He takes Islam out of the Moslem, Judaism out of the Jew, such as Buddhism. Why? It is because religion is the enemy of God; it was religion that cried out against Jesus as he stood before Pilate. Even to this day, its echo can still be heard. *"But they cried out, Away with him, away with him, crucify him. Pilate saith unto them, Shall I crucify your King? The chief priests answered, We have no king but Caesar."* (JOHN 19:15)

Religion will tell you, "Join me, and ye shall be saved." But the Lord Jesus Christ says, *"I am the way the truth and the life, no man comes to the Father but by me."* (JOHN: 14:6) It was not religion that sweated great drops of blood in Gethsemane, it was not religion that was lashed with the cat of nine tails, and it was not religion that died upon Calvary's Cross. It was Jesus Christ. So, let God be true and man-made religion a liar. (ROMANS 3:4)

My conversion influenced others. To what extent, I shall never fully know until I get to Glory Land. Certainly, my mother, just before she died, repented of her sin and owned the Lord Jesus as her Saviour. My mother had a fear of the priest; it was something that was common to that generation, including mine. Well, the night that she came to the Lord, it would be around midnight in a dark hospital ward, I told her, "Mother, from this day forth, your sins are between you and God, you no longer need an earthly priest to confess to. Jesus is now the mediator between you and God. "Do you understand that, Mother?" She looked at me and nodded yes. The next day the priest came up to take her confession and she addressed him, not as father, but as son. "Look son," she said, "my sins are between me and God, no one else; but if you would like to sit and talk, so be it." She told me later that the priest got angry and stormed out of the hospital ward. After her conversion, she was to go on to serve God as a Sunday school superintendent until her death in 1987 she was forty-six years old. Even in my darkest hour, God never left me. My late wife, May, was a Bible-believing Christian. I am now sixty-four years old and have never lacked anything that was needful for this life.

God blessed me with a second wife, Kat, a beautiful Christian lady. I have a wonderful stepson and a beautiful sixteen-year-old daughter who is also saved. I have three children by my first wife: two girls and a boy who are still to come to faith in Jesus Christ. But I live in hope that God will give salvation to my household.

Religion failed me miserably. It failed me because religion has the hand of man in it; therefore, religion has to be flawed. Why? Because man is a sinful creature, born and shaped in iniquity. As the Bible says, *"behold, I was shapen in iniquity; and in sin did my mother conceive me."* (Psalm 51:5)

Papal Rome has changed since I was a boy, but the changes have only been cosmetic. A snake may shed its skin, but it remains a snake and "deadly," and this is something that we must never lose sight of. My testimony is truly called, "Snake Poisoned, then more than Revived."

I thank God, and our Lord Jesus Christ, for my deliverance from sin and Papal Rome. I thank God for taking me out of the hands of blind leaders. If you reject Jesus Christ what are the alternatives for everlasting life? *"Then Simon Peter answered him, Lord to whom shall we go? Thou hast the words of eternal life."* (John 6:68)

—Alexander Lennox

JIM TETLOW

From Religion to Relationship

Catholicism – A Family Tradition

I was raised in a large family, the fifth born of six children. Each week I attended Catholic Church with my mom and siblings. My mom was the overseer of our religious education and Catholic upbringing. Even on vacations, she would faithfully load us up into the station wagon and head for the nearest Catholic Church. She saw to it that each of her children was taught the Catholic faith. She also gave us a Bible in our younger years—though we seldom read it.

While my mom supervised and ensured our religious upbringing, Dad on the other hand was disinterested and seldom involved himself with the family's religious affairs. Though he never protested our involvement with the Church, Dad himself never attended church when I was younger, except for weddings and funerals. I found out why later in life. Apparently, he was disillusioned with the Church after a couple of unpleasant incidents. He may have had other reasons, or perhaps they were just an excuse. Either way, Dad did not attend Mass regularly until the last few years of his life.

My father enjoyed bird watching, and when he was not working overtime on the weekends, he would often be out enjoying God's creation. I recall him explaining to Mom that he felt closer to God in the great outdoors then in any church. This made sense to me—where better to find and communicate with the Creator then out in His creation. Later in life, after he was diagnosed with lung cancer, he told Mom that he needed to go to confession—he needed to repent. From then, until he died, he attended Mass regularly.

Ritual and Superstition

It was my mom who was the one who loyally and diligently made sure that we attended church each weekend and on Holy Days of Obligation.

She also saw to it that each of her six children attended religious education through the twelfth grade. Mom would remind us to say grace at dinner—including a Hail Mary most nights. She also had a large picture of what was supposed to be Jesus in the living room with eyes that seemed to follow you around. I vividly remember coming home drunk one night and looking at that picture and saying—with great conviction—"What are you looking at?" before stumbling down the stairs.

My mom also had me carry a "Sacred Heart of Jesus" card in my wallet. I recall one night at the bar, as I was withdrawing money for the next beer, this card fell out. Embarrassed by the icon, I said to my friend, "I ought to chuck this." To which he responded seriously, "Oh no, I would not do that, your mother is trying to watch out for you." Even though my buddies and I never spoke much about God, we believed in His existence and the supernatural realm. Therefore, certain things were taboo—including throwing out a card that was meant to protect me.

My twelve years of religious education were, for the most part, quite boring. We memorized a number of prayers and became familiar with several stories in the Bible. We were also taught Catholic doctrines from the Catechism. And, of course, we were encouraged to live good lives, love God and our neighbor, and remain faithful Catholics. We were also exhorted to shun the moral depravity and social woes pervading our society.

Notable Memories

A few early events in my Catholic upbringing stand out. I recall the time when some teenagers were outside our classroom throwing rocks at the window. After a few hits, our religious education teacher stopped and began to pray out loud. She prayed, "Evil spirits be gone! Lord, remove the evil spirits!" We all chuckled. She was a nice lady I thought, but totally out of touch with reality.

During my senior year, religious education was held at a private home. We would talk about many life issues. One evening, we even meditated with the lights turned down low. Yet, not once, did we ever read from the Bible. Though I received a New Testament for my Confirmation, I do not recall ever reading from any Bible except a Children's Picture Bible when I was young. The only time I heard God's Word was during the weekly readings at Mass and during religious education when the teacher would relate one of the Bible stories.

My weekend attendance at Mass was rather non-eventful. Usually I arrived late, would leave right after Communion, and heard little of what was said. I do remember when a group of women testified of their experiences at Fatima. Supposedly, an apparition of Mary had appeared there in the past, and miracles were still being claimed. The women pulled out their rosary beads and announced that they had turned into gold while on pilgrimage. Though I was young, this intrigued me—miracles, reported healings, signs, and wonders were to me evidence that there was a supernatural realm.

Other memories included a priest who could say the Mass faster than any other. If we arrived a few minutes late, which we often did, he would have us blessed and out the door in thirty minutes. Then there were the intimidating priests who spoke of hellfire and brimstone, mortal sins that meant sure damnation, and the Devil. Of course, there also were priests who spoke about God's love and how we should be good Christians and follow the commandments to insure our entrance into heaven.

I particularly remember when one priest expounded on the Bible verse which says, *"And if thy right eye offend thee, pluck it out, and cast it from thee: for it is profitable for thee that one of thy members should perish, and not that thy whole body should be cast into hell."* (MATTHEW 5:29) I thought these words by Jesus Himself were quite extreme. Were not my eyes priceless— why would I pluck them out? But down deep, I knew my eyes had caused me to sin. Furthermore, there was something far more valuable then my "priceless" eye, which was my soul—although at the time I did not really understand this inner conviction.

Though I remember certain sermons, several Scripture passages, and a few specific events, to be honest, most of the time I was oblivious to what was being said. Attending Mass was simply the duty of every good Catholic. Though I knew it was important to be a good person, most of the church ritual seemed rather pointless. I jokingly referred to church as Catholic calisthenics—kneel, sit, stand—kneel, sit, stand. This was my way of expressing a deep-seated belief that much of this "church thing" was ultimately a futile endeavor. The truth is, though I knew the prayers and the routine, my heart and mind were usually adrift in other thoughts.

Questioning My Religion

There were moments of questioning. Once, I asked my mom what the difference was between Catholics and Protestants. She told me that some Protestants did not want to follow all the rules. Some wanted the "liberty" to divorce, or violate other rules, and so they started their own denomination. This satisfied me at the time because my Catholic neighbors appeared conservative, while my Protestant neighbors appeared more liberal. As Jesus said, *"Ye shall know them by their fruits,"* (MATTHEW 7:16) and from my point of view, the Catholic "fruit" was superior.

I remember asking a couple priests and religious education teachers questions about evolution, where the races came from, the afterlife, and how we knew for sure that what we believed is true. Their answers seemed weak and unconvincing. I thought, "Perhaps no one really knows the answers to life's most fundamental questions."

During supper one night, I recall Dad talking with Mom about a couple of new co-workers who claimed to be born-again Christians. He explained to Mom, somewhat perplexed, that they were rather lazy and unfaithful at their jobs. He was not sarcastic—he truly appeared puzzled. At that time, I had no idea what a born-again Christian was. However, I could tell from my dad's reaction that they must be people who claimed to be good.

Later, when I was a little older, perhaps sixteen, two of my female neighbors were said to have become born-again Christians. But they also were rumored to have smoked pot and to have loose morals. So, at the ripe age of sixteen I determined, with my very limited knowledge, that they were part of a cult. And certainly, I thought, no cult offered answers to life's most important questions.

As I passed through my upper teen years and into my early twenties, pessimism began to set in. My dad had died and the healing Mass had no lasting effect. Other hopes and dreams seemed unattainable; those that were did not satisfy for long. I remember that even during my dad's battle with lung cancer, the sense of God's presence remained far away. In addition, the sufferings of this world became more personal and chronic.

Furthermore, religion did not seem to hold the answer. I knew there was a God, but He was distant. There seemed to be a gulf that separated me from Him.

The Voice of Conscience

During this time, the only "spiritual" voice that I did perceive was my conscience—that inner voice that tells a person what is right and what is wrong. Yet, even that inner voice was growing ever fainter. Sins that paralyzed me with guilt when I was younger were committed without hesitation by the time I was twenty. Small sins were completely ignored, and justified, while larger ones were easier to commit with each new transgression.

I convinced myself that I could sin in "small" ways, while remaining a "good person." I hoped, at least in this way, I would eventually end up in heaven after a stay in Purgatory. These so-called venial sins included drinking, gossip, lust, and pride. But driving drunk, stealing, and premarital sex were more serious infractions in my mind. These I tried to avoid. Furthermore, I determined to work hard, take care of the environment, help my family, and do good works whenever convenient in order to offset my lesser sins.

At this time, I was unaware that Jesus said, *"Ye have heard that it was said by them of old time, Thou shalt not commit adultery: But I say unto you, that whosoever looketh on a woman to lust after her hath committed adultery with her already in his heart."* (MATTHEW 5:27, 28) Nor did I know that drunkenness, or any other "venial" sin would damn me: *"Know ye not that the unrighteous shall not inherit the kingdom of God? Be not deceived: neither fornicators, nor idolaters, nor adulterers, nor effeminate, nor abusers of themselves with mankind, nor thieves, nor covetous, nor drunkards, nor revilers, nor extortioners, shall inherit the kingdom of God."* (1CORINTHIANS 6:9, 10) I never saw myself as a fornicator or a drunkard until some years later.

Guilt Followed by Penance

This leads me to another routine that I practiced. Whenever I would get overly guilt ridden, I would go to confession. I then would perform the required penance, which usually included saying a couple Our Father's, several Hail Mary's, a Glory Be, and an Act of Contrition, and in some cases, a good work. After penance, I would have a false sense of feeling cleansed.

There was a sense of peace, and for a short while I convinced myself that my conscience was clean. Ironically, I would usually end up at the bar later that same evening with one stipulation: I would only have a couple beers.

On one of those occasions, I recall a friend at the bar asking me why I was only having a couple drinks that night. I explained to him that I had just gone to confession. To which he asked, "Are you not getting drunk any more?" I replied, "Of course, I'll get drunk again in a few weeks, this confession bit only lasts for awhile."

My hope was that when I died my death would occur right after going to confession. This may sound foolish, and I never really thought it through at the time, but I hoped that the Lord might receive me if I had recently confessed my sins. If I could refrain from so-called mortal sin—between when I went to confession and when I died—then I felt my chances were good. And certainly, I thought, confession would shorten my stay in purgatory.

Success and Pessimism

By 1991, at the age of twenty-six, I was a successful engineer with my own house, a nice new car I owned outright, and no debt (not even school loans). I was a driven worker and was able to pay my way through college to earn a bachelors degree in electrical engineering. Once I graduated, I ascended the corporate ladder rapidly.

It was now my fourth year in industry, the sky was the limit, income was good, company awards were rolling in, and offers were regularly presented. Despite this outward success, my cynical outlook on life only grew, and troubles seemed to multiply. My health was failing. In addition, my father's death five years earlier caused family difficulties and pain.

As things went downhill, though from the outside few noticed, I began to think more about the meaning of life and the big picture. Even if I had perfect health and everything else I could dream of—what then? Financial success did not gratify me. Growing fame at work left me empty. Various lusts were never satisfied. Life seemed so shallow and pointless. And worse, I would eventually die and none of it would matter.

As I would soon find out, my assessment of life was identical to what King Solomon had concluded 3000 years earlier: *"I have seen all the works that are done under the sun; and, behold, all is vanity and vexation of spirit... Therefore I hated life; because the work that is wrought under the sun is grievous unto me: for all is vanity and vexation of spirit."* (ECCLESIASTES 1:14; 2:17)

Lust and Frustration

During this season of outward success (but inward despair), my boss hired a young attractive secretary. I was single, and he asked if I approved of the new hire. I did and was delighted! It seemed my boss wanted to retain me so much so that he hired a pretty girl to work near me. What I never would have guessed is how this event would soon change my life forever.

There was a mutual attraction. Though we flirted, we did not date. The reason—she was a new Christian. I assured her that I was a Christian, too. But she would just say, "Jim, you need Jesus." When I finally realized that dating was out of the question, I turned cold on her. I even informed her that she was a hypocrite. She dressed provocatively, and even worse, she never recycled! I told her that both were terribly wrong. Shortly after my accusations, to my surprise, I noticed that this brand new Christian began dressing more conservatively. She even began recycling!

Yet, this did not satisfy me. In fact, her very presence was a source of frustration. I remember on one occasion that a few of us were working late, including her. I could not understand why I detested this girl, and yet I was drawn to her. On this particular night, the copier jammed. I proceeded to air my frustration with a string of curse words. Yet, this girl was silent; she did not even look up. I was fuming. How smug and self-righteous she was. I knew what she was thinking. How dare she judge me! When I returned to my desk, I told another co-worker that she was a great big hypocrite. He replied, "Jim, she didn't say a word to you, why does she bother you so much?"

You Take the Bible Seriously?

Some time after this episode, I began to question this girl about the Bible and Christianity. I asked her many questions. Questions like: If science has proven evolution is true, how can you take the Bible seriously? Do you really believe in all those fanciful tales when scholars have disproved so much of the Bible? What makes the Bible different from the other holy books? How do you know that Jesus rose from the dead? Maybe He was a fraud.

To most of my questions she simply stated, "Jim, I know the Bible is true. You should read it for yourself." Concerning evolution, she laughed and confidently asked, "Jim, do you really believe that nonsense?" She also alluded to biblical prophecies that were fulfilled. But most of the time, she would simply smile and say again that I needed Jesus.

During this time, my health continued its downward spiral. I had always dealt with health issues, but now the chronic dizziness, nausea, sweats, and gastrointestinal problems made my frequent work travel extremely difficult. I even wrote in my medical records that 1992 was the worst year of my life. Again, in 1993, I wrote that "this year" is worse then the worst year of my life. I was seeking every medical specialist I could. It seemed that every week I subjected myself to some new unpleasant test or evaluation—always seeking a cure.

I'm a Hypocrite!

I was also burdened with much soul-searching throughout this time. At one point during those months, I remember asking God something like this: "If the Bible is true and you want to save me, why did you not send somebody who knew the facts—the evidence? Am I not worth sending the best? Why do you not send someone who knows how to answer the difficult questions?" Ironically, though I was blind to it at the time, God had already sent His best to me—His only begotten Son—the Word of God! And this girl was the instrument that God chose to point me to Him. Down deep, I knew she had a relationship with the Living God, but I wanted answers.

Finally, I realized my hypocrisy. I had been playing religion to quiet my guilty conscience, but I was unwilling to read the Bible to see if the path that I was on was true. What if I were wrong? What if I were headed towards hell? If the Bible was truly God's Word, would I have to give up my lifestyle? Though I was descending into more and more misery, there were certain sins that I did not want to repent of—I liked them. No, I loved them. But, were they worth spending eternity in hell? At last, I determined to read the Bible for myself.

Flight from Hell to Heaven

It was early 1994 when I began reading the Bible. During this time, a new warehouseman was hired. Incredibly, he was a Bible-believing Christian! I realized God had now answered my earlier prayer, but it was not until I began to search for Him. Actually, He was drawing me towards Him. This warehouseman was able to help me find answers to many of my questions. In addition, my Christian co-workers suggested that I listen to a local Christian radio station, which I also began doing.

As I read the Bible, the Holy Spirit's conviction intensified, particularly concerning the sin of lust. I knew that God could see my thought life, and though I struggled to stop this sin, I kept returning to it. During this time I was scheduled to go on a business trip to California. Because of my deteriorating health, I dreaded these trips. At one point on this business trip, I was in my hotel room with a Bible in one hand and a remote control in the other. The battle to turn from my sin was so intense that I would shake. One minute I would be reading the Bible, the next minute I would be flipping on a pay-per-view movie.

My flight home was an even worse nightmare. I was sick the night before, missed my early flight, and was in a nauseous sweat for most of the long trip home. When I finally arrived back in New York, I was more determined then ever to study the entire Bible to determine if it was truly God's Word.

I do not know the exact day the Lord saved me, but it was during the first part of 1994 that I truly began calling on the Lord. And as I would read later: *"For whosoever shall call upon the name of the Lord shall be saved."* (ROMANS 10:13) While I had cried out to the Lord to help me on previous occasions, it was during this period that I truly repented and asked Jesus Christ to save me.

Repentance is different than penance. As a Catholic, I would go to Confession and confess my sins to a priest. The prescribed penance, involving certain prayers and good works, was meant to earn God's forgiveness. In contrast, biblical repentance literally means to *change your mind*—to turn from your way and surrender to God's way. It is not only confessing our sins to God, but also turning from them and trusting in the Savior. Repentance is not a bandage to cover sins, nor a bribe to pay for sins, nor a method to appease God. Instead, biblical repentance means acknowledging that my way is wrong and leading to destruction, and then turning to the Lord alone to save me and change me.

Many Infallible Proofs

In the months that followed, I began to discover that the Bible was abounding with internal and external evidence. For example, Isaiah 53 and Psalm 22 contained graphic, detailed descriptions of the crucifixion. The fact that they were penned hundreds of years before the Messiah's advent confirmed God Himself inspired these words. I soon learned that Jesus fulfilled dozens of prophecies written centuries before His birth. These included His precise lineage, birthplace, ministry, the manner of His death, the purpose of His death, and His subsequent resurrection—all prophesied centuries before He was born. Fulfilled prophecy, as evidence of the Bible's divine inspiration, is something that I never recalled hearing while attending the Catholic Church.

As I studied the Scriptures, my confidence in God's Word increased. "Last Day's" Bible prophecies coming into focus in our current generation, offered additional proof. Furthermore, scientific insights foreseen in the Bible presented powerful evidence. For example, 4,000 years ago Job wrote that the earth free floats in space. (JOB 26:7) In contrast, other "holy books" claimed the earth sat on the back of an animal. Moses wrote that blood is the source of life and health. (LEVITICUS 17:11) Yet physicians practiced bloodletting as a cure for disease until recent years. The apostle Paul wrote that each star is unique at a time when the stars were believed to be the same. (1 CORINTHIANS 15:41) Over the years I've also read the Book of Mormon, the Koran (Qu'ran) and an array of other religious writings. What a difference! For example, the Book of Mormon contains no specific fulfilled prophecies and was not even "revealed" until the 19th century. Furthermore, the Book of Mormon declares that Native Americans descended from Jews which has been disproved by DNA research, archeology, linguistics, and a vast array of other evidence.

Specific fulfilled prophecies are also absent in the Koran and Hadith. In addition, the Koran and Hadith include numerous documented historical errors, and contain many myths. The Eastern writings also contradict true science, have no specific fulfilled prophecies, and contain many myths.

As a Catholic, I had never known the many evidences confirming the Word of God. In fact, I was told that the Bible was accurate only in regards to faith and morals. In other words, it was God-inspired when it came to spiritually related things, but we should not necessarily take all the stories as literal history.

Sadly, the Catholic Church defends their dogmas more than the inspired Word of God. Today, Catholic apologetic ministries use Scriptures in an attempt to defend their Church dogmas, instead of defending and proclaiming the inerrancy of God's Word. However, God commands His people to proclaim His Word because: *"All scripture is given by inspiration of God..."* (2 TIMOTHY 3:16) And Jesus warned us not to replace the Word of God with man's traditions. (MARK 5:7-13)

Insights into Life's Ultimate Questions

As I grew in the Lord, all the prophetic and scientific evidence was important to me, but it was the spiritual insights that were the most vital. For example, answers to why we were created, where our conscience came from, and what eternity holds, were all answered in the pages of Scripture.

In the beginning God created everything very good. We find that Adam and Eve had a loving relationship with God. (GENESIS 3:8; EPHESIANS 3:9; REVELATION 4:11) There was no ritual or religion. This is how God intended it to be. However, after man's rebellion, religion emerged. Religion is man's efforts to reach or appease God by his own effort or merit. In contrast, the Creator offers freely the gift of eternal life and a restored fellowship with Him for all those who will place their trust in Jesus Christ. *"For the wages of sin is death; but the gift of God is eternal life through Jesus Christ our Lord."* (ROMANS 6:23)

In the beginning, God warned that the penalty for any sin was death—physical and spiritual. (GENESIS 2:17) But the good news is that Jesus paid our full penalty on the cross. When a person repents of their sins and believes on Jesus, he is freely reconciled back to God based on faith in Christ's finished work on the cross.

God desires to reconcile us back to Himself—as it was in the beginning. Therefore our very purpose in being created is to know and serve God eternally. *"And this is life eternal, that they might know thee the only true God, and Jesus Christ, whom thou hast sent."* (JOHN 17:3)

Besides explaining why we were created, the Bible is also the only book that explains where our conscience came from. Scripture tells us that God has given every man a conscience. *Con* means *with*, and *science* means *knowledge*. Therefore, we each have knowledge of God's moral law written on our heart. This separates mankind from the animals and makes us moral beings, created in God's image. God's Word explains that the moral law is written on every man's heart, bearing witness with each person's conscience that there is a Lawgiver and that we need a Savior. (ROMANS 2:15; GENESIS 2:9; 3:22) Jesus Christ, as Creator and Lawgiver, has revealed this light to every man. (JOHN 1:9)

And the Bible answers many other fundamental questions. For instance, God's Word explains the origin of sin, suffering, and death. When mankind rebelled, suffering and death resulted. No other book offers a plausible explanation. And through Jesus' substitutionary death, restoration with God and a loving, eternal relationship with Him is offered freely to all who will receive Christ! (JOHN 1:9)

Asking My Priest

In those first months of reading the Bible, I still attended the Catholic Church. However, it soon became apparent that I had to make a choice. This was not easy. But I knew I needed to choose God over convenience. When I explained that I was leaving the Catholic Church, my mom asked me to at least meet with the priest before leaving. So I decided to compile a list of biblical questions and then call him for an appointment.

When we met I asked him several questions: "Why does the Church teach us to pray to Mary and the saints? Nowhere in the Bible do we find a believer praying to anyone accept God." The priest had no answer. "Where do we find purgatory in the Bible?" He agreed that purgatory is not specifically taught in the Bible. "The Bible teaches that we are saved by grace through faith in what Jesus did. Why does the Church teach salvation through the sacraments and good works?" The priest said that works were important, but seemed confused. Ultimately, he said we must each find our own way. I asked, "But if the Bible is true, and we can prove it, why are you in a system that contradicts it?" He only repeated that we each needed to find are own way.

Over the years I've spoken with several Catholic prelates and was surprised to find that most do not know the Scriptures very well. Those who do, including several popular Catholic apologists, choose to twist the Scriptures to support Catholic doctrines. Sadly, the apostle Peter warned that there would be some who would twist the Scriptures to their own destruction. (2 PETER 3:16) However, for all those who search God's Word without preconceived bias, they will find the simple and glorious gospel.

Seeking to Establish Their Own Righteousness

God's Word explains, *"But we are all as an unclean thing, and all our righteousnesses are as filthy rags...."* (ISAIAH 64:6) No righteous act on our part could pay the penalty for previous sins committed. The penalty for any sin is death, (EZEKIEL 18:20) and the penalty has to be paid if God is a just judge. The Bible is clear. We each have broken His Ten Commandments and the penalty has to be paid. Using His name in vain even once is blasphemy. (EXODUS 20:7) Having hatred or calling someone Raca (a "fool"—said with hateful malice) is murder in God's eyes. (1 JOHN 3:15; MATTHEW 5:21, 22) One lie makes us liars under the evil one's sway. (MATTHEW 5:33-37) And as James explains, *"For whosoever shall keep the whole law, and yet offend in one point, he is guilty of all."* (JAMES 2:10)

The good news though is that through the cross, God's justice was met and His mercy extended. As a Catholic, I was taught that when Jesus died for us, He opened the gates of heaven and made access "possible." Now it was up to me to keep the commandments, receive the sacraments, and earn the right to pass through those gates. I was also taught that even if I did live a "good" life, I would most likely only enter heaven after a purifying season in purgatory. Purgatory was where my lingering "minor" sins would be expiated (atoned or paid for).

As a Catholic, I was familiar with several tenuous hopes. Catholics, who remained close to the "Saints," and especially the "Blessed Mother," would have an insider as their advocate when Jesus judged them. Catholics, who refrained from mortal sins and remained in good standing with the Church, could minimize their time spent in purgatory. As spiritual descendents of the apostle Peter, Catholics could maintain their valuable heritage by obeying the Church and the pope. There were other claimed benefits to being Catholic, but every one revolved around my own merit or standing within the Church.

How this differed from so many verses I had now read: *"For by grace are ye saved through faith; and that not of yourselves: it is the gift of God: Not of works, lest any man should boast."* (EPHESIANS 2:8, 9) *"And if by grace, then is it no more of works: otherwise grace is no more grace…"* (ROMANS 11:6) *"Not by works of righteousness which we have done, but according to His mercy He saved us…."* (TITUS 3:5) *"I give unto them eternal life; and they shall never perish…."* (JOHN 10:28)

Salvation is a gift from God based on the merits of Christ alone. Jesus' own words confirm this truth: *"For God so loved the world, that He gave His only begotten Son, that whosoever believeth in Him should not perish, but have everlasting life."* (JOHN 3:16) When some Jews asked Jesus how to earn

God's favor through works, Jesus replied, *"...This is the work of God, that ye believe on Him whom He hath sent."* (JOHN 6:29)

I could continue, but suffice to say, I never understood grace until I searched the Scriptures. Every significant doctrine that I even remotely understood in Catholicism undermined the complete sufficiency of Christ's redemptive work on the cross. Said simply, I thought Jesus only opened the gates of heaven, but I needed to deserve (earn) entrance in order to pass through. Yet, Jesus' cry from the cross, *"It is finished,"* (JOHN 19:30) meaning "paid in full," revealed that there was nothing I, or anyone else, could add to His redemptive work.

Now as I searched the Word of God, I found that the Catholic Church was guilty of the same offense as the Jewish religious leaders of Christ's day. *"For I bear them record that they have a zeal of God, but not according to knowledge. For they being ignorant of God's righteousness, and going about to establish their own righteousness, have not submitted themselves unto the righteousness of God. For Christ is the end of the law for righteousness to every one that believeth."* (ROMANS 10:2-4)

The Simplicity of the Gospel

Salvation by works is religion, but God offers a restored relationship through Christ based on faith alone. Though our pride drives us to earn eternal life, only when we humbly submit to our Creator on His terms can we be saved and reconciled back to God.

The Bible's clear and simple message was so different from what the Catholic "religion" had taught me. God's Word commands everyone to repent and trust in Jesus Christ, not in a religion. (ACTS 2:38) The Bible admonishes all to follow Jesus, not a church. (JOHN 12:26) The Scriptures proclaim Christ and His Word, never a denomination or a system. (1 CORINTHIANS 1:23) The Bible commands all to look to God, not any man-made organization. (ISAIAH 45:22) We are exhorted to abide in God's Word, not a Catechism. (JOHN 8:31)

A couple years after being saved, I began teaching the Word of God to young children. What I learned from these five and six year olds confirmed the simplicity of the Gospel. These youngsters naturally understood that they were sinners, that there was a Creator-God, and that they needed His mercy and grace. Their young and tender consciences (which were not yet seared) bore witness to these truths.

By reading the Scriptures, I discovered another clear reason that salvation must be simple, and that it cannot be earned. The Bible declares that God is both holy and loving. I understood God's holiness as I examined His law, the Ten Commandments. And I recognized God's love as I looked to the cross. Jesus, the Creator of all things, died in my place—for me! There was no greater demonstration of love in the entire world. In fact, the Bible plainly states, *"God is love."* (1JOHN 4:16) This means that God in His very nature (essence or being) is love. He is fundamentally and essentially LOVE. (JAMIESON, FAUSSET, AND BROWN COMMENTARY. 1 JOHN 4:8, GOD IS LOVE.)

Yet, I felt these two characteristics were at odds. At first, God's love and holiness appeared to me as conflicting attributes. However, God's Word opened my eyes. If God is perfect love, He also must be perfect righteousness. Therefore, He must always do what is right. For instance, God, Who is love, could never lie. He could never steal, deceive, go back on His Word, or be unfaithful. God as love demands from His very nature that He be perfectly righteous. And His holiness demands that He is perfect in love. These characteristics are inseparable. Anything less and God would not be perfect, nor would heaven be paradise.

Therefore salvation had to be so simple that anyone from anywhere could receive it. And that is exactly what our loving and holy God offers to everyone who has been chosen in Him from before the foundation of the world. (EPHESIANS 1:4) Salvation based on what He has done—freely offered to all who will believe!

Conclusion

God is the source of every good gift. (JAMES 1:17) And salvation is the greatest gift from the Giver of all things. Though it is simple to repent and believe (so simple a child could do it), our pride poses an insurmountable hurdle. To receive this gift means admitting that our way is wrong. It means confessing that our way to heaven is actually leading to hell. It means acknowledging that we have offended our Creator by ignoring our God-given conscience and sinning anyway. It means trusting in Jesus alone and turning from our sin. It means dropping the arrogance of our pride and coming humbly before God. It is then that the hurdle is removed.

Here is our choice: we can continue to gratify our self with all the temporary enjoyments and sinful pleasures this world offers, or we can submit to our Creator—the Giver of every truly good gift, and trust that His way is best.

Shortly after beginning my new life in Christ, this precious girl I mentioned earlier left to work for another company. Ironically, she would again be used in a similar way with a lady who attended the same Catholic Church that I did while growing up. I saw the wisdom in the Lord moving her on because many in my office thought I got "saved" so I could date her. Once she left, they could see that this was not the case.

As I began my new life in Christ, I was hoping for a complete physical healing, though I knew the Scriptures did not guarantee this. In fact, several verses promised hardship and tribulation. Although my health seemed better at times, my physical healing never came. Ultimately, it will in heaven!

Since becoming a Christian, my life has actually been more difficult in many ways, but now I have Jesus carrying me through every storm. Best of all, I went beyond King Solomon and found that life now has purpose and heaven is my destination. Every prayer, every Bible study, every witnessing opportunity, even giving a cup of water in His name, has eternal value. (MARK 9:41) As a Christian, this life is the closest to hell I will ever experience. But for an unbeliever who never comes to faith in Jesus Christ, this is the closest to heaven they will ever experience. Today, eternal life with Jesus motivates me to share the truth whenever possible.

So to conclude, please consider the value of your soul. Count the cost. Realize that nothing is worth forsaking your Creator and forfeiting eternal life. My prayer is that you will trust in the only One qualified to say, *"I am the way, the truth, and the life: no man cometh unto the Father, but by Me."* (JOHN 14:6)

—JIM TETLOW

Jim Tetlow produced a book and video on Marian apparitions entitled Messages from Heaven.

CYNTHIA B. LINDSTEDT

A Matter of Life...and Death

AS LONG AS I CAN REMEMBER, I BELIEVED IN GOD. I WAS BROUGHT UP Roman Catholic and considered myself a Christian. Although I did not attend Catholic grade school, at age seven I was sent to catechism classes in preparation for my First Holy Communion. I did not understand what it was all about, but I figured this "sacrament" was a *big deal* based on the number of youngsters enrolled in the Saturday morning class, the explicit instruction given by the priests and nuns, and the emphasis my family placed on it. I memorized rote prayers and answers from the Baltimore Catechism and, with great "fear and trembling," made my first confession to a priest. At last, dressed in a miniature "bride of Christ" garment with a lacy white veil, I received my First Holy Communion. With rosary, prayer book, and Scapular in hand, I felt as pure and holy as a seven-year-old can feel.

But, even at this young age, it seems God had given me a measure of discernment. I remember questioning our instructor nun as to how the Catholic Church (mere humans) could determine a matter like "indulgences" (specified time off from the "purifying" fires of Purgatory) as a reward for

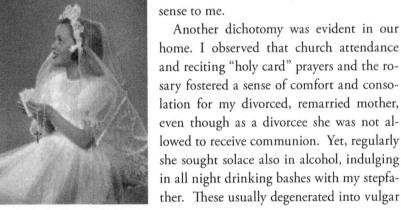

the recitation of certain prayers. It made no sense to me.

Another dichotomy was evident in our home. I observed that church attendance and reciting "holy card" prayers and the rosary fostered a sense of comfort and consolation for my divorced, remarried mother, even though as a divorcee she was not allowed to receive communion. Yet, regularly she sought solace also in alcohol, indulging in all night drinking bashes with my stepfather. These usually degenerated into vulgar insult and belligerence bouts for him, and crying jags for her. Our home was often terrorized by his fits of alcohol-inflamed aggression.

One night when I was around twelve, I awakened to yet another fracas. I tiptoed past their partially ajar bedroom door to view him pointing a handgun at her. To my horror, I heard her mutter, "Go ahead, and pull the trigger. I don't give a (blank)!" I returned to bed terrified, heart pounding, listening for the shot; which thank God, did not come. Often my mother was forced to bundle my younger sister and me into the car in the middle of the night in order to flee my stepfather's inebriated insanity.

An Accident

A turning point occurred when I was sixteen. As the result of a freak car accident, I suffered a brain concussion and skull fracture, permanently losing the hearing in my right ear. Doctors said I had been "lucky," since the basil fracture might have caused death, epilepsy, or paralysis. I soberly pondered God's purpose in sparing me, and began to take Him more seriously. I reflected that perhaps God had "knocked some sense into my head"!

It was a day of emancipation, jubilation, and even trepidation when, at eighteen, I said goodbye to my volatile home life and boarded a train bound for new beginnings: college in a southern state where my real father lived. In the sanctuary of my mind, he had become my "knight in shining armor" through his caring correspondence, birthday and holiday gifts, and now, the prospect of asylum from the environment of my childhood. I had seen him only twice in the fifteen years since my parent's divorce. As the train chugged southward, my mind buzzed with nervous anticipation. I knew I was heading toward the unknown: college in an unfamiliar area and life with a virtual stranger who was also, strangely, my father. Yet, I believed anything would be better than the lunacy I had left behind.

I was wrong. Four months later, my "knight" crashed from his pedestal, shattering my life in the carnage. During Christmas vacation of my freshman year, my "recovered alcoholic" father stormed out of the house in an unprovoked fit of temper, returned with a bottle of whiskey, and then sexually molested me. Incredulity, shame, guilt, silent outrage, heartbreak, and mortification silenced me from telling anyone of the unspeakable incident.

Although I did not yet know the biblical doctrine, this experience, together with my volatile upbringing, was teaching me the harsh reality of mankind's depravity:

The heart is deceitful above all things, and desperately wicked: who can know it? (JEREMIAH 17:9) *As it is written, 'There is none righteous, no, not one: There is none that understandeth, there is none that seeketh after God. They are all gone out of the way, they are together become unprofitable; there is none that doeth good, no, not one. Their throat is an open sepulcher; with their tongues they have used deceit; the poison of asps is under their lips: Whose mouth is full of cursing and bitterness: Their feet are swift to shed blood: Destruction and misery are in their ways: And the way of peace have they not known: There is no fear of God before their eyes.'* (ROMANS 3:10-18)

I returned to college feeling like damaged goods, humiliated and stunned at being so inexplicably betrayed by one I had so admired and trusted. Shortly afterwards, my father unexpectedly died, allowing no opportunity for reconciliation.

During subsequent college years, I struggled to find meaning, direction, and purpose in life, sensing something essential was missing. I regularly attended Sunday Mass, but also visited other churches to see if they had any answers. I especially was drawn to the quiet, contemplative "Time Out" sessions held at a campus Evangelical church when someone would read Scripture or an inspirational piece in the semi-darkened sanctuary. My roommate and I began reading the Bible aloud together at bedtime. Little did I know that through all of this, the Spirit of God was preparing a way in the "wilderness" of my life. (JOHN 1:23)

I graduated from college with a Bachelor of Arts in journalism and returned home to begin my adult life in earnest as a reporter for a daily newspaper. One day, a trusted male coworker covertly planted some shockingly raw pornographic material on my desk. I was stunned, again feeling sexually desecrated. It seemed the world was a sordid, perverted, God-forsaken wasteland. Was there no real "knight"—no one to save me?

My New Knight

Since my junior year, I had been dating a childhood friend. John was an intelligent, "tall-dark-and-handsome" all-American type from my subdivision. I had liked him ever since he had given me rides on his go-cart and taught me how to shoot a bow when we were adolescents. We had ridden bikes together with the neighborhood gang and attended the same high school. John had attended a U.S. military academy and now had returned home to study chemistry. I delighted in his levelheaded common sense, unpretentiousness, and humor. And his family seemed refreshingly "normal."

When John eventually proposed marriage, I believed our union had been ordained in heaven, partly because he surprised me with the exact engagement ring setting I had secretly admired, despite our pact not to spend his limited funds on such "frivolity." We dutifully attended the Catholic "Cana" marriage preparation classes. We had a modest but storybook wedding, and began what I anticipated would be life lived "happily ever after." However, less than a decade later, our heavenly marriage had spiraled into a diabolical pit.

Following John's graduate studies and U.S. Naval submarine duty, we returned to our home state. On the outside, things appeared storybook perfect. By now, we had two children (a daughter and a son), a home of our own, a dog, a steady income, and were active members of our local Catholic parish. John was a hard-working, faithful, dutiful husband and father.

I was occupied part-time in my chosen profession, writing for our community newspaper. Yet, on the inside, I was plagued by a gnawing emptiness. I blamed our marriage. Trying to "fix" things, I dragged John to a "marriage encounter" seminar. When that did not help, I hauled him to a "Christian" marriage counselor, who ultimately had no solutions either, even tendering divorce as a viable option! Disheartened, I began to follow an all-too familiar pattern by anesthetizing my emotional pain with alcohol. John's bewilderment at my disconsolation turned from concern to frustration, then to exasperation, and finally to chilling apathy. He was doing everything in his power to make me happy, but it was not working. My "knight" could not rescue me. The theme song of my life seemed to be the melancholy refrain by Peggy Lee, *"Is That All There Is?"*

It was during this critical period that God intervened in two extraordinary ways. First, in 1975, my editor asked me to interview a local realtor, named Mary, for a feature story. Due to impending deadlines, I conducted a telephone interview. Yet, even through the phone wires, Mary's vibrant faith rocked my world. It was unlike anything I had ever witnessed—not a "Sunday only" kind of religion, but a startlingly authentic, every-fiber-of-her-being certitude in God that struck a plaintive chord deep within me. It was as though she knew Him!

Not long afterwards, my journalistic curiosity was intrigued by a bizarre story claiming evidence of an actual photograph of "Jesus" in the clouds, reportedly taken by a passenger during a potential airliner crisis. Pursuing a "lead," I contacted a woman named Linda to learn more. To my chagrin, I discovered that Linda was a religious *wacko*! She talked incessantly and fanatically about Jesus, punctuating her patter with a bevy of Bible verses. I could put down the phone, go start supper, come back, and she would *still* be talking about Jesus. It was as though she knew Him.

Amazing Grace

"Amazing grace, how sweet the sound that saved a wretch like me..." Who can explain God's sovereign grace? Jesus said, *"The wind bloweth where it listeth, and thou hearest the sound thereof, but canst not tell whence it cometh, and whither it goeth: so is every one that is born of the Spirit."* (JOHN 3:8)

For weeks, Linda, a former Catholic, kept phoning me to talk about Jesus! Trying to be polite, I would listen briefly before making excuses that I had to go. One day she invited me to visit her new church. I thought, No way! Yet, days later, on July 24, 1977, I inexplicably found myself meeting Linda in the church lobby.

During the service, the Spirit of God seemed to settle over me like a celestial comforter. I was deeply moved by the congregation's spontaneous worship, praise choruses, and ardent prayer. It was as though they all knew God!

Then, at the close of the service, the pastor said the words that would change my life forever:

> *Perhaps you have been trying to make your life work out every way you know how...and it is just not working. Maybe you have tried everything in your power to make things better...and nothing has helped. Are you ready to surrender your life to Jesus Christ, to ask Him to be the Lord and Savior of your life?*

The pastor's words penetrated my heart like a divinely directed scalpel. I felt they were spoken to no one in the church but me! How did he know my burden? As tears flowed down my cheeks, I silently cried out for Jesus to be my Lord and Savior.

I had no more understanding of what was taking place (i.e., *spiritual birth*) than an infant understands its physical birth. I did not realize that

Jesus once had told a very religious man: *"...Verily, verily, I say unto thee, except a man **be born again**, he cannot see the kingdom of God."* (JOHN 3:3) I did not know that the Bible clearly states salvation cannot be earned; that it is a gift of God, given by His grace through faith: *"For by grace are ye saved through faith; and that not of yourselves: it is the gift of God: Not of works, lest any man should boast."* (EPHESIANS 2:8, 9) *"But after that the kindness and love of God our Savior toward man appeared, Not by works of righteousness which we have done, but according to his mercy he saved us, by the washing of regeneration, and renewing of the Holy Ghost; Which he shed on us abundantly through Jesus Christ our Savior; That being justified by his grace, we should be made heirs according to the hope of eternal life."* (TITUS 3:4-7)

I also did not realize that by receiving God's gift of salvation I had just passed from having a religion to having a vital relationship with Jesus Christ. Now that I was a believer, I could know Him and fellowship with Him. *"Behold, I stand at the door, and knock: if any man hear my voice, and open the door, I will come in to him, and will sup with him, and he with me."* (REVELATION 3:20)

I also did not know that in that divinely ordained moment, my heart had become radically different than my mother's, my stepfather's, or my father's, whose hearts were still enslaved to sin. All I knew was that my life, which was hell-bent for destruction, needed a savior, and I sought him in Jesus Christ. I sensed an enormous weight had lifted from my life.

The words on the cover of the church bulletin that day read: *"Thy words were found, and I did eat them; and thy word was unto me the joy and rejoicing of mine heart: for I am called by thy name, O LORD God of hosts."* (JEREMIAH 15:16) Only God knew how significant this verse would become in my spiritual pilgrimage.

Spiritual Truths

Linda urged me to begin reading the Bible, starting with the Gospel of John. As I did so, the words seemed like they were written *personally to me!* I did not realize that as a believer, I now had *God's indwelling Spirit* enabling me to understand the very words of God: *"Now we have received, not the spirit of the world, but the spirit which is of God; that we might know the things that are freely given to us of God. Which things also we speak, not in the words which man's wisdom teacheth, but which the Holy Ghost teacheth;*

*comparing spiritual things with spiritual. But the natural man receiveth not
the things of the Spirit of God: for they are foolishness unto him: neither can he
know them, because they are spiritually discerned... For who hath known the
mind of the Lord, that he may instruct him? But we have the mind of Christ."*
(1CORINTHIANS 2:12-14, 16)

My spirit soared as I read of God's great love revealed in the only true
Savior, the Lord Jesus Christ. Through tears of awe, I realized my Savior
had prayed for me: *"Neither pray I for these alone, but for them also which
shall believe on me through their word."* (JOHN 17:20)

I phoned Mary (the lady I had interviewed) to share what had happened.
She rejoiced and directed me to a ladies' Bible study. Appropriately, the
study was on "love." (1 CORINTHIANS 13) I discovered that God's concept of
agapē love was not a feeling but a sacrificial commitment: an unconditional
giving to those loved, despite all. *"For God so loved (agapaō) the world,
that he gave his only begotten Son, that whosoever believeth in him should not
perish, but have everlasting life."* (JOHN 3:16) When I learned God's pattern
for marriage, based on First Peter, chapter three, I comprehended with horror my own contribution to the near destruction of my marriage, and was
brought to my knees in repentance. *"Every wise woman buildeth her house:
but the foolish plucketh it down with her hands."* (PROVERBS 14:1) I begged
God to help me become a wife pleasing to Him and to the husband He had
given me. *"A virtuous woman is a crown to her husband: but she that maketh
ashamed is as rottenness in his bones."* (PROVERBS 12:4)

A Three Strand Cord

Within weeks, I discovered to my delight that a friend from my church,
Jeanne, had also experienced the new birth. She informed me of a unique
spiritual leader who had recently relocated to our church. The day I met
Catherine (not her real name for reasons you will later understand) I felt I
was in the presence of a truly godly woman. A striking, stately, lady with
dark, luminous eyes, Catherine spoke reverently and lovingly of her Lord
Jesus like He was her most intimate companion. Her large, Jerusalem Bible was tattered with use. She had an amazing grasp of Scripture. Most
impressively, she could instantly transition from conversation (talking to
people) to ardent, eloquent prayer (talking to God) using her own words—
not the rote prayers of the Roman Catholic Church. I was awed. Friends
regularly stopped by or phoned her for godly counsel and prayer.

Our threesome began meeting weekly to pray for spiritual renewal in our church. One of the first Scriptures Catherine shared was, *"...a three-fold cord is not quickly broken,"* (ECCLESIASTES 1:12) explaining that she believed God had brought us together for a reason. Our prayer group drew others, and eventually became so large we had to move it to the church. More people came. I learned to strum guitar and lead worship.

I became deeply involved in Catholic parish life, playing my guitar for Mass and teaching CCD (Confraternity of Catholic Doctrine) to teens as preparation for their Confirmation. I used the classes as a springboard to share the gospel. I attended a national conference on Catholic spiritual renewal and was amazed to witness thousands gathered to praise and celebrate Jesus. It seemed God's Spirit was moving mightily, answering our prayers, and blessing our denomination, our local church, and our prayer group with spiritual awakening. But, I soon experienced a Roman Catholic doctrinal "reality check."

As a CCD teacher, I attended a conference sponsored by the Archdiocese. There, I was confronted with a double dilemma. First, I watched the general session begin with a costumed native American Indian, complete with headdress, chanting and dancing on stage around a fire, using an eagle feather to invoke blessings (smoke) to the four corners of the earth! Secondly, I attended a workshop entitled, "A Mediation on the Book of John." The teacher, from a "holistic" health center, directed us to close our eyes and meditate on "the 'third eye' in the center of our forehead" as we listened to a John Denver recording! We were instructed to send "our healing energy" into the world.

However, the biggest shock was that not one of the attending priests, nuns, brothers, or teachers questioned this bizarre, blasphemous exercise. Incensed, I wrote a letter to the Archbishop questioning the orthodoxy of such offerings. Months later, my reply came from the conference director, stating that the Catholic Church "recognizes the validity of other spiritual philosophies." His response left me disconcerted. For the first time, I deliberated about leaving the Catholic Church, and prayed God would make the answer crystal clear to me, because I feared such a move would cause an earthquake in my marriage and family.

A Crusade

Our prayer group was excited to learn that a Crusade was coming to town. Catherine and I took training to lead follow-up groups. Longing for my husband to know Jesus, I fasted and prayed that he would attend the Crusade. My prayers were answered! John not only attended, but to my utter delight, responded to an invitation! As he made his way down the stadium steps and into the dazzling lights of the infield, I followed at a distance. Imagine my blessed amazement when I saw that among the hundreds of people streaming about, the individual who walked towards John to pray with him was the same pastor who had led my prayer of salvation at Linda's church! I rejoiced that now, at last, John and I would live "happily ever after."

But sadly, nothing seemed to change. John showed no spiritual interest beyond Sunday Mass. As Catherine and I led the "Nurture Groups" subsequent to the Crusade, John was among the dozen or so Catholics who attended, but we saw little spiritual vitality among any of them. I bought him a Bible, but it lay unopened. He dodged other believers, calling them dogmatic.

Once for All?

Meanwhile, the more I read Scripture, the more I discovered serious discrepancies regarding Catholic doctrine. While Catholics certainly believe that Jesus is the Son of God and is called a Savior, what that means to them is precariously ambiguous and confusing. There is no clear message of Jesus' mandate to be "born again" (JOHN 3:3) in the Roman Catholic Church. The Catholic Catechism suggests, rather, that spiritual birth is automatic upon water baptism. Moreover, there exists an underlying emphasis on "works" for one's salvation. I saw no biblical substantiation for the doctrine of Purgatory, veneration of Mary, or praying to saints (the New Testament clearly defines all born-again believers as "saints"). I found no substantiation for a priest to "absolve" sins in confession and dole out penance when the Bible clearly assures us: *"Why doth this man thus speak blasphemies? who can forgive sins but God only?"* (MARK 2:7) I saw that the Apostle Peter himself called all believers "priests:" *"But ye are a chosen generation, a royal priesthood, a holy nation, a peculiar people; that ye should show forth the praises of him who hath called you out of darkness into his marvelous light."* (1PETER 2:9) I realized that it was not Peter, but his profession, *"Thou art the Christ, the Son of the living God,"* (MATTHEW 16:16, 18) that was the "rock" upon which the universal church is built.

Most importantly, the Bible refutes the very centerpiece of Roman Catholic dogma, the "Sacrifice of the Mass:"

*Wherefore he [Jesus] is able also to **save them to the uttermost** that come unto God by him, seeing he ever liveth to make intercession for them. For such a high priest became us, who is holy, harmless, undefiled, separate from sinners, and made higher than the heavens; **who needeth not daily, as those high priests, to offer up sacrifice,** first for his own sins, and then for the people's: **for this he did once,** when he offered up himself. For the law maketh men high priests which have infirmity; but the word of the oath, which was since the law, maketh the Son, who is consecrated for evermore."* (HEBREWS 7:25-28)

After I learned this, I could no longer watch Christ being fallaciously "sacrificed" at every Mass. I could no longer utter the phrase voiced during the consecration: "May the Lord accept this sacrifice at your hands, for the praise and glory of His name, for our good, the good of all His holy church." I even questioned whether the consecrated host was the "real presence" of Christ as maintained by Catholic doctrine, or simply a remembrance.

*"...That the Lord Jesus the same night in which he was betrayed took bread: And when he had given thanks, he brake it, and said, Take, eat: this is my body, which is broken for you: this do in **remembrance** of me. After the same manner also he took the cup, when he had supped, saying, This cup is the new testament in my blood: this do ye, as oft as ye drink it, in **remembrance** of me."* (I CORINTHIANS 11:23-25)

About this time, God brought to my attention the existence of a local Christian research and apologetic ministry. Alarmed by my encounter with unbiblical doctrines at the CCD conference, I desired to learn to discern God's truth from aberrant theology. I began volunteering my time with this ministry.

Catherine, who by now had become my closest friend, joined me in this endeavor. Under the wise tutelage of its director, we were taught the dangerous doctrines of the New Age Movement, Latter Day Saints (Mormons), Watchtower and Track Society (Jehovah's Witnesses), and scores of other Scripture-twisting methodologies. I took seriously the words, *"Beware lest any man spoil you through philosophy and vain deceit, **after the tradition of men, after the rudiments of the world, and not after Christ.**"* (COLOSSIANS 2:8)

I readily accepted the Bible as the standard of truth because Jesus declared it to be so: *"Sanctify them through thy truth: thy word is truth."* (JOHN 17:17) I realized I had to apply this same standard to the official teaching of the Roman Catholic Church. I became increasingly concerned about "born again" Catholics who appeared to rely more on experience and popular religious custom (tradition) than on Scripture.

For example, many of my Catholic colleagues unabashedly advocated devotion to the "Virgin Mary." The apparitions supposedly occurring in Medjugorje, Yugoslavia, had captivated many. Some even made pilgrimages to these sites. This troubled me deeply. I knew Jesus had diverted praise of his mother in the Bible. *"And it came to pass, as he spake these things, a certain woman of the company lifted up her voice, and said unto him, 'Blessed is the womb that bare thee, and the paps which thou hast sucked,' But he said, 'Yea rather, blessed are they that hear the word of God, and keep it.'"* (LUKE 11:27, 28)

It became increasingly apparent that much Roman Catholic doctrine was arbitrary, based on human decrees, and often contradicted the Bible. For example, I learned Pius IX had declared the doctrine of the Immaculate Conception of Mary in 1854, maintaining Mary was conceived without sin, which is clearly a biblical contradiction of, *"For **all** have sinned, and come short of the glory of God…"* (ROMANS 3:23) Mary's prayer in Luke also vouches for her having sinned, *"And Mary said, My soul doth magnify the Lord, And my spirit hath rejoiced in God my Saviour."* (LUKE 1:46-47) If she were sinless, she would have no need of a savior. Another example was the dogma of Papal infallibility decreed at the Vatican I Council in 1870. I continued to seek God's guidance, praying, "Lord, if and when I am to leave the Catholic Church, please make it very clear to me." Then in the spring of 1990, during a week John was away on a trip, what I believed were three indicators occurred in rapid-fire succession:

(1) The local Christian radio station aired a series doctrinally critiquing the unbiblical policies of our local archbishop,

(2) The director of the apologetic ministry simultaneously recommended I visit a local Evangelical pastor, with whom he had recently become very favorably acquainted,

(3) A concerned Christian friend gave me a taped message exposing many of the fallacious Roman Catholic doctrines I had already found troublesome.

Come Out of Her

As I prayerfully sought God's direction in Scripture regarding this critical decision, I encountered some powerfully significant passages. *"Wherefore if ye be dead with Christ from the rudiments of the world, why, as though living in the world, are ye subject to ordinances, (Touch not; taste not; handle not; which all are to perish with the using;)* **after the commandments and doctrines of men?** *Which things have indeed a shew of wisdom in will worship (self-made religion), and humility, and neglecting of the body; not in any honour to the satisfying of the flesh."* (COLOSSIANS 2:20-23) *"Howbeit in vain do they worship me, teaching for doctrines* **the commandments of men**... *Making the word of God of none effect through your tradition, which ye have delivered: and many such like things do ye."* (MARK 7:7, 13) *And, most convincingly, "And I heard another voice from heaven, saying, 'Come out of her, my people.'"* (REVELATION 18:4)

I arranged a meeting with the recommended pastor. As we talked, I perceived a refreshing spiritual affinity rooted in the desire for God's truth. I believed God was saying, "It's time... Come out of her, my daughter." That Sunday, I attended the Evangelical pastor's church, believing God was calling me to remove myself from the false religious system of the Roman Catholic Church. It was a bold move, and I knew there would be repercussions, but I did not realize how severe they would be.

When John got home, my "defection" hit him like a slap in the face. He refused to hear my reasons or read explanatory material. The tension in our home became obvious as we began to attend separate churches. Our children, now numbering three, did not know what to believe or where they belonged. "Religion" was a taboo topic. Catholic friends, and particularly extended family, quietly disapproved. I began to understand Jesus' caution: *"Think not that I am come to send peace on earth: I came not to send peace, but a sword. For I am come to set a man at variance against his father, and the daughter against her mother, and the daughter in law against her mother in law. And a man's foes shall be they of his own household."* (MATTHEW 10:34-36) One consolation was that one of my "threefold" friends, Jeanne, left the Catholic Church the same week I did and joined me at the new church.

But Catherine was a different story. Over lunch, I candidly informed her of my decision and reasons, offering some substantiating literature and tapes. She was polite, but soon returned the materials, asking that I not give her any more. My heart sank as she informed me that she intended to stay in the Catholic Church. "It's where my husband is and where God wants me," she said resolutely. I feared this rift would strain our relationship, because I had believed our friendship was based primarily on our mutual love of God's truth. However, more importantly, I feared it would affect her relationship with the Lord.

Life and Death

"There is a way which seemeth right unto a man, but the end thereof are the ways of death." (PROVERBS 14:12) God's truth as revealed in His Word is the dividing line between the "right way" and "the way that seems right" but leads to death. God instructed His people:

> *See, I have set before thee this day life and good, and death and evil; In that I command thee this day to love the Lord thy God, to walk in his ways, and to keep his commandments and his statutes and his judgements, that thou mayest live and multiply; and the Lord thy God shall bless thee in the land whither thou goest to possess it. I call heaven and earth to record this day against you that I have set before you life and death, blessing and cursing: therefore, choose life, that thou and thy seed may live: That thou mayest love the Lord thy God, and that thou mayest obey his voice, and that thou mayest cleave unto him: for he is thy life, and the length of thy days....* (DEUTERONOMY 30: 15, 16, 19)

Following Catherine's fateful declaration, I witnessed with grief the unraveling of her and her family: a family that was greatly esteemed and respected in the Church and community. First, Catherine's husband was diagnosed with a brain tumor. Convinced this was "for the glory of God" and that God would heal him, Catherine intensified her prayers and Catholic pieties such as rosaries and novenas. Her husband's condition worsened. Ignoring judicious counsel, they accepted a job transfer to another state. His condition deteriorated; he became unable to work, and the uprooted family was sadly bereft of support from distanced but caring relatives and friends.

Next, Catherine determined her husband should try alternative medical treatment, necessitating numerous trips to Texas—all to no avail. Within a year and a half, he died. At the funeral, Catherine clung to me, tearfully divulging how she felt like "a general who had lost not only the battle, but the whole war."

Tragically, that is not the end of this story. A year later, I visited Catherine after she had relocated in our area. To my dismay, I observed a woman in an emotionally and spiritually precarious state. This once confident and capable woman expressed frustration, exasperation, and desperation in trying to manage her home and children. She related stories of dating men twice her age and others half her age. She voiced irrational fears regarding the supposed presence of a "poltergeist" in her condominium. Most regrettably, she lamented a disconcerting "spiritual dryness," saying she no longer "got anything" out of Mass attendance.

On a happier note, she expressed gratitude that our friendship had withstood religious differences, revealing that most of her "former Catholic" friends no longer had contact with her. I agreed, but candidly acknowledged that things were not exactly the same. I divulged my disappointment at her not scrutinizing biblically the doctrines of Roman Catholicism, noting I had always believed the banner over our friendship was truth.

I drove home that day deeply disturbed by the confused, defeated woman I had just seen. Catherine seemed adrift in a quagmire of spiritual uncertainty; yet, she was still clinging to the rudder of Roman Catholic familiarity and security. She seemed like the doubtful individual described: *"...For he that wavereth is like a wave of the sea driven with the wind and tossed."* (JAMES 1:6)

Several months later, I awoke one morning with a particularly heavy heart, recalling our conversation and grieving anew over the situation. I wrote Catherine a note, explaining that the reason I had been so forthright during my visit was that I loved her and loved the Lord, and I yearned for her to walk in the light of God's truth. I picked a bunch of Forget-Me-Nots from my garden, sealed them in plastic wrap, and tucked them in the note. On the way to the post office, I prayed that God would open her heart.

That same afternoon I got a call from a mutual friend. In somber, hesitant tones she ventured, "Cindy have you heard about what happened to *Catherine?*" She had committed suicide that very morning! Her teenage son came home from school to find her lifeless, asphyxiated body in their automobile in the garage. She left five fatherless, and now motherless children, and two grandchildren.

Watch Your Doctrine

Does doctrine matter? Paul warned Timothy: *"Take heed unto thyself, and unto the doctrine; continue in them: for in doing this thou shalt both save thyself, and them that hear thee."* (1 TIMOTHY 4:16) As much as I would love to have rescued Catherine, I believe I did what I could. The outcome was ultimately in God's hands: *"And the servant of the Lord must not strive; but be gentle unto all men, apt to teach, patient, in meekness instructing those that oppose themselves; if God peradventure will give them repentance to the acknowledging of the truth; and that they may recover themselves out of the snare of the devil, who are taken captive by him at his will."* (2 TIMOTHY 2:24-26)

The worst onslaught to the gospel of truth was yet to come. Catherine's small, private funeral was only for immediate family and close friends. The celebrant, a local priest, consoled mourners with the *"assurance"* that Catherine was "now at peace in heaven because she had a relationship with Mary, the Mother of God." My spirit recoiled at these deceptive, heretical words.

While in the Catholic Church, I never paid much attention to those who venerated Mary. But lately, I had been involved in investigative research, writing and speaking regarding the megalomania surrounding Marian apparitions such as Medjugoria, Fatima, Guadalupe, Lourdes and countless others. I was horrified to learn the truly demonic underpinnings of this cultic phenomenon that diverted devotion from Christ to "Mary" and espouses *"unto another gospel: which is not another."* (GALATIANS 1:6-7) The Apostle Paul wrote: *"But though we, or an angel from heaven, preach any other gospel unto you than that which we have preached unto you, let him be accursed."* (GALATIANS 1:8)

A "relationship with Mary" is not the way to eternal life. Jesus stated clearly, *"...I am the way, the truth, and the life: no man cometh unto the Father, but (except) by me."* (JOHN 14:6) How much plainer can it be said? As my research disclosed blatantly blasphemous messages, reportedly from "Mary," I anguished over the multitudes (including children) that through the years have been duped by such devilish deceit. I came to understand the significance of Paul's words, *"And with all deceivableness of unrighteousness in them that perish; because they received not the love of the truth, that they might be saved. And for this cause God shall send them strong delusion, that they should believe a lie."* (2 THESSALONIANS 2:10, 11)

I grievously lament the destruction of a life, a family, a testimony, and a witness whose faith was in a religious system that ultimately failed to supply the answers and stability necessary for the storms of life. *"Therefore whosoever heareth these sayings of mine, and doeth them, I will liken him unto a wise man, which built his house upon a rock. And the rain descended, and the floods came, and the winds blew, and beat upon that house; and it fell not: for it was founded upon a rock. And every one that heareth these sayings of mine, and doeth them not, shall be likened unto a foolish man, which built his house upon the sand. And the rain descended, and the floods came, and the winds blew, and beat upon that house; and it fell: and great was the fall of it."* (MATTHEW 7:24-27)

Unless the Lord Builds...

By God's grace, my own marriage was still limping along. Initially, I did all the wrong things, trying to pressure, cajole, and guilt-trip John into spiritual vitality. At last, I realized I could not play the role of the Holy Spirit; John's spiritual destiny was between him and God. I resolved to intercede for him and with God's enablement, try to be the best wife I could be, focusing on my own walk with the Lord. *"Except the LORD build the house, they labour in vain that build it: except the LORD keep the city, the watchman waketh but in vain."* (PSALM 127:1)

It took twenty-two years and three painful trials—John calls them "being taken out to God's woodshed" but glory to God, He captured John's attention, and his heart! In what was a landmark testimony to God's faithfulness, together, we were baptized by immersion, the summer of 2002. During my public testimony, I intimated that God had given me such a spiritual "head start" because He knew John is a quick learner! Praise God, all of our children and their spouses have come into the Shepherd's fold. Apart from God's amazing grace, I have no doubt our marriage and family would have crashed onto the shoals of disaster; but thanks to Him, our foundation is solidly established on the rock, which is one's knowing, trusting, and obeying Jesus Christ.

Jesus Christ did not promise life would be easy for his followers. In fact, He said just the opposite. After teaching about the truth-illuminating ministry of the Holy Spirit and the imperishable "complete joy" that His followers would experience, Jesus warned his disciples, *"These things I have spoken unto you, that in me ye might have peace. In the world ye shall have tribulation: but be of good cheer; I have overcome the world."* (JOHN 16:33)

The Lord Jesus cautioned His disciples to "count the cost" of following Him, *"...whosoever he be of you that forsaketh not all that he hath, he cannot be my disciple."* (LUKE 14:33) As a believer, I soon learned the "cost" of following Jesus. Many times, clouds of dejection pressed in on me after being ridiculed for my beliefs by those dearest to me. But I drew comfort from Jesus' words: *"Blessed are ye, when men shall revile you, and persecute you, and shall say all manner of evil against you falsely, for my sake. Rejoice, and be exceeding glad: for great is your reward in heaven: for so persecuted they the prophets which were before you."* (MATTHEW 5:11, 12)

Suffering for righteousness' sake is part of a believer's life. *"For what glory is it, if, when ye be buffeted for your faults, ye shall take it patiently? but if, when ye do well, and suffer for it, ye take it patiently, this is acceptable with God. For even hereunto were ye called: because Christ also suffered for us, leaving us an example, that ye should follow his steps."* (1PETER 2:20-21)

The way of discipleship is sometimes challenging, but Jesus leads us. He picks us up when we fall and encourages us on toward holiness. *"...But I follow after, if that I may apprehend that for which also I am apprehended of Christ Jesus."* (PHILIPPIANS 3:12) I had learned these lessons.

It has been a remarkable journey learning to possess the "promised land," (DEUTERONOMY 30:15, 16) with many "Ebenezer stones" marking my way. (I SAMUEL 7:12) I have indelibly learned that "Jesus saves" by grace, through faith, (EPH. 2:8) every step of the way: past, present, and future.

Why did God spare my life when I was sixteen? Why did He rescue me from myself and sanctify my marriage? I cannot begin to fathom His mercy and grace, but I know I could not have heard his voice unless He had first opened my spiritual ears to hear His call. (JOHN 8:47)

I know He had work to do in me: *"But we all, with open face beholding as in a glass the glory of the Lord, are changed into the same image from glory to glory, even as by the Spirit of the Lord."* (2 CORINTHIANS 3:18)

I know He had work for me to do. *"For we are his workmanship, created in Christ Jesus unto good works, which God hath before ordained that we should walk in them."* (EPHESIANS 2:10) These "works" have most recently manifested as my pursuit of becoming equipped as a biblical counselor. Yes, *"Thy words were found, and I did eat them; and thy word was unto me the joy and rejoicing of mine heart...."* (JEREMIAH 15:16) It has profoundly been the "joy and the rejoicing of my hear" to realize, minister, and advocate the inerrancy, authority, sufficiency, and supremacy of God's Word as I have endeavored to remove the "beams" from my own eyes and help others to see the "motes" in theirs:

> Judge not, that ye be not judged. For with what judgment ye judge, ye shall be judged: and with what measure ye mete, it shall be measured to you again. And why beholdest thou the mote that is in thy brother's eye, but considerest not the beam that is in thine own eye? Or how wilt thou say to thy brother, Let me pull out the mote out of thine eye; and, behold, a beam is in thine own eye? Thou hypocrite, first cast out the beam out of thine own eye; and then shalt thou see clearly to cast out the mote out of thy brother's eye. (MATTHEW 7:1-5)

The Year of the Lord's Favor

The Lord Jesus opened his public ministry with the words recorded in Luke 4:18-19, citing Isaiah 61:1-2, "*The Spirit of the Lord is upon me, because he hath anointed me to preach the gospel to the poor; he hath sent me to heal the brokenhearted, to preach deliverance to the captives, and recovering of sight to the blind, to set at liberty them that are bruised, to preach the acceptable year of the Lord.*" (ISAIAH 61:1, 2)

To everyone's astonishment, the Lord Jesus then proclaimed: "*This day is this scripture fulfilled in your ears.*" (LUKE 4:21) His words were fulfilled in me when I cried out to Christ for salvation. I was poor and He opened to me the infinite riches of Christ; I was brokenhearted and He healed my soul; I was captive to my own sin nature and He delivered me; I was blind to eternal truths, and He gave me sight; I was bruised by the sinfulness of man, including a false religious system, and He released me. In 1977, He proclaimed "*the acceptable year of the Lord*" (LUKE 4:19) for this lost soul, and made her a child of God.

Thank God, I finally found my true "Knight" in shining armor, my Savior who will never fail me, leave me, forsake me, nor betray me—my precious and eternal Friend with whom I will live "happily ever after."

> Let your conversation be without covetousness; and be content with such things as ye have: for he hath said, I will never leave thee, nor forsake thee. So that we may boldly say, The Lord is my helper, and I will not fear what man shall do unto me? (HEBREWS 13:5, 6)

Because of Jesus Christ I have been able to forgive my father and stepfather, honor my mother, reconcile my past, love and serve my husband, minister to others, and stand steady in the midst of life's storms. In today's vernacular, I came from a "dysfunctional" family; God calls it SIN—and His remedy is Jesus! Because of His redeeming grace, I am compelled to forgive those who sinned against me, since I myself am a sinner. *"For all have sinned, and come short of the glory of God..."* (ROMANS 3:23) *"...He that is without sin among you, let him first cast a stone..."* (JOHN 8:7) The ground is level at the foot of the cross.

Our trials can defeat and destroy us, or they can be God's sanctification seminar. *"For the grace of God that bringeth salvation hath appeared to all men, Teaching us that, denying ungodliness and worldly lusts, we should live soberly, righteously, and godly, in this present world; Looking for that blessed hope, and the glorious appearing of the Great God and our Savior Jesus Christ: Who gave himself for us, that he might redeem us from all iniquity, and purify unto himself a peculiar people, zealous of good works."* (TITUS 2:11-14)

God has a purpose in our difficulties: *"And we know that all things work together for good to them that love God, to them who are the called according to his purpose."* (ROMANS 8:28) The "good" for which God is working "all things" is that we become conformed to the character of Christ. *"For whom he did foreknow, he also did predestinate to be conformed to the image of his Son."* (ROMANS 8:29) Because of God's magnificent plan, my life has purpose: to glorify God by being conformed to the image of His Son, and to serve Him now and forever. *"For in him we live, and move, and have our being."* (ACTS 17:28)

Because of Him, my life's theme song has been transformed to an eternal, glorious refrain: "The LORD is my light and my salvation; whom shall I fear? the LORD is the strength of my life; of whom shall I be afraid?"

(PSALM 27:1) *"I will sing unto the LORD as long as I live: I will sing praise to my God while I have my being."* (PSALM 104:33)

One final note: in the Bible, names are poignantly significant. I cannot help but marvel that my own name, Cynthia is Greek for "of the moon, celestial light." The moon has no light of its own; it merely reflects the light of the sun. My heart's desire is to forevermore reflect the light of the Son Jesus Christ the Lord!

—CYNTHIA LINDSTEDT

JOHN STEWART LINDSTEDT

Three Strikes and You're In!

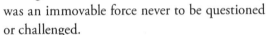

FAITH, I WAS TAUGHT, MEANT TRUSTING IN THE HOLY ROMAN CATHO-
LIC Church, never questioning what you were instructed and never challenging its sacred doctrines. Nuns and priests drilled this dictum into me
repeatedly during my Catholic grade school education. Church hierarchy
was an immovable force never to be questioned
or challenged.

Yet, as I grew into young adulthood, the
very fabric of our society was being challenged.
Change and challenge were everywhere. America
in the 1960's was a place of ferment and change.
This change was dramatic and unforgiving. It
sowed the seeds of a shift in society that we be-
moan today as the degrading of American culture. It was hard to see its significance then, but
forty years later, time provides a lens through
which events may be discerned more clearly.

The seventh decade of the 20th Century had many iconic images: JFK,
the Beatles, Vietnam, hippies, drugs, political assassinations, and moon-
walks. It was a time of extremes, of polarization in many areas, high political ideals, e.g., John Fitzgerald Kennedy's inaugural: "Ask not what your
country can do for you – ask what you can do for your country," contrasted
with three shocking political assassinations: John F. Kennedy, Robert F.
Kennedy and Martin Luther King, Jr.; and a loss of trust in our elected
leadership, which grew out of the war in Vietnam. By decade's end, the
simple, rhythmic rock and roll music of Buddy Holly, Elvis, and the Beatles had deteriorated into drug-induced anti-establishment rantings.

A war raged in Southeast Asia—a war sold as a patriotic struggle against
communism, but fought with constraints by politicians who wanted to san-

itize its brutality, push their political agenda, and satisfy both the generation that fought WWII and their children—the emerging counter-culture.

With the publication of *Silent Spring* in 1962, the "environmental movement" was born, and it attracted many anti-establishment youth. In June of that year, a convention in Port Huron, Michigan captured the spirit of the 60's radicalism with its manifesto (Port Huron Statement)—a bold rejection of America's sanctioned values. In short, the country was corrupt, confused and disjointed. There was a disharmony among the citizenry. People strongly and, occasionally, violently, disagreed. America was a ship at sea in a storm and she had lost her rudder. Grave and critical factions demanding sweeping change were eroding American foreign policy, corporations, race relations, economic relationships, and government. A clamor for personal freedoms, "making love not war," and material goods denigrated society's moral and ethical standards.

This counter-culture faction did not respect the country's institutions, leaders, moral tone, or tolerate gradual reform. Their revolt was against the entire American culture. Yet, America's majority clung to traditional ideals of family, work, and material advancement. Two distinct groups emerged within our society. I chose to side with tradition and work for those ideals that were being tested.

I was appalled by the counter-culture and determined not to be part of it. I resolved to use my education, resources, and skills to create a life that showed the tenants of the "other side" invalid. My plan was to use my education in the sciences (chemistry) to prove the ideologies of the New Left flawed. Science was logical, clear, and precise. There were no gray areas here, no philosophies of society, no drug-enhanced self-exploration, just FACTS—provable, measurable facts. The simplicity appealed to me.

My Life's Foundation

To master science requires work, lots of long, plain, hard WORK; study, study, and more study. I worked at it and excelled. I built a foundation, the foundation of my life: hard work and logic. God was a distant part of the picture, a transcendent Being who had set the Earth in motion and then left humans to run it using the minds He had given them.

My Catholic faith had become nothing but a ritualistic revolving door. Go to church and school and learn the rules. Try, but fail to keep the rules. Realize how you "blew it." Go to confession and admit your sins to a priest. Receive absolution and do penance. Feel cleansed. Go to Mass and Holy Communion and feel sanctified. Blow it again. Go to confession again...etcetera, etcetera, and etcetera! After a while, I did not even bother going to confession because nothing ever changed. I found myself confessing the same sins over and over—and over again.

I even asked a priest about this once while in the confessional. He only compounded my guilt by intoning, "I'd hate to be in your shoes, come Judgment Day!" While I desired to embrace the Church and its teachings, I felt I could never succeed at what was expected of me. I was forever failing and asking forgiveness. What was the use? The whole system seemed hopelessly impotent and expendable. Besides, my own "system" seemed to be working just fine.

While I was in graduate school, the Vietnam War interrupted my "life plan." The first peacetime draft since WWII forced me to enlist in the U.S. Navy. I applied for submarine service and I was selected. I also applied for the nuclear power training program and I was selected.

At this juncture, I encountered the individual who, besides my father, had the most notable influence on my life, Admiral H. G. Rickover, the father of the Nuclear Navy. Rickover was legendary for his leadership and engineering acumen in designing, building, and operating mobile nuclear power generation plants. I learned his foundation was exactly like mine—science, logic, and hard work used to create a safe, efficient engineering system that was second to none. I embraced and excelled at his methodology. It affirmed my worldview but added a new dimension: self-reliance.

Ready to Conquer

In 1974, at twenty-seven years of age, I was a very confident, capable young man, schooled in the sciences, proven in the submarine service, and ready to tackle the world. I had excelled, was not part of the counter-culture, and had done everything through my own efforts, or so I thought. Pride and self-assurance were not in short supply. Add to this a beautiful wife, a budding family, and with my life ahead of me, I was ready to conquer the world. My state of mind could be correctly characterized by, *"Because that, when they knew God, they glorified him not as God, neither were thankful...."* (ROMANS 1:21)

Upon leaving the service to join my father in the family business, I employed my system of logic, science, hard work, and self-assurance with the objective of growing the company and making it the best metal finishing business in the state.

Years passed and the company grew as hoped, both financially and in professional stature. My goals appeared to have been reached. Gross sales were twenty times greater than when I joined the business. The company was known for its expertise in gold, silver, nickel, and tin finishes. I was recognized nationally as an articulate and competent spokesman for the metal finishing industry in its never-ending regulatory struggles with all levels of government. Environmental science in the 1990's had become a political platform for much of the counter-culture of the 1960's. It was gratifying to use my system of science, logic, and hard work to derive science-based solutions to impending regulations.

As my professional skills grew, I disregarded God and increasingly relied on myself. Why not? I was capable of conquering anything set before me. God was "known" to me, but seemed distant; there was no relationship. He was an intellectual curiosity, not a personal Being who could help me, direct me, or desire my trust. Although I regularly attended church, it was merely a dutiful obligation. I could best be characterized as a deist—someone who believes God exists and created the world, but thereafter assumed no control over it or the lives of people.

When Billy Graham came to our town, my wife Cindy coaxed me to attend his Crusade. I listened to his presentation and responded to his invitation to come forward, more out of curiosity than anything. A man prayed with me, but nothing seemed to change. I did not believe I needed more of God in my life. I was absorbed in my own pursuits and did not have time for "religion."

When my wife, who had been studying the Bible, informed me several years later that she could no longer attend the Catholic Church because of its errant teachings, I felt mystified, angry, and abandoned. Although she offered to share information explaining her faith, I was not interested. We began to attend separate churches, and what used to be "family Sundays" now became days of tension and division. During the week and on Saturdays, I was buried in work and my own pursuits, so it was easy to disregard whatever differences we had.

God's "Woodshed"

By 1995, at forty-eight years of age, I was a confident and self-assured entrepreneur at the height of his professional skills. Other than brief passages cited during Mass, I had never read the Bible, so I did not know it says that everything, including wealth and honor, comes from God; (1 CHRONICLES 29:12, 14) that He is the One who provides success and satisfaction in work. (ECCLESIASTES 2:24, 5:18, 19) I thought I had done it all. However, I was about to be taken to the woodshed by the God of the Universe and taught some eternal truths.

That year, a sequence of events began to unfurl that would test my avowed foundation, and prove it flawed.. These trials would demolish my pride and self-assurance. These events occurred over five years as God kept providing a series of trials that would truly test me and finally teach me the central truth of God's Word: *"Trust in the Lord."* I would be drawn into a relationship with God and learn eternal truths that would establish me on the only firm foundation. *"Therefore whosoever heareth these sayings of mine, and doeth them, I will liken him unto a wise man, which built his house upon a rock."* (MATTHEW 7:24)

I have often wondered since then why God wanted me. But He truly did, as the Apostle John states: *"No man can come to me, except the Father which hath sent me draw him: and I will raise him up at the last day,"* (JOHN 6:44) and again, *"...that no man can come unto me, except it were given unto him of my Father."* (JOHN 6:65) God used a series of circumstances that would test my self-assurance and pride. I would be broken and shown the bankruptcy of my belief system, causing me to cry out to Him for help.

Lesson One: Loss of a Friend

The first of these was the loss of my business partner of thirteen years. Eric was more than an associate, he was a friend, one of the few people I trusted and confided in, someone who made me laugh and helped me enjoy life. We had grown somewhat distant recently, but never seriously —I thought. A back injury resulting from an auto accident in 1995 made life painfully difficult for him, especially in the stressful world of job shop manufacturing. One day over lunch, he announced his decision to resign. I was stunned. By our mutual agreement, I was obligated to purchase his shares of company stock. No time is ever convenient to incur a large debt, but it was not the debt that was most difficult for me, it was the perceived betrayal of trust by one who had been like a brother. I was upset and hurt.

The answer to this problem was simple: I would pick up the slack, do his job and mine, work harder, work longer, and solve the problem. The "system" had worked before and it would work again. I would not be weak and defeated by the loss of one individual, no matter how valuable. Therefore, I plunged into the additional duties of sales and customer relations, as well as my customary responsibilities. However, this time, the load was greater than anticipated. I grew tired and frustrated. This fostered irritability and depression, and those closest to me suffered. My resolve hardened—I would not lose!

Lesson Two: A Bolt from Above

Almost one year later, on October 6, 1996, God sent trial number two. A late season thunderstorm struck our city, and a bolt of lightening from above ignited a fire that burned my business to the ground. Lost was eighty percent of my manufacturing capacity! Chemical residues of former finishing lines were puddled among the wreckage left by a three-alarm fire. Heat and 750,000 gallons of water left the work of three generations in a smoldering mess.

That is how I felt inside—a smoldering mess. I questioned, "Why?" Why had this happened to me? I rationalized by using the post-modern mantra: I had never hurt anyone; basically, I was a good person; I did not deserve this. Mixed with my perplexity were anger, confusion, and uncertainty. Due to the catastrophic amount of damage (loss of nearly all manufacturing capacity, and lack of adequate insurance coverage: a $1.6 million shortfall), for the first time I was unsure of what course to take.

Finally, after several late night meetings with my father, we laid a plan in place to restore the company. The building would be reconstructed. Dad and I would finance the capital shortfall. I would start rebuilding the plating building, design the finishing lines, and handle the regulatory requirements of water permits. Dad and our operations manager would handle our customers, insurance, and personnel concerns.

However, this time something was different. My self-assurance was gone. Each week was an emotional roller coaster of highs and lows, punctuated by the day's successes, challenges, problems, and concerns. Worry was my constant companion. I became exhausted—bone weary. Clear, rational thought did not come as easily as before. For the first time in my life, my foundation seemed deficient. I truly wanted help. I needed someone, something. My Catholic religion offered no answers or solace.

The Light Shines Through

A few weeks following the fire, during our critical, potentially lethal, chemical cleanup, I telephoned my wife. In all seriousness I implored, "If ever I needed people praying, it is now!" I was worried about the very real possibility of a fatal chemical mishap during a critical stage of the chemical cleanup, which involved handling cyanide. I dragged myself home that night after a grueling but accident-free day. Cindy handed me an index card on which she had written some incredible words from the Bible; which she said God had comforted her with during her prayer time that day: *"O bless our God, ye people, and make the voice of his praise to be heard: Which holdeth our soul in life, and suffereth not our feet to be moved. For thou, O God, hast proved us: thou hast tried us, as silver is tried. Thou broughtest us into the net; thou laidst affliction upon our loins. Thou hast caused men to ride over our heads; we went through fire and through water: but thou broughtest us out into a wealthy place."* (PSALM 66:8-12)

I read it over and over. The words seemed to penetrate the fog of my helplessness. I read and reread especially the ninth verse, *"Which holdeth our soul in life, and suffereth not our feet to be moved."* (PSALM 66:9) Was God telling me something? Had I been so self-absorbed, so self-reliant, that I had taunted God? Had he sent this trial to get my attention, to turn me to Him—to get my focus off John and onto Him? Could that be the reason why the fire, why the loss of my partner? I carried the card in my briefcase for months.

I began reading the Bible, desiring to understand and get to know this God—the God who created the world with all the order and symmetry that I loved. I wanted to be acquainted with the God who had the awesome power to "lay burdens on our backs" in order to turn our attention to Him. The phrase, "fear of the Lord," suddenly had startling significance. I read the Bible each night for comfort and direction, visiting the Psalms frequently.

Then one evening I read, *"The LORD is my rock, and my fortress, and my deliverer; my God, my strength, in whom I will trust; my buckler, and the horn of my salvation, and my high tower."* (PSALMS 18:2) That was it! I had to trust God and accept His direction for my life. I turned my life over to Him. I had to believe and trust Him as "my rock." The word of God did not return void. (ISAIAH 5:11) My fledgling faith was new, and I did not understand all the fullness of God's gift, that everything is from God, for Him and His glory. However, I did understand that if the company were to be rebuilt, and succeed, He would do it. If the company failed, that was okay ...it was God's plan. I recognized that God was in control of my life and future and experienced a refreshing new peace.

I also began attending Cindy's evangelical church with her. The Bible was preached and taught there, and although I was a neophyte, I began to learn about God's Word and His gift to us, His Son. For the first time in my life, I began to experience God on a personal level. Besides, I thought that Cindy and I had gone our separate spiritual ways long enough. However, I felt guilty about no longer attending the "one true" Catholic Church and knew my [Catholic] family would disapprove. Occasionally, I would attend Sunday Mass, just to touch base with my roots and ease my conscience.

Lesson Three: Refiner's Fire

The company was gradually rebuilt. Many times during the process, I repeated the words, *"The LORD is my rock."* (PSALMS 18:2) Life and the business slowly returned to normal and three and a half years later, I felt "safe." I had weathered the storm. Some of the "old John" had crept back, not as extreme as before but still there: pride, a muted self-assurance. Then, in March 1999, God turned up the refiner's fire with trial number three. Just days before my 52nd birthday, I was diagnosed with prostate cancer! I was devastated.

This time, no amount of logic, hard work, effort, or training could fix the problem. I had only this recourse: to trust God completely. I knew I had slipped, and I asked His forgiveness. Unbeknownst to me, my wife, a few Christian friends, and some folks at our new church had been praying for me. They prayed for a full and genuine conversion to God's way, according to Paul's prayer: *"That the God of our Lord Jesus Christ, the Father of glory, may give unto you the spirit of wisdom and revelation in the knowledge of him. The eyes of your understanding being enlightened; that ye may know what is the hope of his calling, and what the riches of the glory of his inheritance in the saints."* (EPHESIANS 1:17, 18)

Through studying God's Word, I finally realized that man is—that I am a rebellious and self-centered sinner, and that I cannot live God's plan my way. Partial obedience to God is just as damning as total rebellion, *"For rebellion is as the sin of witchcraft, and stubbornness is as iniquity and idolatry."* (1 SAMUEL 15:23)

With dismay, I recognized myself as "the man" in First Corinthians, *"But the natural man receiveth not the things of the Spirit of God: for they are foolishness unto him: neither can he know them, because they are spiritually discerned."* (1 CORINTHIANS 2:14) I did not want to be him anymore. I wanted to be born spiritually, God's way. (JOHN 3:3) By God's grace, I decided to trust God completely—to trust and believe on Jesus totally as my Lord and Savior. Thus it was that I was spiritually born again. I decided to be baptized as a sign of obedience to God and for the powerful symbolism of dying to self and rising in Christ pictured by going down into and coming up out of the water.

In this life God has given me many blessings (including post-operative freedom from cancer) that I want to be used for His purposes as He chooses. I now realize that all that I have comes from Him and not by my efforts. It is a new beginning and a new life...and I am excited about what lies ahead, knowing my future, like my past, is in His hands. *"I trusted in thee, O LORD: I said, Thou art my God. My times are in thy hand..."* (PSALMS 31:14, 15)

—JOHN LINDSTEDT

A. J. Krause

From Darkness to Light

FEW PEOPLE HAVE EVER LOVED OR RESPECTED THE CATHOLIC CHURCH more than me. As we lived just a stone's throw from St. Dominic's Church and school, my sister and I were raised in the church. Members of the Krause family, as far back as granddad could remember, were all good Catholics. We had a proud tradition to follow, and the baton had been handed to me. In no way would I let our tradition down. What confidence I had in this awesome religion! Why, I questioned, was everyone who claimed to be Christian not a Roman Catholic? This was my heartfelt belief. The following is my personal testimony of salvation.

Born Catholic, Die Catholic

My parents thought it very important that my sister and I receive a good Catholic education instead of one from a public or private school. Therefore, I spent my grammar, middle, and high school years being educated by nuns and priests. I was well indoctrinated into the rules and doctrines of Catholicism. I was baptized as an infant, confirmed as a young boy, and received my first Holy Communion at my school and church. I started confessing my sins to priests at an early age. I had received four of the seven sacred sacraments by the age of twelve, and I felt my spiritual quest was headed in the right direction. After all, I was following one of the most organized religions in the world. My Catholic school regularly challenged us to consider the possibility of becoming a priest or nun. Thoughts of dedicating my life to God in this way danced in my soul. What greater career path could I travel? So, I talked like someone who was interested in the path of serving God. Because of my obvious devotion and love for the Catholic Church, the nuns and priests gave me special attention, especially because of my vocal desire to become a Catholic priest. I was taught that the priesthood is the highest calling for a man. I set out in a devoted path, desiring to do all that I thought pleased the Lord.

Devoted Catholics go to Mass as often as they can, and further training taught me that going to Mass everyday would grant me special grace and fewer days in Purgatory (a Catholic doctrine meaning a temporary place after death where the body burns until purged of all smaller sins). I had zeal of God, but the remark made by the Apostle Paul concerning the devout Jews also applied to me, *"For I bear them record that they have a zeal of God, but not according to knowledge. For they being ignorant of God's righteousness, and going about to establish their own righteousness, have not submitted themselves unto the righteousness of God."* (ROMANS 10:2-3) I was ignorant of God's righteousness. I believed that Catholicism was "the way" for righteousness, but the Scripture insists, *"For Christ is the end of the law for righteousness to every one that believeth."* (ROMANS 10:4) Believing on Christ for righteousness is the key. Without confidence in God, in His fidelity, His truth, His wisdom, and His promises, you have no security, as the Scripture maintains, *"...without faith it is impossible to please him...."* (HEBREWS 11:6) However, my faith and confidence were in my beloved religion which "I thought" to be God's righteousness.

My Loyalty to the Mass

An absolute requirement of all good Catholics is the participation in the sacrifice of the Mass. Central to the faith of all Catholics is the Eucharist, i.e., a re-enactment of the Last Supper in the sacrifice of the Mass. In my grammar school years, weekday Mass started at 7a.m. My sister and I considered it a privilege to live so close to the church and to have the opportunity of making Mass and Holy Communion every day. We also ate a special breakfast at the school, because at that time it was a mortal sin (an offense that would send a person to hell) to receive communion if you had eaten any food after midnight. Later, this particular mortal sin was changed to eating no food for the three hours before receiving communion. We liked the special attention we received from the schoolteachers and our classmates when we ate breakfast at our desk during class. I was committed to attending Mass every school day. I rose an hour earlier than my classmates. This was one of the only ways I thought I could please the Lord. If I had studied the Scriptures, the Word of God would have caused me to question my daily practice. Concerning Christ's sacrifice and the continuing of it, the Scripture says, *"By the which will we are sanctified through the offering of the body of Jesus Christ once for all. And every priest standeth daily ministering and offering oftentimes the same sacrifices, which can never take away sins: But this man, after he had offered one sacrifice for sins for ever, sat down on the right hand of God."* (HEBREWS 10:10-12)

This section of Scripture can certainly be applied in reference to the daily Mass. The practice of the Mass, according to the Bible, should never take place; Christ's death on the cross for our sins was a one-time event, not to be ministered repeatedly. However, I, like most Catholics, was knowledgeable of my religion but ignorant of the Bible, and so I followed our tradition.

As a Catholic, I firmly believed what the Church taught: that the Eucharist (the bread and wine) was the actual body and blood of our Lord Jesus Christ. The Catholic Church teaches that the host is actually Christ's body and the wine is His real blood. They called this metamorphosis "transubstantiation." The Scripture teaches, *"...I will even set my face against that soul that eateth blood, and will cut him off from among his people...Therefore I said unto the children of Israel, no soul of you shall eat blood..."* (LEVITICUS 17:10,12) Regarding His Last Supper, it is important to read Christ's own words. His command in the institution of the Last Supper did not initiate a continual sacrifice but declared the institution of a remembrance of His finished work. His words declared, *"...'This cup is the New Testament in my blood: this do ye, as oft as ye drink it, in remembrance of me.' For as often as ye eat this bread, and drink this cup, ye do shew the Lord's death till he come."* (1 CORINTHIANS 11:25-26) The purpose is clearly given: to proclaim and publish His death. It is a remembrance of what Christ has done and suffered. However, in this remembrance, true believers are to declare His resurrection to be their life and the cause of their comfort and hope. "Who by him do believe in God, that raised him up from the dead, and gave him glory; that your faith and hope might be in God." (1 PETER 1:21)

After I received my first Holy Communion, I made a vow to God to never miss Mass on Sunday or any holy day of obligation. Catholic doctrine clearly states that missing Mass without good reason is a damnable sin. I went a step further, no matter how sick I was, or where I traveled, nothing would prevent me from attending Mass. Some Sundays, while running very high fever, I would crawl out of bed so I would not miss Mass. I believed this added to my good works, which were necessary for eternal life. I was the talk of the school making such sacrifices as a young boy. "What a great priest he could be for the Church," people whispered. Local Jesuit priests courted me in my high school years giving me special attention. They enticed me with their private wine cellars in the basement of their rectory and allowed me to play with their champion bird dogs. They even took me bird hunting on weekends. They explained to me how priests received salaries, retirement programs, and ample vacations. This looked like a good life to a high schooler considering a career. Jesus warned the top religious leaders of His day, *"Woe unto you, scribes and Pharisees, hypocrites! for ye compass sea and land to make one proselyte, and when he is made, ye make him twofold more the child of hell than yourselves."* (MATTHEW 23:15) In my early years, I entertained the real possibility of entering the priesthood when I became old enough.

Our Home and Holy Water

As a child, along with my parent's blessings, I gladly took the responsibility of keeping fresh holy water throughout our home. Attached to our bedroom light switches was a cradle that held holy water. It was common practice to dip our hand in this water as we turned on the light switch and then make the sign of the cross. As head altar boy at my parish, I had a good opportunity to obtain holy water. Looking back, this seems like a strange practice, but at the time we were taught to put great confidence in this as protection for our home. There is no such substance as holy water in the pages of the Bible. The traditions of Catholicism bring into the worship of God "holy water," oil and salt, charcoal and incense, and many other physical objects that dishonor the true worship of God.

Mary, St. Christopher, and Medals

The Rosary was another very special part of my life. The "Blessed Virgin Mary" dominated my prayer life. My prayers to Mary were continuous, day-by-day and year-by-year. The Rosary alone has fifty-three exaltations to Mary, and only eight to God. A central truth taught in the Bible is, *"For there is one God, and one mediator between God and men, the man Christ Jesus."* (1 TIMOTHY 2:5) The only way to God is through Jesus Christ, not

Mary. However, our home had several statues of Mary that we used as "aids to worship." I always wore my special St. Christopher medal. It had been purchased at the national Cathedral of the Immaculate Conception in Washington, D.C., and my favorite parish priest blessed it. I strongly believed it had supernatural powers until the pope admitted that there was no historical evidence that St. Christopher ever lived. I continued to wear it, because it also had on the reverse side an image of Mary. She, I reasoned, would protect me. I was ignorantly committing a terrible sin because of my lack of knowledge of the Second Commandment. *"Thou shalt not make unto thee any graven image, or any likeness of any thing that is in heaven above, or that is in the earth beneath, or that is in the water under the earth: Thou shalt not bow down thyself to them, nor serve them: for I the LORD thy God am a jealous God...."* (EXODUS 20:4-5) I continued to break God's Second Commandment every day. Ignorance is no excuse in man's courtroom or in God's judgment. I am attempting to tell you the truth of God's law, not the "commandments of men." This is one of God's blessed Commandments. Do not take my word for it, read it for yourself, even in a Catholic Bible.

Steadfastly a Catholic

While many of my close Catholic friends were questioning their faith concerning the history of the Church and its doctrine, I remained steadfast. Steadfast into my adult years, who was I to doubt or second guess the teaching of the "Mother Church?" However, the history, tradition, and loyalty of the "Saints" humbled me. Even though I studied world history, the Crusades, and the Inquisition (the torturing of Bible believers who spoke against the Roman Catholic Church—many being tortured and burned at the stake), I still would not speak against my Church.

In my world, a priest's word was held in high esteem, especially his opinions and understanding of spiritual matters. I, as all good Catholics, was taught to trust the "priest" to interpret Scripture and the Roman Catholic Church's doctrines. However, the Scripture teaches, *"...in vain do they worship me, teaching for doctrines the commandments of men. For laying aside the commandment of God, ye hold the tradition of men...Making the word of God of none effect through your tradition...."* (MARK 7:7,13)

Mankind loves tradition, and ignorantly, superstition. All ancient religions are steeped in delusions and rituals. Carefully, I asked the Jesuit priests about the millions tortured, killed, or burned at the stake by my Church. Their answers were unsettling, but I wrote it off, because my Church admitted she had made errors in the past. I trusted these men's word. Who was I to ponder or doubt the Church? I believed my Church was started by Christ Himself, Peter being the first pope.

Was Peter the First Pope?

One of the few verses we were taught to memorize in catechism was: *"And Simon Peter answered and said, 'Thou art the Christ, the Son of the living God.' And Jesus answered and said unto him, 'Blessed art thou, Simon Barjona: for flesh and blood hath not revealed it unto thee, but my Father which is in heaven. And I say also unto thee, That thou art Peter, and upon this rock I will build my church; and the gates of hell shall not prevail against it. And I will give unto thee the keys of the kingdom of heaven: and whatsoever thou shalt bind on earth shall be bound in heaven: and whatsoever thou shalt loose on earth shall be loosed in heaven.' Then charged he his disciples that they should tell no man that he was Jesus the Christ."* (MATTHEW 16:16-20)

We were taught to believe that Peter was authorized to start the Church by Christ Himself. We were taught to believe that all other Christian churches, religions, and denominations were offshoots of Roman Catholicism. This gave Catholics a great superiority over other faiths. No other Christian Church or world religion, in my understanding, could rank with my Church. What pride I had in my religion. Catholic teaching states that Peter was the first pope. (Note: The word pope is non-biblical and is a man-made title). The Catholic Church teaches that Peter is the rock in Matthew 16. What does the Bible say about this? This rock is to be the foundation of our faith; so let Scripture define who it is, Peter or Christ?

In the passage, we are taught that the disciples had a distinct knowledge of Christ expressed by Peter on their behalf. The Lord says that this knowledge—that He was "the Christ" and "the Son of the Living God"—was a revelation from His Father in heaven. It is this revelation, the Lord declared, that he was the Rock, or foundation stone, upon which He would build His Church. This was the very concluding subject of the Lord's summons to the disciples, *"Then charged he his disciples that they should tell no man that he was Jesus the Christ."* (MATTHEW 16:20) To hold the view that Peter himself is the Rock is to deliberately pervert the plain sense of the Lord's own words. The word "Peter" by definition means pebble, not rock.

The Bible repeatedly calls God "the Rock" of His people. For example, *"And they remembered that God was their rock…."* (PSALMS 78:35) *"O come, let us sing unto the LORD…the rock of our salvation."* (PSALMS 95:1) *"There is none holy as the LORD: for there is none beside thee: neither is there any rock like our God."* (1 SAMUEL 2:2) *"The LORD liveth; and blessed be my rock; and exalted be the God of the rock of my salvation."* (2 SAMUEL 22:47) The Apostle Paul proclaimed, *"… for they drank of that spiritual Rock that followed them: and that Rock was Christ."* (1 CORINTHIANS 10:4)

Even the Apostle Peter warned of a false "rock of offense," *"Unto you therefore which believe he is precious: but unto them which be disobedient, the stone which the builders disallowed, the same is made the head of the corner, and a stone of stumbling, and a rock of offence, even to them which stumble at the word, being disobedient: whereunto also they were appointed."* (1 PETER 2:7-8)

There is no doubt that the revelation of Jesus Christ, given by the Father, is "the rock" in Matthew 16, not Peter, or any pope. When faced with the truth, a choice has to be made. Ignorantly, I chose my religion over the Bible. I believed that Peter was the first pope and all the infallible teachings of the popes throughout history were equal to the Gospel. There have been over one thousand official edicts of popes. If I were to list some of them, you would be in shock with horror. Ignorantly, I had blind faith in this religious church system. My faith was not in Christ as the Way, the Truth, and the Life. My faith was in the Roman Catholic Church as the way, the truth, and the life.

My parents bought both my sister and me a Catholic Bible. I carried my Bible throughout my high school and college years. As most Catholics, we had great respect and fear of this "mystery book." In my years of Catholic schooling, I cannot remember one time ever being required to read the Bible. Maybe this is because it raised more questions than answers relating to the Catholic Church. Instead, we were taught to trust the priest to interpret the Bible for us. One official catechism declaration that we were required to memorize taught us the Catholic stance as it relates to the Bible and tradition. It states, *"The scriptures and tradition are one in the same but when contradictions arise, tradition is to rule over the Bible."* The Scriptures teach against this position in many places. For example, the final commandment of the Bible, in the final book, and in the final chapter is, *"…and let him that heareth say, come and let him that is athirst come. And whosoever will, let him take the water of life freely. For I*

testify unto every man that heareth the words of the prophecy of this book, If
any man shall add unto these things, God shall add unto him the plagues that
are written in this book: And if any man shall take away from the words of
the book of this prophecy, God shall take away his part out of the book of life,
and out of the holy city, and from the things which are written in this book."
(REVELATION 22:17-19) God uses men to tell other men the good news—and
the bad news—of His Holy Word. I have a responsibility to warn you of
these things as I tell you my story.

My Fellowship with Non-Catholics

My college years took a distinctive career path. I got very involved in
athletics and had an active social life, therefore, my desire to become a
priest dwindled; but my love and devotion of the Church stayed strong.
My first association with Bible-believing Christians, or non-Catholics, was
when I joined the Fellowship of Christian Athletes and Campus Crusade
for Christ at the University of Alabama. It was strange for me to see people
carrying Bibles, quoting Scripture, and having devotions around Bible passages. This was a peculiar lifestyle for someone whose only exposure was
the Catholic faith. I could see a zeal for God at these get-togethers where
genuine openhearted prayer abounded. It is usual for Catholics to recite
from a book of prayers rather than pray from an open heart—directly to
God. This new form of worship fascinated me.

I started going regularly to the Christian fellowships but also continued
to attend Mass. I can remember many Bible believing Christians asking
me why I was Catholic and I jumped at the chance to defend my faith and
exalt my Church. Although a few people did make me question my faith
in my religion, a few words with a priest always comforted and led me
back into their fold. The Church teaches that the priests must interpret
Scripture for us. They were the experts and I was taught to trust their interpretation. After all, were they not the vicars of Christ? Many years of
schooling and special training convinced me to trust them. After talking
to a priest, his words would reinforce my faith and keep me loyal. Christian speakers on the campus pricked my heart with Bible-based messages.
My soul longed for what they had; surely, I could search and find that kind
of faith and peace in the Church. Some Scripture verses which impressed
me were: *"...hath he [Christ] quickened together with him, having forgiven*
you all trespasses," (COLOSSIANS 2:13) *"...and the blood of Jesus Christ his Son*

cleanseth us from all sin." (1 JOHN 1:7) Another was, *"Therefore being justified by faith, we have peace with God through our Lord Jesus Christ: By whom also we have access by faith into this grace wherein we stand, and rejoice in hope of the glory of God."* (ROMANS 5:1-2)

How could these verses be true? I believed it was necessary to confess sins to a Catholic priest before someone could be absolved from sin. What about a forgotten sin? Bible-based Christians claimed to have forgiveness of "all" sins. They professed to be born-again and to already have obtained salvation. I reflected on the confidence and freedom they seemed to possess. I had to keep record of my sins for confession. After one campus meeting, I was bold enough to ask if I could talk with the speaker. I felt compelled to meet him afterwards in his hotel room. He questioned me about my salvation and put me in conviction for a short while. He showed me in the Bible where it says, *"For whosoever shall keep the whole law, and yet offend in one point, he is guilty of all."* (JAMES 2:10) I asked, "You mean one small sin is like committing murder or adultery?" "Sin is sin" was his answer. The Bible does not teach such a thing as mortal or venial sin. This is a man-made concept, created by religion.

A Challenge from a Christian Girl

I started dating a Christian girl who had love and zeal for the Lord Jesus Christ like none I had ever seen. She questioned my faith and my salvation. "When were you saved?" she asked. "Saved" was a strange word to me; it was not found in any Catholic vocabulary, even though it is used over two hundred times in the Bible. This girl gave me my first Christian Bible. She highlighted key verses, and I challenged myself to read. There is power in God's Word; I felt the conviction of the Holy Spirit as I read it. What a testimony this Christian girl was when she stopped dating me because I was not a true believer. The Bible teaches, *"Be ye not unequally yoked together with unbelievers: for what fellowship hath righteousness with unrighteousness? and what communion hath light with darkness?"* (1 CORINTHIANS 6:14) That passage, later in my life, gloriously guided me to my wife and later to my business partners. I now understand what it means to be equally yoked together with Christ at the helm.

Most Catholics consider themselves spiritual people, as did I, but now looking back, I was on the outside looking in. I now understand I was imitating the Christian life. Catholics tend to believe their faith is a private thing, not to be examined, but the Bible says: *"Examine yourselves, whether ye be in the faith; prove your own selves. Know ye not your own selves, how that Jesus Christ is in you, except ye be reprobates? But I trust that ye shall know that we are not reprobates."* (2 CORINTHIANS 13:5-6) Now I realize that in my former faith I was a reprobate. When have you examined yourself in the light of God's Word and not man's religion? The Holy Spirit will lead you to only one truth.

I often caught myself in a wrestling match with others trying to convince them I was a good Catholic and that all good Catholics were saved. Bible-based Christians continued to doubt my salvation. This greatly troubled me, but I still kept faith in my Church and tradition. Jesus said, *"...full well ye reject the commandment of God, that ye may keep your own tradition," "...Making the word of God of none effect through your tradition."* (MARK 7:9,13) Verse 13 has been quoted twice in this testimony for a good reason, for there was where I lived.

A Christian Business Couple Led Me to the Bible

My adult years provided me success in private business. I recruited and trained many talented people who marketed health products throughout the country. One of my most talented managers was a preacher who had a rare zeal and excitement about life and the Bible. As I spent time with him, he questioned me about my salvation. He always seemed to carry a Bible wherever he went. That was strange and uncomfortable for me. After a business meeting, I found myself at his home with him and his wife. Unknowingly, they had been praying for an opportunity to witness to me about my salvation. Only a few times had someone taken out a Bible and showed me "truth." They took me to Scriptures such as: *"Brethren, my heart's desire and prayer to God for Israel is, that they might be saved."* (ROMANS 10:1) It was their desire for A. J. Krause to be saved! I had a zeal but not according to Bible knowledge. I had looked for righteousness in a religion and not in the Person of Christ Jesus. *"For Christ is the end of the law for righteousness to every one that believeth."* (ROMANS 10:4) I was under the law and this verse spoke to my heart. I was under rules and rituals, imposed by a religion, to gain "my" righteousness. I was keeping the law for "my" righteousness. My faith and confidence was partly in Christ and partly in keeping the Church law and in living a good life, not "solely" in the finished work of the Savior on the cross. Nowhere in the Bible did it teach me to go to Mass or any church in order to have eternal life. It declared the opposite, *"Not by works of righteousness which we have done, but according to his mercy he saved us."* (TITUS 2:5) Salvation and eternal life are God's gift. *"For by grace are ye saved through faith; and that not of yourselves: it is the gift of God: Not of works, lest any man should boast."* (EPHESIANS 2:8-9) Listen, once I could boast in my supposed good works. I had had great pride in my faith. However, having a strong faith in any religion will send a person to hell. Only faith in Jesus Christ will save a person.

My Day of Salvation

This Christian couple witnessed to me out of the Scriptures, but I quoted to them a memorized catechism statement. The words of the catechism, however, could not match the Word of God. Verse after verse revealed that my religion and faith were not based on the Bible. This totally stripped my faith in my Church. I had always believed my Church was biblically based, now I saw that this was not so. The choice was clear, either my salvation was in my religion, or my salvation rested on Christ and His sacrifice on the cross. It could not be both. I went home to a lonely house and that night lay in bed looking up at the ceiling. I truly examined myself, realizing I had never in my life had a time where I put "all" my faith and trust in Jesus Christ alone. My confidence was always in my good works and the sacraments of the Roman Catholic Church. I especially had confidence in Holy Communion and in keeping the Commandments. I had hoped to persevere with enough grace at my death to obtain heaven. But there before my eyes were the words of the Lord, *"...'Verily, verily, I say unto thee, Except a man be born again, he cannot see the kingdom of God.' 'Verily, verily, I say unto thee, except a man be born of water and of the Spirit, he cannot enter into the kingdom of God.'"* (JOHN 3:3,5)

At that time, four verses stood out in my mind. I had been shown them in the Scriptures, *"Moreover, brethren, I declare unto you the gospel which I preached unto you, which also ye have received, and wherein ye stand; By which also ye are saved, if ye keep in memory what I preached unto you, unless ye have believed in vain. For I delivered unto you first of all that which I also received, how that Christ died for our sins according to the scriptures; And that he was buried, and that he rose again the third day according to the scriptures."* (1 CORINTHIANS 15:1-4) Christ had died for my sins. All my sins! The heart of the Gospel is contained in these five words, Christ died for my sins! I was always worried about having them confessed. Another verse that stood out in my mind from the Scriptures was one of the most quoted verses in the Bible. *"For whosoever shall call upon the name of the Lord shall be saved."* (Romans 10:13) "Whosoever shall call," did that mean even me? In the privacy of my bedroom, between God and myself, I called upon the Lord Jesus Christ believing that He would save me. Why? Because I had His Word on it, not religion's word or man's word, but God's Holy Word.

January 22, 1981 was the day I received the salvation God had provided me. God saved me! *"We then, as workers together with him, beseech you also that ye receive not the grace of God in vain. (For he saith, I have heard thee in a time accepted, and in the day of salvation have I succoured thee: behold, now is the accepted time; behold, now is the day of salvation.)"* (2 Corinthians 6:1-2) Nothing did I do but put my faith in what He had done for me. I trusted Christ's sacrifice as payment for my sins. The Bible teaches there is a day of birth, a day of death, and a day of salvation. Remember the eternal commandment, *"Ye must be born again."* (John 3:7) When was your day of salvation?

Seek the Lord and His Peace

The Bible says, *"…the peace of God, which passeth all understanding, shall keep your hearts and minds through Christ Jesus."* (Philippians 4:7) I now have that peace. *"Therefore if any man be in Christ, he is a new creature: old things are passed away; behold, all things are become new."* (2 Corinthians 5:17) All things are new, now! This is my heart's desire for you! Why would I take the time to put this in writing? Many of you have a love and zeal for God like I did, but unknowingly, not according to Bible knowledge. *"In the beginning was the Word, and the Word was with God, and the Word was God…and the Word became flesh."* (John 1:1,14) Put your faith in the Word, i.e., the Lord Jesus Christ, and not in the word of any man. *"…it pleased God by the foolishness of preaching to save them that believe."* (1 Corinthians 1:21) *"Believe on the Lord Jesus Christ, and thou shalt be saved, and thy house."* (Acts 16:31) *"Trust in the LORD with all thine heart; and lean not unto thine own understanding. In all thy ways acknowledge him, and he shall direct thy paths."* (Proverbs 3:5-6) Ask God for the truth! His Word is His promise! That is why His Word, Christ Jesus, became flesh!

When a man desires truth, seeks God for answers, and is willing to forsake all, God will lead him into His truth. The Lord said in the Scriptures, *"If any of you lack wisdom, let him ask of God, that giveth to all men liberally, and upbraideth not*; and it shall be given him."* (JAMES 1:5) This was my plea. I asked God and He answered my search. A man can "know" that he has eternal life while living on this side of eternity. The Lord's word in Scripture says, *"These things have I written unto you that believe on the name of the Son of God; that ye may know that ye have eternal life, and that ye may believe on the name of the Son of God."* (1 JOHN 5:13) I had never known with confidence I could have eternal life. Now, I know. A personal testimony will be required of all men at the Judgment Seat of Christ. Christ Jesus Himself is my surety! My eternal destiny hangs on my faith in Christ's perfect sacrifice…and only that has made me right with God. Your eternal destiny likewise must rest secure, for *"…it is appointed unto men once to die, but after this the judgment."* (HEBREWS 9:27)

—A.J. KRAUSE

*Please feel free to call me with any questions,
toll free: 1-888-643-7374, or email me at: AJKrause1@aol.com*

---

* 'Upbraideth not' means that God will not scold us on the contrary, He will give without reservation.

LAURA M. GORECTKE

Accepted in the Beloved

MY FAMILY HAS ALWAYS BEEN CLOSELY KNIT TOGETHER. I ALWAYS KNEW my parents loved me and wanted the best for me. However, they were my parents; they were supposed to love me. Sundays were family days; we would get all dressed up and attend Catholic church together. Mass was only one hour in length, but it seemed longer to me as a child.

Being Catholic was just part of who we were; it was never something I questioned. However, growing up I had mixed feelings about the religious rituals associated with being a Catholic. Both of my parents were raised Catholic and they were determined to raise their daughters in the "one true church." Since I learned that all of the rituals were necessary, I never outwardly complained or rebelled against participating in them. However, inwardly I would dread the time spent at church. The ten-minute homily by the priest seemed like it lasted forever. When my sister, Allison, was born, I liked the fact that we could go into the crying room and look at books. We did not have to be on our best behavior since it was segregated from

the main congregation. As I got older, I would daydream during the homily, to make the time go faster.

Sacraments and Tradition

My First Communion was a special event. I truly enjoyed participating in the sacrament for two reasons. First, communion is the most important part of the Mass, and participation is essential for Catholics. It made me feel grown up, since you had to be at least seven years old to participate. Second, I was also excited that I was able to wear a special dress. A young girl's dream came true when she wore a dress that resembled a wedding gown! I thought I understood the significance of the event at the time, but I really understood only what people told me. A nun that helped us prepare for the actual taking of the host* mentioned that it would taste differently for our First Communion because the priest blessed it; therefore, it would be the body of Jesus Christ. We practiced with unconsecrated hosts. The day of my First Communion, I was convinced the host had a different taste.

My "First Reconciliation," or my first time at confession, was a somber time for me. I had no problem realizing I had sins to confess; I was just scared about talking to the priest. I also worried about what penance he would give me to make up for my sins. The actual sacrament was much easier than I expected, but it was not like the enjoyable experience of First Communion.

Holidays and holy days required extra church attendance. I did not realize until I was older that my parents did not make us go to all of the required holy days. However, Easter and Christmas meant attendance at Mass was mandatory. I enjoyed the Christmas Eve service because the church geared it toward children and it included a skit and a "parade" with homemade drums for baby Jesus. I dreaded Easter week with Mass attendance that lasted for four days straight, including a two-hour Mass Saturday evening. It seemed endless!

Our family members and most of our friends were Catholic, so I did not have a lot of exposure to other religious backgrounds. For the most part, I enjoyed my time with other Catholics. One main exception was the time I spent at Catholic school in first and second grades. I was a shy child, and although I had friends, I never adjusted to the snobby attitude of a majority of the students. I was more comfortable with my neighborhood friends. After I switched to public school, I found myself enjoying school much more.

Through my religious upbringing, I learned that there was a God out there somewhere. I learned that He was holy and that I was not. Since I was not holy, I had to do numerous works through the church to earn God's grace. Although I knew Christ had died on the cross, I did not real-

* The wafer offered at communion

ly understand what that had to do with salvation. I focused more on what actions were required of me. In my view of God, I did not think He cared about someone as unimportant as me. I figured He was too big to care about the details of my life.

Need for Acceptance

As I grew older, I began to feel the need for acceptance. I wanted the kids at school to notice and accept me. I tried to get their attention by wearing the right clothes and doing what they liked. In fifth grade, I wanted to break my leg and be on crutches. My parents could not figure out that desire. What they did not realize was that one of the really popular girls had broken her leg and was on crutches. The crutches brought her even more attention, attention I craved. If my peers did not see me as someone special, then I believed I was not a special person. It did not matter

what my family thought, because they were supposed to love me.

These feelings of inadequacy caused me to question a lot and try new things. I had always been a good student, and I continued to excel in academics because that was one area I felt confident. In middle school I tried athletics and choir, and while I was not a natural at either, I enjoyed the activities. My friendships also changed as we all started growing up, and that brought a new level of uncertainty. My parents were willing to let me occasionally attend other churches with friends and I found myself listening. It was a time of much searching, but few answers.

One of the more drastic things I tried was getting involved in a Catholic group called *Opus Dei*. I did not really understand what I was getting into; I just knew the group made me feel good. It was essentially a group for "super" Catholics; i.e., lay people who wanted to do a better job of living out their faith. Through this group, I spent time in service projects and religious lessons. I also spent time at a home they had downtown. In the

home was a chapel that people considered holier than most local churches because the Pope had ordained the officiating priest. His ordination
was considered more significant than priests who were just ordained by
bishops. The other thing this chapel had was a black cross that had been
blessed by the Pope. Each time you left the chapel, if you kissed the cross,
it was five hundred less days in purgatory. I was not sure if I believed this,
but I remember kissing the cross just in case. In fact, sometimes I would
kiss it twice in the hope I would get one thousand days less! The problem
with my involvement with *Opus Dei* is that the good feelings would not
last. It did not solve my problem. I had to keep doing more good works
to keep feeling good.

None of what I tried truly solved my problem. I struggled with feeling
inadequate through the early years of high school. I hid it well at times, but
the self-doubt always seemed to surface again. Then, "good news" changed
the way I looked at myself.

Exposure to the Gospel

My parents knew I was questioning a lot in my early teen years. They
also knew that sometimes it helps to talk to someone other than your parents. One Sunday afternoon, mom invited a woman over to talk to Sarah
(my sister) and me about religion. Mrs. Mierow was a person we babysat
for as well as our neighbor. Our family had a lot of respect for the Mierows.
Surprisingly, Mrs. Mierow was not a Catholic. My parents were questioning enough about the Catholic Church at this point that they were open to
hearing about other denominations and allowing us to do the same.

Mrs. Mierow came over on March 26, 1988. I dreaded the talk because
I thought religion was boring, and I had already sat through an hour of
church that morning. However, from the moment she began, I found
myself listening intently. What she shared was nothing like what I heard
in our church. She told me that God loved me and had a plan for my life.
This was good news. For the first time, I realized that the God that was out
there somewhere cared about me and thought I was important. She then
went on to point out that we have a problem; man is sinful and separated
from a holy God. She shared a verse from the book of Romans, *"For all
have sinned, and come short of the glory of God."* (ROMANS 3:23)

I had no problem believing I was a sinner because I was well aware of the
many times I had fallen short. Mrs. Mierow explained that sin separates

us from God and that He could not allow anything imperfect into heaven. Because of my sin, I deserved to die. *"For the wages of sin is death...."* (ROMANS 6:23A) This part scared me. If what she said was true, I realized I would not go to heaven because of the sins I had committed. I also realized that eternity is a long time, and I did not want to spend eternity in hell!

I think she sensed my fear, because she went on to explain that God still loved me, even though I had sinned. In fact, He loved me so much that He sent His Son, Jesus Christ, to die on the cross and pay the penalty for my sins so that I could be reconciled to God. She then read the entire verse, *"For the wages of sin is death; but the gift of God is eternal life through Jesus Christ our Lord."* (ROMANS 6:23B) She also read, *"But God commendeth his love toward us, in that, while we were yet sinners, Christ died for us."* (ROMANS 5:8)

All I had to do was place my trust in the Person of the Lord Jesus Christ who had died on the cross to pay the penalty for "my" sins, and then by God's grace, and His grace alone, I would be saved. *"For God so loved the world that He gave His only begotten Son, that whosoever believeth in Him should not perish but have everlasting life."* (JOHN 3:16) Mrs. Mierow had me insert my name into the verse to emphasize that this was true for me: For God so loved Laura that He gave His only begotten Son, that if Laura believes in Him, she will not perish but have everlasting life. In order to be saved, it is necessary for people to place their full trust in the Lord Jesus Christ and His substitutionary death, which paid the penalty for their sins, excluding any good works.

At that moment, I realized I would spend eternity in heaven with God! None of the works I had done—going to church, participating in sacraments, even kissing a cross—would do anything to save me. *"For by grace are ye saved through faith; and that not of yourselves: it is the gift of God: Not of works, lest any man should boast."* (EPHESIANS 2:8, 9) In fact, all my works were like dirty rags to God. *"But we are all as an unclean thing, and all our righteousnesses are as filthy rags."* (ISAIAH 64:6A) I had never heard anyone talk about God the way Mrs. Mierow did. She talked about having a personal relationship with Jesus Christ, rather than trying to earn His acceptance. It was so appealing compared to the works salvation on which I had been raised. It made perfect sense after all my searching. I knew I needed Christ in my life because I did not want to be separated from God. That day by God's grace, I believed on the Lord Jesus Christ alone as my Savior. I thanked Him for His gift of salvation. I was fourteen years old and a freshman in high school. Along with Mrs. Mierow's explanation, Sarah shared that she had been saved the summer before at a Christian camp.

Walking Slowly

My walk with the Lord started slowly. My family was still attending the Catholic Church, and in my newfound faith I was yet unable to discern that the salvation message at the Catholic Church was not the same as what I now believed. I think I just thought I had missed hearing it during all those years. In fact, I did not realize that my parents were not saved! Mrs. Mierow had encouraged me to read the Bible and pray in order to grow in my faith. However, I had never really read the Bible before, and I was not sure where to begin. Most of the time, I did not even try. Through some encouragement from my family, I started attending a youth group, and during the summers, Christian camps. Although my parents were not yet saved, they had started to question the Catholic Church. Besides, they wanted their daughter to hang out with the "good" kids who would be a positive influence.

At youth group and Christian camps, discussion centered on the Bible, and the students seemed excited about what it said. Most of the kids even knew where the books of the Bible were located and how to find their favorite verses. I was amazed! They got me excited, and I tried it. I began to read the Word of God more, and more often, and I realized it had a lot to say about me. The most important thing I learned was that it did not matter if other kids accepted me, because God had accepted me. He had created me to be a special person with a special purpose. As challenges arose, my favorite verse became, *"Nay, in all these things we are more than conquerors through him that loved us."* (Romans 8:37) It was so reassuring to know God is sovereign and in control of all circumstances.

Questioning Roman Catholicism

My junior year in high school was the year I started confirmation classes at the Catholic Church. My parents taught one class, and I attended another. Little did we know that the classes would be life changing for our family. Confirmation is an important sacrament in the Catholic Church. By participating, you are saying you agree with the doctrines of the Catholic Church and, as a result, the church accepts you as an adult in the faith. The classes quickly brought many questions to mind. We had been given Catholic Bibles to use in the classes. In one class, the teachers asked us to look up our favorite Bible verse. I was the only one who could find a verse. In another class, the instructors spent time debating with two girls who proclaimed to be atheists. What bothered me the most was that none of this, had an effect on the outcome of the classes. As long as you participated, atheist or not, the church would confirm you in the faith. What you actually believed did not have any bearing on the matter. I began to question from where some of this teaching came. My parents started having some of the same questions in their class. They had also started reading their Catholic Bibles and attending some Christian Bible studies.

While fighting against a sex education curriculum in our public school, my parents were getting to know more Christians and the impact of biblical thinking. Because of these new contacts, they had two believers come as speakers for their confirmation class. During this time, my parents were saved, and my youngest sister, Allison, was saved soon after them. My questions only added to the questions my parents were having about Roman Catholicism. Never one to make an important decision without researching the issue, my dad decided we would attend a more conservative Catholic church first. That did not last long, because the same questions kept popping up. He ended up finding a thick book on Catholic doctrine. He studied it to make sure what we were finding in the local Catholic churches was what the true Roman Catholic Church taught. What he found was a clear picture of salvation by works, completely contrary to what the Bible said about salvation. *"Now to him that worketh is the reward not reckoned of grace but of debt. But to him that worketh not, but believeth on him that justifieth the ungodly, his faith is counted for righteousness."* (ROMANS 4:4, 5) Finally, he realized our family needed to leave the Catholic Church if we were going to grow in our faith.

Growth

After their salvation, my parents offered me the option of attending a nearby private school where my sisters would end up going. With one year of high school remaining, I decided to graduate from public school. Besides, the more I learned, the more I desired to share Jesus Christ with my unsaved friends. I was so zealous that I often did not share my faith very graciously. I know I offended several friends. Thankfully, they were gracious towards me. They realized that something major had happened in my life to stir up this kind of excitement. Although they recognized a change, I did not find too many people willing to hear more about the gospel. However, I did find encouragement in the Christian friends I was getting to know in youth group.

Following high school, I decided to attend a Christian college. Grove City College is a small Christian college in western Pennsylvania. I had not planned to go that far from home, but God directed me there and really used that time in my life. He stretched and grew me through many experiences. Not only was my faith strengthened, but I also learned to be more outgoing, and I discovered that my faith could be shared in a non-combative way. I took two mission trips during my college years, which reinforced these lessons. The Christian classes were also a blessing. Although I majored in accounting, I still took several Bible classes and learned a lot through the Christian perspective emphasized in all classes. For example, biblical ethics were taught as part of my accounting classes.

The Lord also used my Roman Catholic background when I met Catholics that also attended the school. Because of my time in the Catholic Church, I was able to more effectively witness and have fruitful discussions about the gospel. I led several Bible studies in my dorm room that were helpful for all involved. We would look up topics or discuss issues of the faith using the Bible as the standard. I was learning how to defend and share my newfound faith by relying on the Holy Spirit and using the Word of God.

Discernment and Baptism

God saved everyone in our immediate family within a three-year period. We now realize what a miracle that was. At the time, I believe the Lord used this to encourage us and help us grow in our faith. We were faced with many challenges as new believers. Two major ones were negative reactions from relatives, and the other was unclear teaching. Our Catholic relatives did not take well the news that we were leaving the Catholic Church. They were offended, and some went so far as to tell us we were going to hell for leaving the "one true church." We found ourselves excluded from family events and purposely distanced. It was hard, but it only made us cling to each other all the more.

After we left the Catholic Church, we had trouble finding a good Bible church. The first church we attended was extremely legalistic. It seemed comfortable at first, because legalism was not that different from the works salvation we were used to. However, we eventually realized their view on some issues was not biblical. For example, the pastor told us we did not need baptism as believers because we were baptized as infants. He present- ed baptism as part of a covenant relationship within the family and not as one of the things a believer was required to do. He never clearly presented it as an outward sign of our inward faith.

As we became more aware of the legalism, we left that church and again began searching for a Bible church. It was a difficult search – in and out of a number of churches when doctrinal error revealed itself. We discovered that the majority of churches today do not teach clearly from the Word of God. In the meantime, the Lord put our family in contact with sound Bible teaching through an out-of-state tape ministry and solid local Bible study. Audiotapes from these teachers, and occasional Bible conferences, enabled us to grow in our faith until the Lord brought us to a church home. Through our own study, we understood what the Bible teaches on a number of topics, including baptism. It became obvious that baptism was an outward sign of inward faith, and therefore could only take place after someone was old enough to "understand and believe" the gospel.

During my sophomore year at college, while preparing for a mission's trip, I thought about how I had never been baptized as a believer. It was something I wanted to do before I went overseas for the summer. During a phone call with my parents, they mentioned that they too had been think- ing about being baptized. They decided to talk to my sisters and see if they were also interested. They were, and on May 23, 1993, we were all baptized together. It was a memorable experience, for the first time we all had to write and talk about our testimonies. We realized just how much the Lord had been working in our family to bring us all to a point of salvation in such a short time. It was one more way the Lord encouraged us.

Rebellion and Uncertainty

After graduating from college, I returned to Milwaukee for work. I wanted to be near my family, though I knew I would miss my college friends. The first few years after college brought a major challenge to my faith. I had a job that essentially took over my life, and I was trying to establish myself as an adult outside my parent's home. Part of how I tried to accomplish this was by resisting my parents when they tried to share how they had grown in their faith while I had been away at college. I was also trying to fit in at work, once again seeking acceptance. Since being a Christian would have made me stand out, I hid that fact pretty well. I pushed the limits of what was acceptable behavior in order to fit in. I started pulling away from church and Bible study more and more. It was the wrong route to take, but because of my stubbornness, it took several years for me to realize it.

Two things helped me see the problem with the way I was living. First, I met a believer at work. She showed me how you can live your faith and still survive in a competitive work environment. Second, I was lonely and missing true fellowship with believers. On a couple occasions, my parents had challenged me to take my walk with the Lord more seriously. Although I hated to admit it, they were right. I started attending a Bible study in my parents' home. I went sporadically at first, mainly because I did not want my parents to think they could now tell me what to do. I also had many other "things" filling up my schedule. I changed jobs and gradually made time for this Bible study and personal time with the Lord. More importantly, I realized how much I was enjoying the teaching and fellowship. Once again, I had the peace and joy of growing in my walk with the Lord!

Blessings

The Bible study group eventually became a church, and the Lord used it to bless me. The doctrinally sound teaching helped me build a foundation for my faith on the Rock—Jesus Christ. Things like the importance of a clear gospel message, eternal security,* and learning to really dig  into the Word of God have been invaluable. Although we had met previously, I got to know my future husband, Mike, at church.

---

* Knowing you will never lose your salvation

All the teaching has helped us with our newest challenge—raising our children: Katie and David. Although they are young, we want them raised with the knowledge of our Lord and Savior, Jesus Christ. We love them and want them to spend eternity with us!

My life has not been easy since I became a Christian. In fact, Christ guarantees it will not. *"Yea, and all that will live godly in Christ Jesus shall suffer persecution."* (2TIMOTHY 3:12) My family and I have trials and testings, and we stand out as different from the world. However, I have learned that the other option, hiding your faith, removes the peace and joy the Lord produces in the lives of those who honor Him. *"Therefore, my beloved brethren, be ye stedfast, unmoveable, always abounding in the work of the Lord, forasmuch as ye know that your labour is not in vain in the Lord."* (1CORINTHIANS 15:58) The Lord Jesus Christ gave everything for me, the least I can do is respond in thankfulness that my life can now be used to serve Him, fulfilling the perfect plan He has for me. *"For we are his workmanship, created in Christ Jesus unto good works, which God hath before ordained that we should walk in them."* (EPHESIANS 2:10)

—LAURA GORECTKE

Please feel free to email me at: mlgorectke@yahoo.com

MICHAEL F. SCOTTO

Do You Read the Scriptures?

I HAD NEVER SERIOUSLY STUDIED THE SCRIPTURES AND DID NOT KNOW anyone who did. I had seen my brother reading a Bible in his bed when we were boys, but when I had tried to read it, I often found myself more confused than before I began. However, there I was, looking for answers, stuck in chapter 46 of Isaiah, and torn between two worlds.

> *Bel boweth down, Nebo stoopeth, their idols were upon the beasts, and upon the cattle: your carriages were heavy loaden; they are a burden to the weary beast. They stoop, they bow down together; they could not deliver the burden, but themselves are gone into captivity. To whom will ye liken me, and make me equal, and compare me, that we may be like? They lavish gold out of the bag, and weigh silver in the balance, and hire a goldsmith; and he maketh it a god: they fall down, yea, they worship. They bear him upon the shoulder, they carry him, and set him in his place, and he standeth; from his place shall he not remove: yea, one shall cry unto him, yet can he not answer, nor save him out of his trouble. Remember this, and shew yourselves men: bring it again to mind, O ye transgressors. Remember the former things of old: for I am God, and there is none else; I am God, and there is none like me, Declaring the end from the beginning, and from ancient times the things that are not yet done, saying, My counsel shall stand, and I will do all my pleasure: Calling a ravenous bird from the east, the man that executeth my counsel from a far country: yea, I have spoken it, I will also bring it to pass; I have purposed it, I will also do it. Hearken unto me, ye stouthearted, that are far from righteousness: I bring near my righteousness; it shall not be far off, and my salvation shall not tarry: and I will place salvation in Zion for Israel my glory.*

I was twenty-five years old and a respected Religious Education teacher in my parish. I had a Catholic pedigree and a list of accomplishments longer than anyone else I knew my age. Why did this passage in Isaiah trouble me so? I thought it had the comforting words I sought. I longed to be sure that God was surely in control of my life and that He could certainly *"declare the end from the beginning."* (ISAIAH 46:10) I had done everything right, and yet, I found the world around me collapsing and my mind sinking into despair. Was I being "stouthearted"? Surely, God would answer the cries of one who had diligently studied the doctrines of the Church of Rome as I had. Bad things are not supposed to happen to good people. Is that not right?

What was all this about bowing down before idols? What did God mean by *"I bring near my righteousness"?* (ISAIAH 46:13) I had never read the Scriptures like this before. For nearly ten years, I had read the Scriptures solely to defend the religion into which I was born.

After three years together, suddenly my fiancé was gone. We had planned our futures, from our wedding in her parents' new church, to how we would raise our children. Then one day she announced it was over and that she never wanted to see me again. What was this? It made no sense. I had served God, had been a voice for morality, had defended the One True Church, and supported all the right causes. I desperately needed answers.

This strange trip into introspection resulted in a schismatic attempt to join two opposing worlds. My first reaction was to delve more deeply into my faith. I began dedicating most of my free time to the veneration of the Saints and spent countless hours lighting candles and praying before the altar in my parish. I stuffed cash into the collection boxes under the statues of the Saints.

Looking for Answers

In my desire to achieve peace, I found in the Virgin Mary my greatest hope. I began praying to the statue of her in the churchyard and vowed to say the Rosary every day. I began to attend Friday morning Rosary prayer meetings in the church and sang the songs I had learned as a boy for the May Day Procession. I placed my hopes and dreams in Mary's intercessory powers, and not willing to leave any stone unturned, I went to confession and studied the efficacy of a Novena.

I then tried to solidify my faith by studying the Catholic Encyclopedia and the textbooks I had taught others from in my Religious Education classes. I rediscovered the tape series I had that featured Scott Hahn and Father Mitchell Pacwa which laid out a Catholic apologetic approach to the Evangelical Christian's argument—a tape series I had purchased after my many run-ins with "born-again" Christians in college.

I befriended a priest who noticed my devotion at the noon Mass. I usually stayed after Mass to light candles and pick up literature that had been left in the pews by The Knights of Columbus. Despite all these efforts, my faith was no more solid.

The other part of my journey involved reading the Scriptures. My brother had bought me a Bible for Christmas when I was twelve. I used to read it during the endless hours of kneeling before the Monstrance during Perpetual Adoration (a week long "grace-laden" worship of the Eucharist). We occasionally opened the Bible in religion class, but we never strayed too far from the stories known to most students of western civilization.

Resting on My Laurels

I had been warned as a child that I was not to study the Bible on my own. I was certainly to avoid such things as the book of Revelation. The Roman Church teaches that the Pope and the Magisterium are the sole interpreters of Scripture. However, I needed answers, and I needed them fast. I had lost focus of a future, which days before had been bright; everything else in life, compared to this, seemed trivial. I filled every waking moment with religious pursuits. When I was not at the church, or reading from the Scriptures, I was seeking religion on the radio and on television. While at work, as I sat at my desk, I tuned in Bible teachers on the radio like Oliver B. Greene, J. Vernon McGee, Donald Grey Barnhouse, and Woodrow Kroll.

I had always been wary of Evangelical Christian preachers and viewed most of them as charlatans who preached a free ticket to heaven for personal gain. These men on the radio, however, were teaching something quite different. They were expounding the Word of God as though it were a living document. Their knowledge of all the Scriptures, from Genesis to Revelation, was impressive—for Protestants. They spoke with authority, reflecting their stated belief that the Bible was the absolute, infallible, and direct Word of God. They taught that the Bible was accurate in every way.

This opposed everything I had been taught—and none of them asked for money!

This was significant, because I had just finished a semester at our parish teaching that the Bible had historical and scientific errors in it.[1] This was nothing new; I had learned to marry the Bible to evolution in Catholic school. The Paulist Order (in a book by Richard Chilson) taught that atheists and agnostics could be admitted to the Kingdom so long as they "tried to love others."[2] I knew that these were not necessarily authoritative books, although Chilson's book carries the Imprimatur of the Archbishop of Newark. However, I did not trust the Paulists, a more liberal Order. I had attended grade school and served as an altar boy in the Archdiocese of Philadelphia under the auspices of John Cardinal Krol, and due to his influence, I considered myself a Papalist. Although at Vatican II the Church had approved of the Host's placement into the hands of the faithful in the Liturgy of the Eucharist, I had refused to change. Even as a boy, I preferred to take the Host by mouth and only from the hand of a priest.

Rescuing the Diocese of Charlotte

My family's move to North Carolina a number of years before my crisis of faith, and our membership in a more liberal Paulist parish there, strengthened my resolve to defend the exclusivity of the only church that I considered to be the true church, the one I believed was founded by Christ Himself.

I had dropped out of my ninth grade Religious Education class because I found the teachers to be unlearned and the subject matter simplistic. The next year I joined the tenth grade class and proceeded to be the class "correction officer," questioning the source and validity of the lessons taught. I had avoided the parish youth group. I found it to be just as sophomoric as my classes. I had also accepted a role as an acolyte,[3] not exactly a position that stirs up admiration from fellow teenagers.

In the eleventh grade, I was urged by my mother to attend a beach trip with the youth group. The social outlet was attractive to me since I had not assimilated well into southern culture. The youth group was a mix of

1   *Developing Faith Series*, Kieran Sawyer; Notre Dame, IN: Ave Maria Press, 1978.
2   *An Introduction to the Faith of Catholics;* Richard Chilson, New York: Paulist Press, 1975.
3   A person assisting a priest in a religious service

native Carolinians and children of northern transplants. After only a few youth group meetings, I was urged to attend an intense diocesan youth retreat called Search. I attended the weekend retreat and returned with a new outlook, captivated by the loving, open environment. I wanted to combine the emotional softness displayed at the retreat with the conviction of a devout, loyal Catholic.

My focused devotion, knowledge of church dogma, and a desire for spiritual growth, led me to be elected as the youth group's Spiritual Director. For a shy kid who viewed himself as an outsider, to be elected to one of the most visible positions among the youth, was a real feather in my cap. I relished the role and took it very seriously. I became immersed in diocesan activities and attended a weeklong summer retreat for youth leaders called Christian Leadership Institute. I attended training sessions to be a Search leader and presenter. My senior year was filled with church activities. In addition to my duties as a diocesan youth worker, I was elected Youth Representative to the Parish Council and Vice President of our youth group.

During my second weekend as a Search presenter, I was informed that the Bishop of Charlotte, North Carolina, would be coming by to observe. He was scheduled to visit during my presentation, making me almost as nervous as I was proud. My performance went over well. If only he knew my years of preparation in Philadelphia, I thought, he would be even more impressed.

Becoming more politically active, I attended a Washington, D.C. anti-abortion rally and began supporting pro-life organizations and candidates with the little money I was earning. I had also become aware of several conservative Catholic Orders. I thought they embodied the Papalist agenda I supported. I began to support the Priestly Fraternity of St. Peter and the Legionaries of Christ.

Confidence in the Flesh

My devotion to my Catholic faith only deepened when I enrolled at North Carolina State University in Raleigh, North Carolina. Upon arrival on campus, I joined the College Republicans and the campus Catholic organization. My exposure to evangelical Christians in high school had primarily been confined to a few Baptists who pestered some of my friends in the youth group. We would mock them as deficient Christians and dismissed them as simple-minded Protestants who knew nothing of history, tradition, or the deeper things of God. Now, in this new environment, they seemed to be everywhere.

I stayed in touch with the diocese and served as a young adult leader for several events, and while in Raleigh, I attended the parish of two of my friends from the College Republicans. It was a conservative parish with a traditionalist pastor. After only a couple of meetings, he was so impressed by both my knowledge and my zeal that he asked me to teach a high school confirmation class. Of course, I gladly accepted the position, wanting to pass on my enthusiasm to yet another group of young Catholics.

I felt secure in my faith and found power in my convictions. I was admired by older Catholic students in the Catholic center, was a popular confirmation teacher, and was still in high demand at the diocesan level. I had met several evangelical Christians who were active in the College Republicans group, but a more direct encounter was just around the corner.

I was walking across the brickyard at N.C. State when I saw this sign: Do You Know if You're Going to Heaven? I was incensed! From my earliest days as an altar boy I had been taught to fear such a presumptuous thought. No man can know, I thought. How dare they? I was so angered that I approached the table they had set up for their literature and asked them in quite an indignant manner if they claimed to know their eternal fate. Much to my surprise and chagrin, they answered, "Yes," without the slightest hesitation and even with great conviction. The leader, of this group, called Maranatha, opened up his Bible and read passages such as, *"Verily, verily, I say unto you, He that heareth my word, and believeth on him that sent me, hath everlasting life, and shall not come into condemnation; but is passed from death unto life."* (JOHN 5:24)

This young man, my contemporary, continued to quote a number of other verses from both the Old and New Testaments when the discussion spilled out into the open air. I was not as well versed on the Scriptures as this student, but I certainly had history and tradition on my side. A small crowd gathered as I barked out the verses I knew. I left the scene angry and frustrated. How could anyone presume to be worthy of heaven? Not even the Pope makes such a prideful boast!

I was determined to combat this heresy and searched every Catholic apologetic book I had at my disposal. Lastly, I searched in my Bible for verses that would support my conclusions. I took my new arsenal of information and began to challenge the open-air preachers that frequented the brickyard. Small crowds would gather as I chased every historical rabbit and church document that I could find. The crowds would invariably be behind me, patting my back and cheering my retorts. They had little interest in Roman Catholicism; they just hated these Evangelists.

The men were quite reserved. As I ranted and changed topics at will, repeatedly they kept quoting Scripture. I left these encounters with pride on my face but with trouble in my soul. I knew my Roman Catholicism better than any lay Catholic I knew, so seeking my argument's bolster through answers from my Catholic peers was a waste of time. As with most Catholics, they were blissfully unfamiliar with most church doctrines and documents. I had to work this through on my own.

Almost Persuaded

An evangelical campus group had started a Bible study in the study room of my residence hall. I joined to try to learn more about what these people believed. During one discussion, I quoted from the Apocryphal Book of Wisdom to a room full of blank stares. After that awkward moment, the group moved on. I took my pride and determined in my heart to never attend one of these studies again. I was still intrigued by the devotion of these students and their knowledge of the Scriptures. If salvation is a gift, and they were assured of heaven, why then were they so devout? To what end was all this activity? Since my youth, my religious activity was designed to either earn indulgences, to shorten my time in Purgatory, or to show devotion to the church and her Saints in order to garner favor from the spirit world. I was maintaining my "state of grace," but what on earth were they doing?

Sitting in my room one afternoon, two of these evangelical Christians paid me a visit. They used a small whiteboard and presented the "gospel... unto salvation"[4] from the book of Romans. *"For all have sinned, and come short of the glory of God."* (ROMANS 3:23) Of course I could agree to that, all men were sinners. It was the Scriptures that followed with which I took issue. *"For the wages of sin is death; but the gift of God is eternal life through Jesus Christ our Lord."* (ROMANS 6:23) Now I understood where they were going with this. They were going to focus on the "gift." They showed on their whiteboard how our good works fall short of God's standard. *"Now*

4 Romans 1:16. *"For I am not ashamed of the gospel of Christ: for it is the power of God unto salvation to every one that believeth; to the Jew first, and also to the Greek."*

to him that worketh is the reward not reckoned of grace, but of debt. But to him that worketh not, but believeth on him that justifieth the ungodly, his faith is counted for righteousness." (ROMANS 4:4, 5)

It was all I could stand. I was being nice, but now they were "twisting" Scripture! They were going to try to tell me that all my works, my life of morality, and my religious activity were worthless! I could be "saved" and just cruise on through life with the full assurance of eternal life. I had heard it before. Such thinking was absurd to me. It made no sense! I wrestled with those Scriptures and searched selectively for myself to find verses to contradict the notion that our works are not salvific or essential to our salvation. In Scripture I was well aware of James's teaching that "faith without works is dead" and wanted desperately for that to satisfy my soul; but upon reading the text, it raised more questions than it provided answers. I wanted to understand their argument without admitting my interest, so I took a trip inside one of their meetings, unbeknownst to my friends, to shed some light on my confusion. Not knowing any of the songs they sang, I must surely have looked out of place. The freedom they had! This love and devotion, seemingly to God, and yet designed to accomplish nothing, frightened me. I thought there was something cult-like about the whole thing. Without the threat of hell, or even Purgatory, why practice such strict moral constraints? I was weary, confused, and longed for familiar surroundings.

In Full Retreat

During the summer, after my freshman year, I retreated to the safety of my home parish where I was honored by the diocese by being asked to be a paid seminar presenter at the massive diocesan youth conference. My topic was "Faith." Unlike most of the other presenters, I had limited my examples of faith to the pages of Scripture because I was becoming familiar with more of the Bible. My encounters on the campus had honed my skills at finding select verses I could use in my debates.

After the fall semester of my sophomore year, I transferred to The University of North Carolina at Greensboro (UNCG), even though it was a far more liberal school with a corresponding more liberal College Republican Club and Catholic Center. Being closer to my home parish, I was able to help with the youth group, and by then I was splitting my time between the parish activities and the Catholic Center on campus. I participated in the Bible study led by the campus priest. He was a rank liberal and the experience drove me to a more traditional parish near campus. I still attended campus events at the Catholic Center, but I was through with the liberal nonsense as I saw it.

Shortly after transferring to UNCG, I joined a fraternity. I was attracted by the code of chivalry and the emphasis on honor I found in the recruitment material. Unfortunately, I soon discovered that most of the activities that surrounded the fraternity had little to do with either chivalry or honor. In an attempt to temper the excesses of my fraternity brothers, I ran for, and was easily elected, chapter chaplain. It was mostly a ceremonial position, but it did carry some weight during certain discussions. I was quickly dubbed "the conscience of the fraternity," a title I proudly encouraged.

"Religious" Education

In 1987, my pride and assurance was even more solidified after a trip to Vatican City in Rome. I was overwhelmed with the history of St. Peter's Basilica. The Catholic luminaries represented there, including Peter's supposed grave, filled my mind with awe. My only regret was that the sealed doors, which promised special indulgences, were still closed and not to be opened for another thirteen years. In my state of euphoria, I took a few moments to light a candle for my brother, Joe. Shortly before we moved to North Carolina in 1980, my brother (whom I had seen reading his Bible in his bed when I was young) had left the Catholic Church. At his wedding in a Baptist church the previous year, I had made an overt show of "the sign of the cross" after each prayer. My family and other spectators were going to be assured that, despite the setting, I was still firmly entrenched in the camp of Rome.

Joe had spent several summers smuggling Bibles into Eastern Europe in the early 1980s. Certainly, that was admirable but, outside the Catholic Church, he had no direct access to the grace of God found only in her sacraments. This is clearly taught. His only hope of securing the graces necessary to alleviate his sufferings in Purgatory was for him to return to Rome. It was to that end that I prayed and lit the candle, believing it was the most powerful thing I could do for him.

I returned from my trip to Europe more enamored with Roman Catholicism than ever. Removed from the confrontational environment of North

Carolina State, I continued to become increasingly more comfortable in my faith. The episode in my dorm room seemed like a distant, unpleasant memory. I returned to my home parish and began to teach Religious Education classes. My classes were quite popular and I became something of an unofficial spokesman for the teachers. At one point, there developed a parents' revolt of sorts against the whole program; I was asked to address the angry group in lieu of classes one Sunday evening. Most of the rage was directed at the Religious Education Director. To be more personal, we split into smaller groups where, during one exchange in particular between a parent and another teacher in my group, the parent stated that all she wanted was for us to "Teach my children how to be good people." And, as she said those words, out of nowhere, a thought ran through my mind: "good people go to hell." The thought took me completely by surprise, and I do not remember anything about the meeting after that. This was a foreign doctrine to Roman Catholicism. I had no idea where that thought had come from.

Vatican II had clearly laid out the road to salvation—even for Muslims. They too could achieve their salvation by striving to lead a good life. Ancient papal bulls[5] had stated that apart from submission to the pope no one could be saved, no matter how blameless. But, statements like that had been clarified in the continual revelation found in Sacred Tradition. What on earth was I thinking? "Good people, go to hell?" Where did that come from? It sounded like something those evangelists from North Carolina State might say.

The education wars ended. I was secure in my position as a teacher. The strange thought had passed, and I could continue with my class on the Sacraments. I had graduated from UNCG, had met the girl of my dreams, had become a shaper of young Catholic minds, and my life was planned. I was in a position to combat the liberalism that had infected my parish by directly influencing the youth. I felt safe, sound, and secure.

And the Rain Descended

It was at UNCG that I met my fiancée, Mary, in the cafeteria, but it would take a few months for us to come together. The process advanced quickly when I discovered she was an Irish Catholic from Pennsylvania.

5 Papal bulls are decrees or "solemn edicts" granted by the Vatican.

I was an Italian Catholic. The Irish Catholics and Polish Catholics were seen as more seriously devout than other groups, so this seemed like the perfect match—as though arranged by the Saints themselves! While in Rome, I prayed God would give me a wife. Mary was certainly the answer to that prayer, I thought.

During our nearly three years together, Mary became a part of my family. She was readily welcomed at all family functions and became a fixture in my parents' home. I had been to her parents' home in Pennsylvania on a couple of occasions as well. The idea of a life without Mary was unfathomable; there was no question that we would be anything except husband and wife. Then Mary left me. The Religious Education teacher, the voice of morality, and defender of the Catholic faith found himself suddenly with no answers. Her rejection of me was what triggered an earnest search for the truth. The utter devastation led me to search out the Scriptures and struggle with the message of Isaiah 46. This loss of control thrust me into two contradictory theologies: the Roman Catholicism I had vigorously defended inside and outside the Church of Rome, and the gospel of the free grace of God through faith in His Son, Jesus Christ.

So there I was, diving deeply into my Roman Catholicism as never before while rediscovering the intrigue the Evangelicals at North Carolina State had ignited. However, as noted earlier, I was trying to reconcile two different tracks that would never, and could never, meet.

At the time, I was working at UNCG in the Admissions Office and was traveling extensively in the Northeast. I had a lot of free time in the evenings, which I spent reading the Scriptures, praying, listening to teaching tapes and Christian radio. But, simultaneously, I visited a grotto in Connecticut to pay homage to the Virgin Mary, seeking her intercession. I lit candles and left written prayers. The next night, I attended a Pentecostal healing meeting. During the day, I listened to J. Vernon McGee; I read Catholic tracts at night. I would pray the Rosary, and then I would sit in a dark hotel bathroom and pray for hours on end to the God of Isaiah 46.

I returned to North Carolina for a week, between recruitment trips. As my dual spiritual life continued, I would walk to the parish church and spend hours at the altar, and I would then spend hours listening to gospel preachers, all day at work and through the night.

In my despair, I nearly became suicidal. One Saturday morning, ready to end it all, I had it all planned—had even written the letter. However, an unexpected Saturday morning phone call from my sister interrupted my plans, allowing me to regain control of my thoughts. Desperate calls to my brother, asking him to assure me that God was in control, kept me sane after that. According to Isaiah 46, God declared the end from the beginning. He brought things to pass. I clung to that like a personal promise, which is the reason I fell in love with Isaiah 46.

Day after day, I listened to Oliver B. Greene hammer away at my Catholic faith with the gospel of peace. I became familiar with many verses and clung to them as I had to Isaiah 46. The verses from Romans, which I had heard years before, again came to mind as Dr. Greene repeated them. I would meditate and find hope in the Scriptures, wanting desperately to find peace with God. But, there was no room in my thinking that all my good works were worthless. It just could not be so.

I had been an excellent student in religion, attended multiple Friday morning Masses, made all but one Sunday Mass or Holy Day of Obligation from the time of my confirmation in the fourth grade through my first year in college. I gave time and money to conservative Orders, was an altar boy and an acolyte. I believed in celibacy before marriage, was pro-life, and a defender of the One True Church in many settings. I was the most moral student of any of the young adults that I knew. I prayed the Rosary, said Novenas, and believed I was in a state of grace! I had performed all required penance, had adored the Saints, and I had read Canon Law and the Sacred Councils. I knew more Catholic doctrine and Sacred Tradition than any lay Catholic I knew. How could all of that be worthless?

Everything I knew, and every apparatus of the Roman Catholic Church, is built upon the "unfinished" work of Christ. In the final analysis, it all came down to the Church, her "Saints," the sacraments, and me. I was now confronted with the work of Christ on Calvary. Was it complete? Was it sufficient? Was it finished? What about Canon Law? If Muslims,

Hindus, atheists, and even agnostics could merit heaven, of what value was Christ's work? Were the good works of St. Francis, which could rescue me from Purgatory, more meritorious than the work of Christ on the cross? What was the value of faith? Now, since Christ was being exalted in my heart through the Scriptures, my theology of works was collapsing like a house of cards all around me, one doctrine at a time.

Halt Between Two

I was directly confronted at that time by Oliver B. Greene's series on the wrath of God. He started in Genesis (which he took as absolute truth and history) and traveled all the way through the book of Revelation. Man had no righteousness. There is no one that does good. (ROMANS 3:12) Even man's best efforts and righteousness are filthy rags to God. (ISAIAH 64:6) Salvation was either of grace or of works; it could never be of both or maintained by both. (ROMANS 11:5, 6) What was I to do with these and scores of other passages?

"*Therefore being justified by faith, we have peace with God through our Lord Jesus Christ: By whom also we have access by faith into this grace wherein we stand, and rejoice in hope of the glory of God.*" (ROMANS 5:1, 2) "*...God was in Christ, reconciling the world unto himself, not imputing their trespasses unto them...For he hath made him to be sin for us, who knew no sin; that we might be made the righteousness of God in him.*" (2 CORINTHIANS 5:19, 21)

I determined that I would rather die than continue as a double-minded man. As I lay in bed waiting for death to consume me, I was suddenly consumed with something else: my sin. I was struck suddenly with the fear of meeting God in my sin. I had just been to confession, but it offered no solace. Sins from my childhood, from my teen years, and now the present, had swept across my mind. I screamed into a pillow so my roommate would not hear me. I was terrified of the wrath of God and prayed that the verses and promises of Christ Himself were true.

I told God that I had no other hope. In that moment, I believed the finished work of Jesus Christ on my account, understanding that His finished work alone was my only hope. It was all I had left. I suddenly began to understand what those students at North Carolina State had been talking about. The seed of the Word of God, which they had planted, finally came to fruition.

I took out the Bible my brother had given me years before; I read a number of the Psalms and realized that now I had something for which to

live. In complete contradiction to my musings of years earlier, it now made
sense to me why Christians pursue holiness. It is not to obtain from God
a debt, which He is required to answer; it is to radiate the "new creation's
holiness," [6] which God has already wrought. It is understood that in holiness is peace and joy.

For several weeks, I tried to reconcile my new faith in Christ with my
Roman Catholicism. I searched her doctrines to try to make them com-
patible; but by then, I knew too much. The Treasury of Merit, the Brown
Scapular, Purgatory, Indulgences, Holy Days of Obligation, and scores of
other core Catholic doctrines made obedience to Roman Catholicism difficult and eventually impossible. I found myself "bowing before idols," a
phrase that for most of my life had meant nothing.

Coming Out from Among Her

I never looked for a way to leave the Catholic Church. Being my home
since birth, it was the last thought I had. I had met thousands of Roman
Catholics: priests, nuns, and teachers, all of whom had meant something
to me. I would not leave without good cause. I had given so much to the
Church. She was all I knew.

Shortly after my new birth in Christ, having trusted in Christ's finished
work on the cross, I found myself at a Sunday Mass. When the time came
for me to go forward for Holy Communion, true to form, I was in the
priest's line. As he held up the Host before me and said, "The Body of
Christ," for the first time in my life I could not say the word, "Amen." I
did not agree.

Christ was not on an altar or in a perpetual sacrifice as I had been taught
as a child; He is sitting at the right hand of God, having already obtained
eternal redemption for me. The fact that His sacrifice never had to be repeated was scriptural evidence of its efficacy. (HEBREWS 7:27; 10:1-14) I left
the Roman Catholic Church that day and never looked back.

> *...when he [Christ] had by himself purged our sins, sat down on
> the right hand of the Majesty on high."* (HEBREWS 1:3B) *"For the law
> having a shadow of good things to come, and not the very image of
> the things, can never with those sacrifices which they offered year by*

---

6 Christ's righteousness now lived through me

year continually make the comers thereunto perfect. For then would they not have ceased to be offered? because that the worshippers once purged should have had no more conscience of sins." (HEBREWS 10:1, 2) *"But this man [Christ], after he had offered one sacrifice for sins for ever, sat down on the right hand of God; From henceforth expecting till his enemies be made his footstool. For by one offering he hath perfected for ever them that are sanctified."* (HEBREWS 10:12-14) *"Neither by the blood of goats and calves, but by his own blood he entered in once into the holy place, having obtained eternal redemption for us."* (HEBREWS 9:12)

From Genesis to Revelation, the Scriptures are filled with promises and word "pictures" of the finished work of Christ. There is no room in that book for compromise. I knew the doctrine of transubstantiation, and I knew the basis upon which that doctrine was constructed. As hundreds of thousands before me had done for sixteen centuries, I had to come out of the Roman Catholic system of works and rituals in order to find rest in the finished work of Christ.

It all had to go: the Treasury of Merit, Indulgences, Holy Days of Obligation, and the like, all contradicted not only the Scriptures but the very work of Christ Himself. I could not truly honor and serve Jesus Christ while outwardly displaying my lack of faith in His work on Calvary—by maintaining a presumed "state of grace"—and seeking forgiveness of sins through rituals and faith in the work of the "Saints" on my behalf.

"Faith without works is dead." (JAMES 2:17, 20, 26) What we do reflects what we truly believe. I could not say that I had faith in Christ and continue to act in a manner that suggested a faith in myself. If my hope of heaven and the forgiveness of my sins were obtained in indulgences, prayers to Saint Francis, Mass cards, and "doing my very best," then my faith was in me. Our works clearly show where our faith rests.

I have not recounted all my good works here, nor have I disclosed all my experiences in the Roman Catholic Church: the countless arguments, the countless sacraments, and the countless self-sacrifices offered to God. Neither is it possible to list here all the complexities and voluminous dogmas of the Roman Catholic religion that keep its faithful trapped in a system that offers no solutions. I rest in the knowledge that the complexity can be cast aside in the light of the *"simplicity that is in Christ,"* (2 CORINTHIANS 11:3) and in the pages of Scripture which are able to make even a little child wise unto sal-vation. (2 TIMOTHY 3:15) Salvation is not a "do my very best" or "hope so" con-cept; it is a gift (EPHESIANS 2:8, 9) which can be known! (JOHN 5:24; 1 JOHN 5:13)

I understand that the documents of Vatican Council II state that there is no salvation for those who either "refuse to enter in" or for those who "will-ingly leave" the Roman Catholic Church.[7] I know that missing Mass is to commit a "grave sin" meriting a loss of my "state of grace" (out of which meant: no hope of eternal life).[8] However, once I found rest and satisfac-tion in the finished work of Christ, coming directly from God the Father in heaven, Who Himself had granted permission; there was no fear in the pronouncements of mere men. However, I am filled with compassion for those still trapped in the Roman Catholic religious system.

Today, I have a small music and teaching ministry to try reaching Ro-man Catholics with the gospel of the "free" grace of God. I spend much of my time educating Catholics con-cerning the doctrines of their own church. Most of these lay Cath-olics are blissfully unaware of the councils, decrees, dogmas, canon laws, and the rest of the tenets that define Roman Catholicism. These doctrines are then contrasted with the simple gospel and the Word of God—a weapon that is stronger than any two-edged sword. In the

Michael and his beloved family

end, as those fellows at North Carolina State had done, I seek only to plant the seed of the Word of God. It is God who saves and God who gives the increase. To God alone be the glory!

—MICHAEL SCOTTO

If you wish to contact me, please do.
My email address is: michaelfscotto@gmail.com

---

7   1964 Dogmatic Constitution on the Church

8   See Catechism of the Catholic Church, Para 2181

GEARÓID MARLEY

A Testimony of God's Sovereign Grace

LIKE MOST BOYS IN THE REPUBLIC OF IRELAND IN THE 1980S I WAS brought up a Roman Catholic. My parents taught me to live a good life, say my prayers, and attend Mass every Sunday. I believed there was a God, but I did not know Him personally. I prayed as my mother taught me, but I never knew whether God was really listening. I attended confession monthly and did many penances. Conscious of my sinfulness, I hoped that God would accept me into Heaven if I did enough good works. I tried to live the best life I could. It was like balancing the accounts, hoping that my credits (good deeds) would cancel my debits (my sins). Zealous to please God, I was eleven years of age when I decided to become a Roman Catholic priest. I went to the local priest but he said I would have to wait until I was eighteen years of age before entering the seminary.

During my teenage years, I got involved in much sinful behaviour. I rebelled against God and disobeyed His Commandments. I loved my sin, but I hated that miserable life and started to cry out to God. I realise now that God was working in my heart. He showed me I was a sinner. I longed to be right with Him. This became the focus of my life. I knew that I needed to be saved from my sins. I went on a pilgrimage to a famous Catholic shrine. I ate oatcakes, drank black tea, and crawled on my knees around the Stations of the Cross over three days to do penance for my sins. I fasted and meditated but never knew pardon for sin. I wanted to know forgiveness, but how?

Training for the Priesthood

In 1993, at the age of nineteen and after checking different religious organizations, I finally decided to join the Society of Missions to Africa (SMA). They are a society of priests who live together in small communities in different parts of the world, seeking to convert pagans to the Roman religion.

Gearóid on his Catholic Confirmation day

I entered the Roman Catholic Seminary located in Maynooth, County Kildare, Ireland. I began training for the priesthood. During my two years in the seminary, I learned about religion and philosophy but there were no biblical studies. I attended daily Mass and monthly confession. Alas, there was no teaching on forgiveness for sin. We had set times of prayer as a community—at morning, evening, and night. I heard many talks that were focused on pleasing God by doing charitable works and buying favor with God through the church. I also heard a lot about how to use psychology to spiritually counsel people. Not once did I hear how to be reconciled to God through Christ who alone could forgive my sins!

I began to read the Bible. As I read it, I asked the priests serious questions about the religious rituals in the Roman Catholic religion, but they could not show me the scriptural basis for much of the superstition and traditions. I discovered that the Bible does not promote the veneration of Mary as practiced in the Catholic Church. The official teaching of the church is that Mary does not necessarily answer prayers but rather intercedes on the Catholic's behalf and prays for us. However, the Bible implies she is a sinner: in the famous "Magnificat" she is found praying to God her Saviour. (Luke 1:46-47) Mary knew she had sinned and here she is found rejoicing in God her Saviour, who was conceived in her womb; i.e., Jesus Christ her Lord.

I realized that rosaries and prayers to the saints have no scriptural basis. Mary is addressed in Catholic prayers, (e.g. "O Mary, conceived without sin, pray for us who have recourse to thee") but the Savior teaches us to pray to the Father directly. (Luke 11:1-4) Indeed, the Bible warns us against ritual prayers. This described me exactly: outwardly very holy and pious, but inwardly my heart was sinful and corrupt.

Also, the Church teaches its followers to pray to the saints. There is a saint for almost every circumstance: St. Christopher for travel, St. Anthony for lost things, Martin de Porrés for healing, St. Joseph for the dying, St. Vincent de Paul for the poor, and St. Jude for lost causes. I asked the priests many questions about religion. I could not find anything in Scripture to support this teaching. I was told that these Church traditions could not be questioned.

I was conscious of my sin and longed to have assurance of salvation. I asked the priests but I was told that we could never be sure of salvation until we died! I was instructed to attend the priest for auricular confession, but I did not find that in Scripture either. In Scripture, one is urged to confess his sins to God, not to human priests. *(1John 1:9)* I also realized that as a priest I would have to hear people's confessions and absolve them. I was confused—how could I forgive other people's sins, when I did not even know forgiveness myself? I now realize that the Lord was lifting the veil from my eyes to show me that true faith and forgiveness for sin is in Christ alone.

Eventually, I left the Roman seminary in 1995. The society had decided I was not suitable, but the Lord showed me through His Word the errors of Catholicism and that I should leave the priesthood as well. I had entered the seminary thinking that I would find the answer to forgiveness of my sins. When I left, I thought that I was finished with God—but He was not finished with me!

For the next two years I lived in Dublin and continued my search for God. I went to various Protestant churches and also met people from different cults. One cult told me that if I were baptized again, then I was born again. This sounded too much like the Roman Church and its teaching of justification by works, so I left them as well.

England

I went to London to work in preparation for nursing studies. On the first night I met a man who told me how I could know forgiveness for sin. He gave me a leaflet that emphasized the need to trust in Jesus Christ alone. I read this leaflet many times, but still had no peace with God. I became depressed in my spirit, although I was well physically.

I knew that I was condemned if I were not converted. The Bible says that if I did not believe then *"the wrath of God abideth upon him* [i.e., me]." (John 3:36) Then I read *"There is therefore now no condemnation to them which are in Christ Jesus, who walk not after the flesh, but after the Spirit."* (Romans 8:1) This was a constant challenge to me. I was alone in a huge city with no one to turn to for spiritual advice. O, how my heart yearned to be right with God!

I met some students on my nursing studies that seemed to know God. I attended their church where the Bible was central to the whole service. The sermon was preached from the Bible. That was something completely new to me. Deep down I knew these people were genuine Christians. I asked many questions and started to attend the church regularly. About this time, a small Christian group was meeting in my halls of residence. I went along aiming to disrupt the meetings, but slowly began to be drawn to Christ. I saw that they had something that I did not have: peace with God and a real love for Christ. They knew the reality of *"therefore being justified by faith, we have peace with God through our Lord Jesus Christ."* (ROMANS 5:1) I asked them many questions and one of them gave me a book called *Knowing God* by J. I. Packer. I read this book and saw that I too could know God in a personal way.

My Conversion

One Sunday morning, the 8th of February 1998, I was listening to a sermon from Luke 10:30-37 about the Good Samaritan. The preacher spoke of Jesus Christ being like the good Samaritan: coming to help us in our wretched sinful state, while revealing that the Holy Spirit gives new life to lost sinners. (1 PETER 1:23) He also urged the listeners to repent of sin and trust in Jesus Christ alone for the forgiveness of sin. I called on Jesus Christ to save me, *"for whosoever shall call upon the name of the Lord shall be saved"* (ROMANS 10:13). Right there and then I knelt down in my room and prayed, "O God, I know that you have sent your Son Jesus Christ into the world to save sinners. Will you save me? I trust in Christ alone and ask that you would come into my life by the power of your Holy Spirit and make me new." I felt a huge weight of guilt and sin taken from my heart. As soon as I opened my eyes a deep sense of peace came over me. At that moment I knew that I was a Christian and truly forgiven of all my sins. The Bible became the living Word of God and He was speaking to me as I read. I realised that we were not saved by works but by grace, *"For by grace are ye saved through faith; and that not of yourselves: it is the gift of God: Not of works, lest any man should boast"* (EPHESIANS 2:8-9). I was baptised in London in September 1998. After my baptism I struggled with temptations and trials, but the Lord was my constant refuge—*"God is our refuge and strength, a very present help in trouble"* (PSALM 46:1).

My Life as a Christian

On my first visit back to Ireland, I did not know of a Christian church, so I went to Mass with my parents. I realised the priest was re-enacting a sacrifice that was accomplished once and for all on the cross of Calvary. The Bible says in 1 Peter 3:18 *"Christ also hath once suffered for sins, the just for the unjust, that he might bring us to God, being put to death in the flesh, but quickened by the Spirit."* For this reason, I could not attend the Catholic Mass any longer.

When I was a young Irish man swearing was second nature to me. Very soon after my conversion this dried up! Worldly pursuits, drinking in pubs and going to nightclubs, ceased. Prayer and communion with God became a whole new area of experience. I had learned formal rote prayer as a young boy, but now as a Christian I began truly to pray from my heart. This is still an amazing experience to me: to be able to lift my heart to God as my Father and know that He is listening and will answer my prayers according to His will!

My family was upset that I had left the Roman Catholic faith. At first they thought it was another religious phase I was going through, but they soon realised that this was different. However, the Lord gave me opportunities to share the true gospel with them. About a year later my youngest brother was converted! What joy filled my heart!

Since my conversion, the Lord has taught me so much from His Word. I am especially thankful to one man from the church in London who helped me to study the Bible. We did a complete overview of the Scriptures as well as an in-depth study of the doctrines of grace. The glorious truth that God is sovereign in salvation and reaches out in mercy to sinners is truly humbling and amazing. That God, the Creator and Sustainer of the world, should call and choose wretched polluted sinners to Himself shows His grace. Yet the Bible says: *"he hath chosen us in him [Christ] before the foundation of the world"* (EPHESIANS 1:4). God saves sinners through Christ and He preserves His people through all trials. What a joyful day it will be when all His people are united with Him in Heaven!

Christian Service and Work

About a year after my conversion I was seeking the Lord about serving Him. One evening after the Lord's Day service I was praying to the Lord asking Him where He wanted me to serve. I read 2 Timothy 3:16 to 4:5 and was profoundly challenged. I had never studied this portion of God's Word before. It was impressed on me that this was how the Lord wanted me to serve Him.

I graduated and worked for a year in the National Treatment Centre for Alcohol and Drugs. Some of the patients were hardened criminals; others were involved in many sordid areas of society due to their addictions. I realised the psychological treatment was not dealing with their real problem: their unpardoned sin. I could not witness openly to the patients but some patients enquired what kept me through the difficult times in my life. I told them that it was my faith in the Lord Jesus Christ, and they were amazed.

My housemate and a Roman Catholic friend were converted and baptized during this time. It was a great privilege to see the Lord use even me to win sinners to Christ. I conducted a Bible Study in Colossians with some Jehovah's Witnesses. They began to seek Christ but the leaders visited and put an end to it. I pray for these people that the Lord would open their eyes to His truth! As I taught young boys in Crusader Class I soon realized that children could be taught the deep truths of Scripture in a simple understandable way.

Pastoral Studies

The Lord amazingly opened up a way for me to go to a full time seminary (London Theological Seminary). I was interviewed and commenced the course one month later. How great our God is! His ways are past finding out. The lasting memories of my seminary days are of the nightly prayer meetings with fellow students and of the godly men who taught us theology and prepared us for the pastoral ministry.

Joys and Trials

Elizabeth (now my wife) and I had been courting for four months when I suddenly fell ill. From December 2001 until April 2002 my health deteriorated. During those months, I was bed-bound for six weeks. Despite numerous tests the doctors could not diagnose the cause. I had to leave the seminary for two months but by God's grace I was able to keep up with the studies. These trials taught me that God's people do suffer and there is a purpose in our sufferings: to bring us closer to God and make us more like Christ. The Lord taught me about my weaknesses and His strength. The verse *"My grace is sufficient for thee; for my strength is made perfect in weakness"* (2 CORINTHIANS 12:9) became very real to us.

The Lord drew close to us and we were conscious of His help and strength. I realised during this time that the Lord had brought us togeth-

er to do a work for Him. We were married in 2003 after graduation and
are now living in Birmingham, England.

The Pastoral Ministry

In October 2003, I was called to be the assistant pastor of a Reformed
Baptist Church in Birmingham, and the following year was inducted as
the full-time pastor. The words from 1 Samuel 7:12 were precious at my
induction service: *"Hitherto hath the Lord helped us."* What an amazing
thing, a Roman Catholic seminarian converted and called to preach the
gospel of Jesus Christ!

Conclusion

I pray that you, dear friend, whether Roman Catholic or not, would read
the Bible and pray to the Lord to lead you to the truth. The Lord promises
that those who seek Him with all their hearts will find Him: *"And ye shall
seek me, and find me, when ye shall search for me with all your heart"* (JEREMI-
AH 29:13). I urge you, friend, *"Seek ye the Lord while he may be found, call ye
upon him while he is near"* (Isaiah 55:6).

The Bible says we need to *"repent ye and believe the gospel"* (Mark 1:15).
Leave behind your works—they are unable to buy pardon of sin. Trust in
Christ who is *"the way, the truth, and the life"* (JOHN 14:6). We do not need
a human priest: *"For there is one God, and one mediator between God and
men, the man Christ Jesus; who gave himself a ransom for all"* (I TIMOTHY 2:5-6).
Trust in Him alone. Please do not delay another moment! Seek Him with
all your heart and you will find Him, just as He promised. May He lead
you to Himself that you too would be saved!

—GEARÓID MARLEY

*Please email with any comments or questions
that you may have: gsmarley@yahoo.co.uk*

Kirk Patrick Haggerty

The Turning Point

I was born and raised in a suburb of Los Angeles, California. My father's ancestors came from Ireland and we still have the original family name. My father was a steel worker and a Marine Corp veteran of the Korean War. My mother was a full-time homemaker and mother of seven children. We attended St. John Vienney Catholic Church in Hacienda Heights.

The church was across the street from Los Altos High School, where my siblings and I attended. The church, St. John Vienney, was named after an eighteenth and nineteenth century French priest. It was a modern building, and the priests were progressive minded as well. Our main pastor at that time was Msgr. James O'Calligham, an old Irish "rock" who preached fire and brimstone. The church seated hundreds of people and there were several Masses every Sunday in order to accommodate the large crowds who attended. There were Masses in Spanish to provide for the large Mexican/Latino community.

My mother was a very devout Catholic. Her parents were divorced and did not practice any form of religion. Converting to Catholicism while a teenager, she became instrumental in the conversion of my father and her brother. She sought to provide all her children with a proper education in the Catholic faith.

I remember going to Mass with my mother when I was a young boy. The priests were consecrating the host, and the altar boys were ringing bells at their sides while standing next to the altar. I asked my mother what was happening, and she told me to be quiet because Jesus himself stood before us in the form of the bread host. I did not understand what she meant. I could not see Jesus. I only saw the priest holding the host high in the air. Jesus, to me, was a picture of a man I had seen in a children's Bible not long before.

My mother taught me to say my prayers at night. She told me to pray for dead relatives so God would take them out of purgatory to heaven. On some occasions, she would make me go to bed early so that we could get up the next morning and go to Mass for a "Holy Day of Obligation." I remember giving up things such as candy for Lent, and we ate fish sticks on Friday evenings.

My Teen Years

I have never understood how my parents, especially my mother, could be so devout in the Catholic faith and yet never arranged to have me baptized as infant. Yet, they never did. Perhaps it was the stress of moving into a new house the month I was born. Whatever the reason, I was not baptized as an infant. I can remember hearing the priest say during Mass that it was important that we be baptized. Baptism, he said, washed us of our sins and allowed us to go to heaven when we died. I knew that I had never been baptized, and the thought of what would happen to me if I died that day disturbed me greatly. This line of thinking continued until my father died of cancer in November of 1977. He battled the disease for two years before he died. I was thirteen years old at the time.

In the spring of the following year, my mother thought I should attend catechism to prepare me for my first communion. During the first session, I told the nun that I had never been baptized. The nun was shocked and informed both the church staff and my mother. Why, they asked, was a young teenager who had never been baptized attending catechism for his first communion? They placed me in a special catechism for baptism.

A few weeks later, my sister and I were baptized. My uncle served as our godfather. We recited the "Profession of Faith" and "holy water" was poured over our heads while we leaned over a metal water font. Like all young Catholics, I believed that this sealed my destiny and guaranteed my soul for heaven. Later in the year, I had my first communion. I was confirmed a year later. What more could I have wanted on a spiritual level? My uncle gave me a Catholic Bible for my confirmation. Ironically, this was the best thing he could have given me, because once I started, I never stopped reading and studying the Bible. God and His Word planted seed in me that would eventually lead me to a truly saving knowledge and faith in Jesus Christ.

We had a family Bible in our home. My mother had received a big, thick Douay Rheims Catholic Bible as a wedding present. It was too large to be carried about and was more for display than anything. We assumed that the Bible came from the Catholic Church. It was God's holy word, but for us, whatever the Catholic Church told us seemed more holy and acceptable than God's word alone. It was an unspoken premise in our minds that whatever the Church said had authority over everything, including the Bible. Given my background, how did God ever do a saving work in my life? He intervened and challenged my faith. Otherwise, I would never have changed.

I heard rumors about "Protestants" and "born-again Christians," as well as "Bible" churches in our area, but my mother was very protective and defensive against them. I saw Christian tracts by Jack Chic Ministries from Chino, California, and they must have had some impact on how I saw my Catholic faith. The Catholic Church responded to these ministries and the people who attended them by labeling them as "enemies of the Church," or as poor deluded souls who are sincere in what they are doing, but misunderstand the Catholic faith. I accepted this teaching at face value for some time.

Intellectual thinking did not start me questioning my Catholic faith, but a personal event. When I was nineteen years old, I was involved in a Catholic teen retreat called "Turning Point." We were planning a seminar for outreaches when one of the girls attending the retreat asked us a question. Her name was Rose, and she had recently become a born-again Christian. She asked the group, "Who is Jesus?" She then asked me, "Who is Jesus?" I could not give her an answer. I was stunned. After years of going to retreats, attending Sunday Mass, and reading my uncle's Bible, I could not say who Jesus was. Rose provided her own answer by saying, "Jesus is my Savior." The whole concept of Jesus as savior was new to me! I had never heard that before. What did it mean?

My College Years

The next phase in my spiritual pilgrimage occurred while I was in college. I attended California State Polytechnic University in Pomona. One day, in the fall of 1986, I saw some elderly men passing out little green books to the students. Most of the students did not take them or left them lying all over the campus grounds. I found one of them on a bench, so I looked at it. It was a Bible. More specifically, it was a New Testament and Psalms (King James Version) printed by the Gideons. I found it interesting, so I placed it in my book bag and went on my way.

A couple of months later, I found myself facing a variety of trials. I had little money and had to work to pay for college. My mother had to work hard to make ends meet, and my older brother had become very rebellious. Life in the household became very difficult. Nothing seemed to be right. In addition to my financial struggles, I wrestled with what I should do with the rest of my life. All in all, it was a very difficult time.

Shortly after Christmas, I was sitting in my room thinking about all the problems whirling around me and feeling very sad and dejected. I opened my book bag and found the little green Gideons' Bible. I thumbed through it, and in the back found something like a "Romans Road" tract. It was a simple four-point presentation of the Gospel using passages from the Book of Romans. It talked about God's love, (ROMANS 5:8) our sin and condemnation, (ROMANS 3:23) Jesus' death for our sin and salvation, (ROMANS 6:23) and our need to receive by faith Jesus as our Savior. (ROMANS 10:9-13)

I suddenly remembered Rose's statement about Jesus who was in her life. At first, I thought it looked too easy. As a "good" Catholic, I had to admit that I was a sinner, but at the moment, none of my good actions were helping me very much. There was a signature line at the bottom of the page where I could acknowledge Jesus as my savior. I hesitated, but thought to myself, "Yes, this is what I want to do. It is not what my mother wants. It is not what the church wants, but what I want." So, I signed it!

At first, nothing happened. For several months, nothing happened. Deep inside me, I somehow began to feel a calling from God. There is no other way of explaining it. I was still going to Mass and doing all the Catholic things. I thought God was calling me to be a priest.

In October 1987, God opened another door in my spiritual journey. He led me to a Christian meeting at the student center. Here was something entirely different; it was completely new. The students wanted to know and worship God. They wanted to study about Him in the Bible. I liked it so much that I kept going back. I joined one of the Bible studies that met once a week to go over the basics of the Christian faith. At this point, I was still very confused. My Bible study group knew I was a Catholic, but I never told them I was thinking of becoming a priest. I saw the dynamic, active faith in, and knowledge of, Jesus that these non-Catholic believers possessed. I still believed that the Catholic Church was the true church, and I thought that God was calling me to take these principles with me to seminary and ultimately to the Catholic Church as a priest.

Now I know how wrong I was, but it led me at the time to approach my parish priest and tell him I wanted to go to seminary. Little did I realize I was setting myself on a collision course? I had three unforeseen problems. First, the Catholic Church would never accept me as a priest if I were to apply and preach the biblical principles I was learning at this Christian organization. Second, I was going into the priesthood to escape problems when God wanted me to deal with them. Third, I was not prepared to live the celibate life of a priest. I had dated girls since high school and had a girl friend at the time. God had already introduced me to my future wife, but I did not know it at the time. Her name is Elisabeth, and she was an exchange student from Germany. Elisabeth had become a believer during her first visit to the United States. We met while playing guitars together at the Christian meetings in 1988-89. She stayed in California for several months and came back for a couple of visits. We wrote letters to each other after Elisabeth returned to Germany.

The Upper Room

In August of 1988, my mother died, and a year later my older sisters de-cided to sell our home on Gembrook Avenue. This left me without a place to live, but once again God provided me a place. I lived in a rented house in Diamond Bar near the university with four other student men. All of them were Christian men who were active with Bible studies on campus. We nicknamed the house "the Upper Room" after the place where Jesus and his disciples had the last supper. (LUKE 22:12) It was during this time that one of my roommates, Don, approached me about the Catholic Church. He was convinced that the church was apostate and cult like. It taught, he claimed, a works salvation, an unbiblical priesthood and sacrifice, and an idolatrous worship of Mary and the saints. He also claimed the church was led by a pope who was accountable to no one. At first, I was very angry with Don. I tried to defend my Catholic faith, but I had no good counterarguments. Don told me, "Kirk, I can see your sincerity, but I am convinced that you are sincerely wrong." He challenged me to prove him wrong by comparing Catholic doctrine with the Bible.

I graduated from college in 1990, and that same summer I decided not to apply for seminary. By now I had learned that all believers in Christ are priests, (1 PETER 2:4, 5, 9) and they all have direct access to God. (ROMANS 5:1, 2) Furthermore, I had concluded that Jesus made the final sacrifice for sin on the cross almost two thousand years ago. A constantly repeated priestly sacrifice of the Eucharist is unnecessary and unscriptural. (HEBREWS 10:11-18)

I began attending both a Evangelical Free Church near the "Upper Room" and a local Bible study. About the same time, I broke up with my girlfriend, lost my job, and seemed to have nothing positive happening to me. The only person, except Jesus, who expressed love and acceptance to me, was Elisabeth in Germany. God had me right where He wanted me. I worked at odd jobs to help pay the rent for the Upper Room. Frequently, I corresponded with Elisabeth. In the spring of 1992, she came to California to visit me. It was obvious that we were in love, and one of us needed to move in order to get married. Since Elisabeth had not yet completed her studies, and I had money remaining from the sale of my parents' home, I decided to take a leap of faith and fly to Germany. We agreed that I would stay for three months and see what God had in mind for the two of us.

Move to Germany

I arrived in Germany on July 17, 1992, following an eleven-hour flight. Elisabeth was there to greet me, show me the sights, and introduce me to her parents. I had no knowledge of the German language. I knew only a few basic phrases from a tourist cassette tape.

From my first day in Germany, I fell in love with the land and the scenery. It was completely unlike Los Angeles. There were small towns and villages separated by large fields and forests of tall pine trees. Every village had church towers that rang their bells daily. Many of the buildings were older than the United States itself, and their architecture was beautiful. Of course, all the road signs were in German and all measurements were metric. Everyone spoke German; I could not understand anything people were saying. It did not matter. I was already in love with the land and with the woman that I wanted to marry. I knew I did not want to go back to America. I knew God was saying to me that this was going to be a new chapter in my life.

Soon the euphoria calmed and Elisabeth and I began the paperwork to arrange for my stay in Germany. I was allowed to work in the business that Elisabeth's parents owned. Arrangements were made for me to attend a language school to learn basic German. Elisabeth knew of an English-speaking church in Munich that we could attend on Sundays. I was given a room above the small workshop where I would work, while Elisabeth lived with her roommate in a nearby apartment. It really seemed that God was opening all the doors for me to stay in Germany.

Elisabeth and I were married on June 19, 1993, in the small village of Viehbach, north of Munich. I worked for her parents in their little air-conditioning shop for several years.

Spiritual Life in Germany

I was happy to be in Germany, and in the town of Bayern, which is in the state of Bavaria. The spiritual life was much different for me, making my own growth difficult. Bayern is primarily Catholic. Most of the churches you see in the villages are Catholic. Unlike the Catholic churches I had seen in Los Angeles, the churches in Germany are filled with elaborate statues, paintings, carvings, rococo altars, and relics.

During the village Masses, the men sit on one side of the center aisle and the women on the other side. The services are mechanical and lifeless. Young people, generally, do not attend Mass for that very reason. The few Lutheran churches I have seen are not so elaborate or rigid, but also suffer from spiritual deadness.

Catholicism created a problem with my in-laws as well. My mother-in-law, Maria, and her family are devout Catholic. Maria's older brother, Hubert, has been a priest for decades and was for several years the Bishop of Essen, a city in northwestern Germany. Uncle Hubert seemed open enough to accept the fact that I was an American with no knowledge of German and I needed to attend an English-speaking non-denominational church for expatriates. Out of an act of love and goodwill, we were married in the Catholic Church and asked Uncle Hubert to perform the ceremony.

Even though we were attending an English-speaking biblical church, spiritual growth for me was slow until 1994, when a new pastor arrived at the expatriate church in Munich. His name was Lars Larson, and I had never met anyone like him before. He was conservative, reformed, Calvinistic, and a preacher! His teachings were intense and fascinating to learn from. He preached expository sermons and often exhorted the listener to repent from sin, believe on Jesus for salvation, and order one's life according to God's will.

Elisabeth and I visited Lars and his family often. They lived in Starnberg. We told him that we came from Catholic backgrounds and became born-again believers in Los Angeles. I remember our first meeting with Lars. He pulled out a Bible and showed me from the Gospel According to Mark where Jesus accused the Pharisees of subverting God's truth with their own religious traditions. (MARK 7:1-13) He then made an analogy with the Catholic Church and showed how the Gospel is smothered by layer upon layer of traditions that have accumulated through the centuries. This impressed me very much and I wanted to learn more from him.

Believers' Baptism

When Elisabeth and I saw that Lars baptized new believers at the church, we found it interesting and wanted to talk with him about it. He arranged a special Bible study in his home about the biblical teaching concerning baptism. We read copies of sermons from pastors on the subject. We read men like John Gill (18th century) and Charles Spurgeon (19th century). Lars emphasized the symbolic nature of baptism. He taught us that:

1. In every instance of baptism in the New Testament, the baptism followed a conscious decision on the part of the believer after they had come to an awareness of sin, felt the need for a saving faith in Christ, and repented of their sin. (MARK 16:16; LUKE 3:8-14; ACTS 2:36-38; ACTS 16:25-34; ETC.) In most instances, the baptism was a public proclamation by a sinner coming to faith in Jesus.

2. Although baptism represents a washing away of sin, its meaning is most powerfully demonstrated as a participation in the death, burial, and resurrection of Jesus. In the Bible, a believer who is baptized is *"Buried with Him in baptism, wherein also ye are risen with Him through the faith of the operation of God, who hath raised Him from the dead."* (COLOSSIANS 2:12; ROMANS 6:3, 4)

3. Although the Bible does not teach that baptism is necessary for salvation, baptism is still written of in the form of a command. (MATTHEW 28:19, 20) Following faith in Jesus, baptism also completes a

command to fulfill all righteousness (Matthew 3:15) and is the pledge
of a good conscience. (1 Peter 3:20, 21)

After a period of study and prayer, Elisabeth and I decided to receive
believers' baptism. In March 1995, we were baptized along with a small
group of other believers in the Olympic swimming pool in Munich. Shortly afterwards, Elisabeth told her mother about our believers' baptism. Maria was devastated. She saw this as a slap in the face to her and her Catholic
faith. For years, Maria had kept the original baby clothes that Elisabeth
had worn at her infant baptism, including the baptismal candle. When she
heard that we had received believers' baptism, she gave them back to Elisabeth, saying that they were of no use to her since Elisabeth saw her infant
baptism as worthless. The tense atmosphere between Maria and us lasted
for months. We continued to build up the relationship as best we could.
Elisabeth encouraged her mother that her upbringing in the Catholic faith
was a starting point that God used to bring her to a saving faith in Jesus at
the proper time. Elisabeth also tried to encourage her mother to compare
Catholic teaching to the Bible.

When our first son, Fabian, was born in 1996, we arranged a baby dedication at a local German Free Evangelical Church near our home so that
Elisabeth's relatives could attend. We did this so they could see for themselves that there is an alternative to the Catholic ritual of infant baptism as
a means of salvation. They could also see the biblical pattern that Jesus gave
us when He blessed the little children. (Mark 10:13-16)

By God's grace, Elisabeth's parents, her brother, and an aunt attended
the baby-dedication service. After the services, while having lunch at a
restaurant, our aunt approached Maria and said to her, "You know Maria,
it is an interesting concept to bless the baby now and wait until he is old
enough to understand his faith, and choose to be baptized on his own." We
saw this as God's words coming out of her mouth!

As the years have passed, our Fabian has grown in the grace of God.
Through prayer, instruction at home, and Sunday school, Fabian does show a
love for God and for people. My mother-in-law has also noticed this and has
slowly accepted the baby dedication of our other two children, Jeremia (correct
spelling) and Felix. We are not perfect parents. Parenthood can be stressful,
but it is rewarding. We trust that God will bring our sons to a saving faith in
Christ; in our lives together, we will continue daily to teach them the Gospel.

Conclusion

I have been in Germany for twelve years, and Elisabeth and I have been married for eleven of those years. My German skills have continued to improve, and we are now attending a German evangelical church near our home, outside of Munich. God has shown me many things

in my growth as a Christian, and I am confident that Jesus will guide us daily by His grace until one day in great joy we see Him face to face.

For Catholic readers who perhaps want to know more, I would recommend the following books for study: *The Gospel According to Rome* by James McCarthy, *Faith Alone* by R.C. Sproul, and *Far from Rome, Near to God* by Richard Bennett.

There may be much confusion to the Catholic once he or she has believed in Christ alone for salvation just as it happened to me. There are many teachings in the Catholic mindset that could take years to work out. Catholics who are recently born again may still have a performance attitude stuck in their mind, that is, they may not completely understand God's perfect love, grace, forgiveness, and acceptance for the sinner who pleads to Jesus for mercy in prayer and repentance. To some Catholics, deep down inside, they still need to do something, or perform in order to be saved, loved, and accepted. Communication with other Christians involved in biblical churches is essential for former Catholics to grow. Don't be afraid or ashamed to be honest with other Christians and say to them you are confused over many things concerning Catholicism and the Bible. In my early years as a Christian, I hesitated for a long time before I was able to open up and get help. Because of this, my spiritual growth was stifled. In my case, it was not "head knowledge" that finally made me decide to leave the Catholic Church; it was personal relationships with Christians who love and care. Remember, as a "new believer" you need to be reminded daily of the following biblical facts:

1. You are deeply loved,
2. Completely forgiven,
3. Fully pleasing,
4. Totally accepted, and
5. Complete in Christ! Amen

Notice that Catholics cannot accept all of these facts in their hearts—not until a work of "saving grace" is done by God to bring them to utter distress and despair over their sins. Once they trust Christ alone for salvation, and have renounced Catholic teaching, they can then freely accept these eternal facts. They cannot be changed, manipulated, or altered by you the believer. God has done these things, and God will see to it that He keeps you in this state of perfect love, forgiveness, and growth until you see Him face to face one day in perfect and eternal joy.

Epilogue: More Information on Germany

Germany, the birthplace of Luther and the Protestant Reformation, is today in spiritual disarray. Germany legally recognizes only two churches: the Roman Catholic Church (Roemisch-Katholische Kirche) and the Lutheran Church (Evangelische Landeskirche). Both churches suffer from spiritual deadness. Traditionally, the Catholic Church is predominant in southern and western Germany, while the Lutheran Church is predominant in the northern and eastern parts. This was due because of the Treaty of Westphalia, which ended the dreaded Thirty-Years War over three hundred years ago.

In 1999, the Catholic and Lutheran Church signed a document in Augsburg called the Joint Declaration on the Teaching of Justification. The document compromised the biblical teaching on "Justification by Faith Alone" so that more unity between the two confessions could be made.

Tolerance, pluralism, and post-modernism are commonplace here in Germany. According to a report in 1995, there were more registered witches than pastors! In 2001, the German parliament (Bundestag) legalized homosexual marriage, which later was upheld by the German Supreme Court in 2002. Christian bookstores are not that common and only exist in the larger cities.

However, there has been a steady growth among Evangelical Christians in the past few years. Christian radio stations like "Evangeliums Rundfunk" have tirelessly broadcasted the Gospel in German for many years on short wave and medium wave frequencies. Tent evangelism sponsored by churches like the "Frei evangelische Gemeinde" is still active every year throughout the country. In 2002, Germany broadcasted its first 24-hour Christian television program called "Bibel TV" with a musical format similar to MTV. Every year more Bible-based churches take root in Germany and there is a small handful of Bible colleges and seminaries.

For several years, Germany has been suffering from an economic recession. Unemployment is high in many parts of the country, national debt is high, and the government can no longer afford to support a welfare state that has been around since the post-war republic was founded. It has become a bloating bureaucracy. Painful reforms are underway, but it will take years before results can be seen. However, the spiritual side of the equation is still not being considered.

In 2004, a popular book was published in Germany, written by a Peter Hanne, a TV news commentator who is a Christian. In this book, *Schluss mit Lustig*, (Enough of Being Funny) Hanne criticizes both politicians and citizens for their secular attitudes. He believes politicians need to put God back into politics and the citizens need to rely on God instead of the defunct German welfare state! The timing of this book could not have been better.

Germany truly is a mission field today! Although you can see some evidence of spiritual growth, it is still on a small scale. I would encourage churches worldwide to consider supporting existing German ministries and sending missionaries to Germany for both short-term and long-term work. There are many non-German ethnic groups living and working here —especially from Eastern Europe and Turkey that also need to be reached with the Gospel. Too often the local German churches are not adequately equipped to minister to these groups.

Please, pray for Germany! It was once a spiritual beacon, and with God's help, it could be again!

— KIRK HAGGERTY

You are encouraged to contact me if you wish:
Ringstrasse 6, D-85777 Viehbach, Germany
haggerty@t-online.de

ARNOLD URBONAS

From the Kingdom of Darkness into the Kingdom of Light

As a former devout Catholic, I am writing this testimony to point you to the light, which is Jesus Christ the Lord. Having been a Catholic believer when I was growing up, I thought that the way to salvation was obedience to the Roman Catholic teachings, which was not resting my confidence in Christ, but rather in a church system that had presented a veneer of righteousness, denying in its very doctrine the righteousness that is by faith of which the Scriptures speak, and God commends. (Hebrews 11:6)

God the Father, through Jesus Christ sent a number of people in my life nudging me closer to Himself. My journey to full faith in Christ Jesus as my Savior took many twists and turns.

The Early Years

When I was of preschool age, I remember my mother saying some prayers in the Lithuanian language. When I questioned her about what she was doing before going to sleep, she told me about God, Jesus, and heaven. I pondered this for a considerable time, catching bits and pieces about faith and God as I was growing up. In my childlike heart, I said that I would follow God according to the light that He would give me. Later I was to learn that, *"without faith it is impossible to please him: for he that cometh to God must believe that he is, and that he is a rewarder of them that diligently seek him."* (Hebrews 11:6)

I briefly attended an Anglican church in a rural Alberta town in Canada in the late 1950s because there was no Catholic church in my hometown. I heard some preaching but, at that time, it did not fully make sense to me. However, to this day, I remember the congregation reciting the Apostles' Creed outlining what they all believed. In the early 1960s, I broke my elbow in a bicycle accident and was taken to a Catholic hospital where some nuns gave me a prayer book. In my childlike way, I viewed my broken elbow as a good thing coming from God, because I was in some sense growing in the faith, as Scripture states, *"And we know that all things work together for good to them that love God, to them who are the called according to his purpose."* (ROMANS 8:28)

A few years later, our family moved to Toronto where my mother, sister, and I attended Catholic Mass weekly; to the point where my parents wondered why I was so religious. Starting in the seventh grade, I attended a Catholic school. This paved the way for me to attend a Catholic high school where I felt very privileged. While at high school, I learned the enjoyment and value of serving others in many ways. My high school motto, "Teach me goodness, discipline and knowledge" was close to my heart. During my high school days while watching the movie, *The Brothers Karamazov*, I was struck by a scene: that if I would call myself a Christian, I should read my Bible every day, which I began to do, one day learning that, *"All scripture is given by inspiration of God, and is profitable for doctrine, for reproof, for correction, for instruction in righteousness."* (2 TIMOTHY 3:16)

When I was in my first year at university studying chemistry, I was challenged by a classmate who asked me, "Are you a Christian or a Catholic?" Although I said that I was both, the underlying purpose of her question caused me to examine my faith. As Scripture states, *"Examine yourselves, whether ye be in the faith; prove your own selves. Know ye not your own selves, how that Jesus Christ is in you, except ye be reprobates?"* (2 CORINTHIANS 13:5)

Into the Kingdom of Light

After completing my Bachelor of Science in chemistry, I felt led to teach math, physics, and chemistry in Africa for two years as a volunteer. I had a tremendous peace and joy teaching boys working in Benin City, Nigeria for two years. While in Nigeria, I met some Christians who invited me to join them to go camping in England after my two year volunteer service was over. Although I was expecting canoeing, hiking, and the great outdoors of England, I found that I was actually attending an Evangelical camp listening to biblical teaching by Jay North. I actually enjoyed listening to sound biblical teaching, although I cringed when the various speakers attacked the Roman church.

While at this camp, I was struggling within myself about the step of baptism. But one thing I understood: to declare my belief and commitment to Jesus Christ, I chose to be baptized identifying myself with Him, as *"we are buried with him by baptism into death: that like as Christ was raised up from the dead by the glory of the Father, even so we also should walk in newness of life."* (ROMANS 6:4)

My brothers and sisters in Christ instructed me to attend a Bible-preaching church upon my return to Canada to get grounded in God's Word; as it states, *"to present you holy and unblameable and unreproveable in his sight: If ye continue in the faith grounded and settled, and be not moved away from the hope of the gospel, which ye have heard."* (COLOSSIANS 1:22-24)

I attended a Baptist church in Toronto, Canada, close to where I was living at the time. I made friends with the young people there, although I still felt the moral obligation to attend Mass. I attended the Baptist church for a year, in addition to Catholic Mass. After that, I realized that I could not keep this up because I recognized that I was being pulled in two directions. *"And have no fellowship with the unfruitful works of darkness, but rather reprove them.."* (EPHESIANS 5:11) Doing some soul searching, I realized that I was not growing in the Catholic Church as I was in the Baptist church; remembering the words of Scripture, *"but you, dear friends, build yourselves up in your most holy faith and pray in the Holy Spirit."* (JUDE 1:20)

At one point, I wrote a letter to the Bishop asking to be excused from attending Mass, but I never mailed it. I made the difficult decision to stop attending Mass. It was difficult because I had made attending Mass a commitment many years earlier. However, my commitment to follow Christ was strengthened, and this gave me more strength than ever attending Mass, as Scripture states, *"I can do all things through Christ which strengtheneth me."* (PHILIPPIANS 4:13)

One of my personal struggles was committing acts of personal impurity. Going to Confession year after year, I was always struggling with this same sin for over a decade. Penances, prayers, and personal effort had no effect on ridding me of this bondage. One day I just cried out to the Lord from deep within my heart that I was in bondage, and would God please free me from this bondage. God heard my cry and delivered me from this bondage. *"The sorrows of death compassed me, and the pains of hell gat hold upon me: I found trouble and sorrow. Then called I upon the name of the LORD; O LORD, I beseech thee, deliver my soul... The LORD preserveth the simple: I was brought low, and he helped me."* (PSALM 116)

Having attended many funerals of family and friends in the Roman Catholic Church, I felt an emotional tug to "come back to the familiar."

However, most of the time there was a sense of morbidity in the Catholic funerals, while Evangelical funerals reflected a positive celebration of life.

Since I started to read testimonies in the book, Far From Rome Near to God, written by a number of former priests who have become born-again believers I began to understand the harsh and tyrannical nature of Roman Catholic Canon Law, especially regarding the Inquisition. *"Beware lest any man spoil you through philosophy and vain deceit, after the tradition of men, after the rudiments of the world, and not after Christ."* (COLOSSIANS 2:8)

Catholic seminarians study Greek philosophy at great length, between two and three years. When I endeavored to study at a Catholic seminary many years earlier, just after graduating from university, biblical courses were almost non-existent. Although I still believe in the benefits of a disciplined life, which is often characteristic of a Catholic upbringing, only a biblical upbringing will ultimately bear fruit for eternity, as our Lord Jesus said, *"I am the vine, ye are the branches: He that abideth in me, and I in him, the same bringeth forth much fruit: for without me ye can do nothing."* (JOHN 15:5) God is all holy; this is the distinguishing factor of His nature. Thus, this is the reason why I needed to be in right standing before Him. By His grace, I turned to Him in faith for the salvation that He alone can give. I knew that I was a sinner. As a result I believed on Jesus Christ for salvation, as Scripture states, *"For by grace are you saved through faith; and that not of yourselves: it is the gift of God: Not of works, lest any man should boast."* (EPHESIANS 2:8-9)

In 1982, I attended Northwest Baptist Theological Seminary in Vancouver, Canada for two years, graduating with a Master of Divinity. After graduation, I had hoped to become a Bible translator, but I ended up moving to the prairies with my new bride, Shirley, where I began my career as a chemist while serving in children's ministries at the churches that I attended. The Lord Jesus said, *"Suffer [permit] little children to come unto me, and forbid them not: for of such is the kingdom of God."* (LUKE 18:16)

Although Evangelicals and Catholics may use the same words, it was at seminary, and afterwards, during my personal study that I learned their concepts and definitions are often completely different. The Catholic Church emphasizes good works to commend believers in Jesus Christ to God. Then the Catholic Church presents her seven sacraments as the inherent means of obtaining the grace of the Holy Spirit. Thus, its official teaching states the following, *"The Church affirms that for believers the sacraments of the New Covenant are necessary for salvation.*" (CATECHISM OF THE CATHOLIC CHURCH, PARA 1129) Such teachings as these come under the Lord's curse of perverting the Gospel of Christ. (GALATIANS 1:9) Then Catholic priests use sacraments to mislead Catholic people. The Catholic Church teaches its priests "*have received from God a power that he has given neither to angels nor to archangels...God above confirms what priests do here below.*" (CATECHISM OF THE CATHOLIC CHURCH, PARA 983) The New Testament established pastors and elders to lead the Church, not priests! Why? Priests daily offer sacrifices on behalf of the people although Scripture states unequivocally, "*we are sanctified through the offering of the body of Jesus Christ once for all.*" (HEB 10:10)

I encourage you to study the following terms: sanctification, salvation, justification, and grace to understand the difference between what the Roman Catholic Church teaches and

what the Bible teaches. Linacer, who was a distinguished physician during the reign of Henry VIII, picked up the New Testament. "Reading it for a while, he tossed it from him with impatience and a great oath, exclaiming, 'Either this book is not true, or we are not Christians.'" He saw at once that the system of Papal Rome and the system of the New Testament were directly opposed to one another; no one who impartially compares the two systems can come to any other conclusion.

God has opened up doors of ministry to me in a variety of areas. When my father passed away, I was able to present the gospel message to family members. In 1991, God blessed me with an opportunity to visit Lithuania, the land of my forefathers, where I explained the gospel to my extended family. God has blessed me with a shared pastorate at a local ethnic church. "*And they departed, and went through the towns, preaching the gospel, and healing every where.*" (LUKE 9:6) The Lord has also opened up an electronic outreach on the Internet as I mentor younger men from around the world.

Conclusion

In my experience, most Evangelical Bible teachers have always encouraged their students to be "good Bereans," always confirming what is being taught by searching the Scriptures. Many Roman Catholic teachers do not trust the Scriptures to be clear enough for the people. However, the Bible says, *"These were more noble than those in Thessalonica, in that they received the word with all readiness of mind, and searched the scriptures daily, whether those things were so."* (ACTS 17:11)

A noted Bible teacher has also cautioned against being personal followers of a particular teacher. To listen to a multitude of Bible teachers is a safeguard against extremism. *"Where no counsel is, the people fall: but in the multitude of counselors there is safety."* (PROVERBS 11:14)

Having been a devout Catholic, I know from personal experience that listening to anyone attack my former church would immediately raise an emotional wall blocking communication. My brothers and sisters in Christ who have come from the Roman church into true faith in Christ know better than to attack what is dear to the hearts of a people. The better approach is to present the historical facts and the biblical account and let the Holy Spirit lead the people to make their own decision.

John the Baptist said, *"He must increase, but I must decrease."* (JOHN 3:30) But the Roman Catholic Church has exalted itself at the expense of our Lord Jesus Christ, to whom belongs all the glory, honor, and praise. As the bride of Christ, we seek to honor our Lord Christ Jesus and not seek our own glory.

Praying that you be reconciled with God, I finish with the words of the Apostle Paul, *"And all things are of God, who hath reconciled us to himself by Jesus Christ, and hath given to us the ministry of reconciliation; To wit, that God was in Christ, reconciling the world unto himself, not imputing their trespasses unto them; and hath committed unto us the word of reconciliation. Now then we are ambassadors for Christ, as though God did beseech you by us: we pray you in Christ's stead, be ye reconciled to God."* (2 CORINTHIANS 5:18-20)

—ARNOLD URBONAS

If you wish to contact me, please do so.
My email is: urbonasa@hotmail.com

Jackie Alnor

From Ritual to Relationship

As a baby boomer, I was raised in a large Roman Catholic family during the 1950s and 60s in Los Angeles County, USA. I have many fond memories, and painful ones as well, of growing up Catholic. I was the middle child in a large close-knit family of nine children, and we were all educated in Catholic school. My dad was our church's choir director, and my mom was the local president of Catholic Daughters. We had a Mary shrine in a grotto in our back yard, and there was a crucifix hanging on the wall in our living room filled with holy candles, holy water from Lourdes, and oil, which I was told was kept in case of an emergency.

My Catholic indoctrination focused on the so-called "mysteries of the Church." I was taught to believe Catholic dogma, whether it made sense to me or not, because the Pope had the keys to the kingdom, and what he says goes. Catholic mysticism had a superstitious tone in my upbringing. My Catholicism was a hodgepodge of sacraments and superstition, the sort of thing that the Catholic Church winks at but does not fully condone. My family would never miss Mass on Sundays and holy days for fear of staining our souls, and yet we saw nothing wrong with following horoscopes and using Ouija boards for fun and games.

I remember attending Mass as a youngster and being trained to whisper and show utmost respect for the mysterious presence of the Lord in the tabernacle. I would get goosebumps during the High Mass when the incense would fill the church. In my child-like understanding, the priest was closer to God than we who were in the pews. I had a fascination with religious sacramental statues, icons, and relics. They were both seductive and repelling to me. One of my earliest memories was walking into a neighbor lady's house to be greeted by a life-sized, bloody "Christ" hanging on a cross amid lit candles. I always got the heebie-jeebies visiting over there.

I remember my mother taking me to a strange Catholic celebration, the May Crowning, held at the Los Angeles Coliseum. I recall being afraid of the crowd of people there in the packed stadium. All eyes were on a larger-than-life statue of the "Virgin Mary" that was being carried in procession up to a podium where she was crowned with a wreath of beautiful roses. The crowd, hushed with a sense of awe, some with tears in their eyes, was reciting the rosary while staring transfixed at the statue. I was hot, tired, and happy to get out of there; yet, I was puzzled at what all of this meant.

My dad would sometimes take me to a church in Los Angeles where he would attend Mass on his way to work. It was called St. Vibiana's Cathedral. It looked like something right out of the Middle Ages. The place was dark and empty, and while my dad knelt at the altar to pray, I stared up at the strangest site above the altar. There was a glass case with the body of a beautiful dead lady inside. He told me that the body was of St. Vibiana, and her body never saw corruption, i.e., it would never decay. Dad said it was a miracle, however, they had to encase the body in wax to help preserve it better. That was the biggest relic I had ever seen, and I was awestruck being in its presence. When I saw the film "House of Wax," I thought of St. Vibiana during the scene where the madman, played by Vincent Price, was about to encase the beautiful leading lady in hot wax to preserve her beauty for all eternity.

When I was in the first or second grade, the nuns showed us a film in our school auditorium. It was a "so-called" true story of a young boy, Saint Marcellus. This boy was an orphan raised by monks somewhere in Europe. He was always in trouble, mostly because of being misunderstood. As a mischievous child myself, I really related to him. He used to sneak into the "attic" library, where he was not allowed to go, so he could look at a life-sized crucifix. As the story goes, one day a scorpion stung him, and he managed to get into some other trouble. He ran up to the attic where he felt comforted by the statue. That day, while he cried at the foot of the cross, the statue came to life and came down from the cross. It held and comforted him.

I was profoundly affected by this story, wondering why Jesus would do that for him and not for me. I, too, was a victim of being misunderstood. So, I would go to the altar of our church where a bigger-than-life sized crucifix hung above the altar. This "Jesus" of mine was made out of gold. In addition, I would pray to it and ask it to come to life and talk to me. However, it was all to no avail! Then, in the fourth grade, my mother was directing a school celebration of the Feast of the Immaculate Conception. She cast me in a little skit that depicted the Fatima Marian apparition appearing to the three children. I was able to play one of them. A statue of Mary was put high on a podium and the other children and I knelt onto kneelers*, and we were to pretend to be in a trance state with our hands folded in prayer. We were to

stare up at the lady while the choir sang the Ave Maria. I was struck with the story of Fatima and hoped for an apparition to appear to me.

I used to wear a scapular** around my neck because one of the Marian apparitions had promised that if you die wearing one (with Mary's image on it), she would get you out of the fiery Purgatory the first Saturday following your death. I also had a "miraculous medal" of Mary, and I think that one promised to spring me out of Purgatory after only three days. However, just to be sure, I still prayed all the little novena prayers that promised me some indulgences, i.e., time off from my purgatorial sentence.

One ritual in the Catholic Church that intrigued me was the Stations of the Cross. This is a ceremony held every Friday during Lent where more Scripture verses are read than in any other Catholic ritual. We would follow the "Passion" of Christ, showing how He was brutally scourged, mocked, and nailed to the cross. One of the twelve stations showed St. Veronica wiping Jesus' face with her veil and an image of his bloody face miraculously appeared on it. I never could find the Bible verse that told that part of the crucifixion story. However, my heart would be touched so deeply

---

* A Kneeler is a cushion or bench for kneeling.

** A scapular is a necklace that hangs down both in front and in back, with a small, flat rectangular pendant at each end. A scapular is worn under clothing in an inconspicuous manner. Traditional scapulars are made out of brown cloth similar to that worn by Carmelite nuns. They can also be made out of leather, various colored cloth, vinyl or plastic. Small scapulars can represent a certain devotion or spiritual idea from a community. These scapulars have two pieces of cloth (generally about an inch square), connected by cords and worn over the head. It often has a picture or a particular color, depending on the spirituality it stands for.

while reading the Gospel accounts that I would walk away from there with a real sense of remorse that He had to suffer for my sins.

Unanswered Questions

My first memory of questioning what I was being taught by the adults in my life was when I was around ten years old. Walking home from school with my sisters, wearing my uniform, some kids from the public elementary school began teasing us for being Catholics. I approached one and asked, "Why don't you like us? What have we done?" The little boy responded, "You worship statues and light candles to them, and one of the Ten Commandments says not to make any molten images."

I was flabbergasted. I ran the rest of the way home, went straight to my mom, and asked her if that was true. She said that we do not pray to statues, but only to what they represent. I asked about the commandment, and she explained to me that they did not list it as a commandment because it is the same as the first commandment: to love the Lord God. I was somewhat relieved, but I still felt something was not quite right.

I could not understand the meaning of the daily Mass, especially since I learned the liturgy in Latin. I could say every response, yet I had not the slightest idea of what I was saying. I took pride in myself that I could say those mysterious words so well. I felt I was doing something religious when I would have to fast for three hours before communion and when I would abstain from eating meat on Fridays. Then of course, it was a sin, and I did not want to have any black stains on my soul.

At the age of twelve, during the time I was being prepped for receiving my Confirmation, Vatican II changes began to take effect at our church. I was told it was no longer necessary to fast before communion, and I could now eat meat on Fridays, except during Lent. The Mass was now said in English instead of Latin, therefore it seemed to lose some of its mysteriousness.

I was filled with doubts and suspicions. I asked myself, "How can truth change, and how can something send you to hell one week and not the next?" I wondered, "What about those who were already in hell for committing the sins that are no longer sinful?" I could not reconcile these things in my mind. It was at this time in my life that I began to mistrust all adults in authority.

Vatican Council II, in essence, said to me that the Catholic Church authorities were admitting they were wrong about something and that their claims of infallibility were a cosmic joke. I knew that truth does not change, although I had never heard the Scripture verse: *"Jesus Christ, the same yesterday, today, and for ever."* (HEBREWS 13:8) I no longer had any confidence in their teachings since I knew the teachings could change with the next Church Council.

When the day of my Confirmation came, and I was to have hands laid on me by the bishop, my doubts were nagging at me. I did not want to go through with the ceremony, but I did not have any choice in the matter. The bishop also wanted my Confirmation class to take an oath never to drink alcohol, and we were told to stand up and swear not to ever drink. I stayed seated, as did a few others, because though I was not interested in drinking booze, I knew my dad drank, the priests drank wine at Mass, and I did not want to promise something I might not be able to keep. Nevertheless, I never did acquire a taste for alcohol.

The Dark Ages

By the time I was in high school, I wanted nothing whatsoever to do with church. My parents insisted that I go to Mass as long as I lived under their roof. Therefore, I would walk into the church, grab a bulletin, leave, and then show them the bulletin when they asked me if I went to Mass. I told them I got nothing out of going, but they did not care. I still had to go.

I lost all confidence in my parents and the Catholic Church, and I am sure those attitudes contributed to my rebellious nature. At the age of seventeen I left my home, located in a Los Angeles suburb, to join my hippie friends in northern California. I wanted nothing at all to do with religion, although I still had an interest in Ouija boards and astrology. I was also advancing into other occult practices, such as tarot cards and palm reading.

It did not take long for me to fall into great trouble and despair. I ended up pregnant by my hippie boyfriend who was already trying to distance himself from me before I discovered my condition. My first impulse was to run to "Mother Church." Since I was miles from home, alone, and scared, I sought refuge in a Catholic church in San Jose, California, where confessions were being heard. I confessed my sins and told the priest what peril I was in, being 17, pregnant, far from home and without a job, money, or a high school diploma. I was astounded that the priest did not want to discuss my problem; he dismissed me with a penance of ten "Hail Marys" and five "Our Fathers."

I never did the penance; I was devastated! I went home to southern California where I was sent to St. Anne's, a Catholic home for unwed mothers in Los Angeles. I was given a pregnant nun as a roommate. As a nun, she had taken a vow of silence, so she was not much company. I gave birth to a beautiful baby girl, and I was forced to give her up for adoption because nobody would take us in.*

I continued to nominally believe in the Lord Jesus Christ, but I felt let down by His church. I would go to Mass on Easter and midnight Mass every Christmas for the next ten years. I had some sort of strange connection to "Mother Church," however, my many questions about the truth of its teachings prevented me from any further involvement; but it was the only religion I knew. I pushed the questions out of my mind and filled the emptiness in my life with partying and drugs.

I became an avid reader and belonged to the "Book of the Month Club." I looked forward to reading anything I could get my hands on if it was exciting and spooky. Stephen King was my favorite author. However, one day I got a book in the mail called, "Michelle Remembers." It was supposed to be a true story given by a girl while under hypnosis. It tells of her recalling hidden memories of a childhood of satanic, ritualistic abuse. As she gave the gruesome details of watching human sacrifices and mutilations while in a trance state, she would manifest ugly welts on her skin in the shape of the devil's tail. The book included photographs of this phenomenon.

This book really scared me. I had just finished reading a book called "The Entity," which was another "true" story of a Los Angeles woman being sexually assaulted by unseen demons, and between these two books, I was convinced of the existence of the devil. I said to myself, "If the devil is real, and I believe he is, then there must be a God."

From Futility to Faith

I went to the local Catholic bookstore and bought a Catholic Bible. I began reading the Old Testament. I thought I knew the New Testament already, but I was only slightly familiar with the four gospels. The Bible began to be a source of encouragement to me and I was becoming convinced that it was truly God's word to man. I felt comforted knowing that God was real too; that the devil was not stronger than God.

* We found each other 26 years later. We are friends, and she is a Christian. Praise the Lord!

However, my life did not change much just because I was again open to matters of faith. I was going through a difficult time at the close of a bad relationship, and I was facing another Christmas alone. At twenty-seven years of age, I felt like an old maid. Most of my sisters and friends had married and divorced already, and I was always the proverbial "brides-maid." Christmas was particularly hard because everyone would gather at my parents' house with their spouses and children, and I would be alone in their midst.

So, for the first Christmas in my life, I attended a Christian church instead of Mass for Christmas. I went to the only church I knew of that taught the Bible, and that was Calvary Chapel of Costa Mesa. The pastor, Chuck Smith, taught that day on the pagan roots of Christmas that originated from the winter's solstice of Saturnalia. I was very much amused by it and amazed by what he was saying. I was impressed. The people did not look at all like the Jesus Freaks I had envisioned. I held on to the bulletin, put it in my nightstand drawer, and forgot about it.

I periodically read the Bible until a personal crisis brought me to the end of myself. I came under intense conviction of my sinfulness while reading the Gospel of John. I cried out to God to save me and I was determined under the convicting power of the Holy Spirit to forsake my way of life and turn the reins over to Jesus Christ. However, I did not know how to pray. It was three o'clock in the morning, and I felt disgusted with myself, but I did not know how to present my petitions to the Lord.

I opened my nightstand drawer and pulled out the Calvary Chapel bulletin. Here it was, the Fourth of July, and I had held onto it since the previous Christmas. It had the phone number of a 24-hour prayer hotline. I dialed the number expectantly. The first words out of my mouth when the guy answered was "Help me! I want to pray and I do not know how. I have been a Catholic all my life and we always recited Hail Mary's and other prayers, but that will not do for me now. I want to know how to pray in the right way."

I was choked up and found it hard to speak. There was silence for what seemed like an eternal minute on the other end of the line. May-be the guy did not know if I was for real. However, he led me to the sixth chapter of Matthew and said, "When Jesus gave the Lord's prayer it wasn't meant to be recited by rote." He read, *"But when ye pray, use not vain repetitions, as the heathen do: for they think that they shall be heard for their much speaking. Be not ye therefore like unto them: for your Father knoweth what things ye have need of, before ye ask him. After this manner therefore pray ye…"* (MATTHEW 6:7-9)

As he read the Lord's Prayer, I followed along in my Bible and saw the words "Our Father" as if for the very first time, as though blinders had been removed from my eyes. He prayed with me, and I wept with the most cleansing tears ever shed in my life. From that moment on my spiritual eyes were opened and I began to read the Bible with understanding. Every verse I read revealed more about God and His Son, Jesus, and I could not get enough of this life-giving manna from heaven. For several months, whenever I spoke to others of what Jesus had done for me, I could barely hold back my tears of gratitude.

Family Reaction

The first person I called to share the excitement was my mom. She listened to my testimony, and my words brought her to tears. I found out later that she had assumed that I was going to come back to "Mother Church" now that I was taking the Lord seriously. However, I had no inclination to darken the doorway of a Catholic church again. I had not found the truth in that system. Even as I read my Catholic Bible, I refrained from reading the footnotes of the Catholic interpretations it contained. I wanted to hear directly from God, not from man's opinion of God. I wanted truth—the truth—God's truth! I knew the reality of deception since I had been deceived already. Moreover, I did not want to end up in any religious cult or under any man's control. I had to know the mind of Christ, and I could only do that by reading His word.

As I studied the "Catholic Bible," so many Scripture verses would condemn ideas I had been taught growing up. I discovered Bible verses that would outright condemn such Catholic ideas as Purgatory, Transubstantiation, indulgences, prayers to saints, Mary worship and the like. However, what frightened me the most was when I read the seventeenth chapter of the book of Revelation. I could not deny the familiarity of the description of the Mother Harlot: *"arrayed in purple and scarlet colour, and decked with gold and precious stones and pearls, having a golden cup in her hand full of abominations and filthiness of her fornication."* (REVELATION 17:4)

I felt such a sense of betrayal by Rome. I mourned over her for a long time, but I had to put her out of my life—she was an imposter! I tried not to let my disgust with Rome affect my love for my parents and other well-meaning Catholic relatives.

The Lord is My Shepherd!

As I reflect on my life, I see the Lord's hand on me from the beginning. He directed my steps even when I was not aware of His presence. My salvation is based on Christ's finished work on the cross of Calvary. That is, He died to pay the penalty for my sins. I can add "nothing" to that great atonement. Sure, my life is lived in a more pure manner as a Christian than it ever was as a Catholic, but none of my selfless works adds to my worthiness before my perfect Savior. He has given me a gift—one I did not earn.

I love Jesus so much because, like the woman in the Bible who had the alabaster box, those who have been forgiven much—love much. (LUKE 7:36-50) There are several verses of Scripture I have held onto since I first was saved. These passages helped to establish me in the faith, *"once delivered to the saints."* (JUDE 1:3) Romans 10 is one that I have returned to again and again since my born-again experience that took me from darkness to light on that Independence Day, 25 years ago. I leave you with its wisdom, *"The word is nigh thee, even in thy mouth, and in thy heart: that is, the word of faith, which we preach; That if thou shalt confess with thy mouth the Lord Jesus, and shalt believe in thine heart that God hath raised him from the dead, thou shalt be saved. For with the heart man believeth unto righteousness; and with the mouth confession is made unto salvation. For the scripture saith, whosoever believeth on him shall not be ashamed."* (ROMANS 10:8-11)

—JACKIE ALNOR

If you wish to contact me please do so.
My email address is: jackie.alnor@gmail.com

JOE MIZZI

The Weight of Responsibility to Accountability in Christ

I WAS BORN IN 1966 ON THE TINY ISLAND OF MALTA, IN THE MIDDLE OF the Mediterranean. My dear parents were hard-working people. Although my father was employed full-time, his salary was not sufficient to support the family, so he also worked as a farmer. My mother not only took care of the house and the family, but during her rest, she knitted woolen cardigans to earn some extra money. They cared for six children. There were my two brothers, three sisters, and I.

My parents were God-fearing people, and they made sure to teach all of us the Catholic faith. Apart from the daily religious instruction at school, they also sent me to catechism after school hours in preparation for the communion. When I was older, I went to classes for the sacrament of Confirmation. Attendance to Mass on Sunday was obligatory; my mother encouraged us by word and example to attend church daily. Every evening, my father used to gather all the family for the recitation of the rosary.

Proud to be Catholic

As a young teenager, I was a proud member of the Catholic Church—believing it to be the one true church of the Lord Jesus Christ. I did not know much about other religions, but the priests at the bishop's seminary where I studied told us that Greek Orthodox and Evangelical churches were breakaway bodies guilty of serious sin due to separating from the Catholic Church.

We were taught about the Lord Jesus and His death on the cross. However, it was emphasized that we had to make our own contribution to our salvation. Doing good works and living a moral and religious life were necessary to increase personal righteousness and keeping us on the way to heaven, and finally gaining eternal life. Of special importance were attending Mass and participating in the Eucharist for spiritual nourishment and freeing us from our daily faults. Failure to attend Mass on Sunday would be a grave sin that if left un-confessed would send me to hell—forever.

Confession was an intricate part of my life. I confessed my sins to a priest after which he would prescribe some works of penance to make satisfaction for my sins. Usually the penance would consist of saying the Lord's Prayer and Ave Maria (A Catholic prayer addressed to Mary) for a definite number of times. I was left in no doubt that my heart remained stained with sin until I performed penance. I did not recite those prayers because of my personal faith in God but as a "form of punishment."

The feast of our Lady of Sorrows is a very special occasion in my country. Solemn processions are organized in many towns and villages, which are attended by a good portion of the population. Our family was no exception. It was a day of fasting, and in the evening we would join the penitential procession saying the rosary and other prayers while we walked behind the statue of Our Lady. We were happy to be doing something—fasting and praying—to cancel our sins. We performed those religious works to make ourselves fit for heaven, for we knew that we were not yet good enough. As a Catholic, I did not rest my salvation in the hands of Jesus, rather, I was striving to to merit, or earn, eternal life by obeying the commandments, participating in the sacraments, praying, and fasting. Just one mortal sin at the end and I would lose all my merits and my soul. So, although we saw salvation as somehow related to Jesus and His cross, it was equally clear that the crucial factor that determined where I would spend eternity was my own personal contribution of good deeds. I had a definite part to play to achieve forgiveness and to be accepted by God.

Weight of Responsibility

At home, at church, and on street corners there were images and statues depicting "souls" in the flames of purgatory. They were a constant reminder that we needed to do more and more good works to prepare ourselves before we died. The mind of a young boy would remain impressed by the scene of men, women, and children in the agony of fire. The horror of that picture can only be surpassed by the Roman Catholic doctrine of purgatory itself. The faithful must pay a debt of punishment by penance and good works on earth, and failing to do so, they must finish paying the debt of their sin by personal suffering and torment in purgatory, or worse, the eternal fire of hell.

Looking back, I can see what a heavy burden my parents felt as they strove to rescue all their children from the torments of purgatory. They too feared the possibility and consequences of failure. I felt very troubled and concerned. I took seriously my duty to say prayers, confess sins, do penance, and perform good works to decrease the torment awaiting me after death, and to keep my soul on the path to heaven and ultimate happiness.

A Strange Question

When I was 14, my brother came home one day and asked me a very strange question: "Do you realize that we are saved by faith in Christ, and not by our good works?" His statement shocked me. He was denying the faith that we cherished so much. At that time, I did not know that the religious conversation that followed would mark the beginning of a dramatic change in my life. I could not believe that such a tragedy as this had happened to our family, and I was determined to convince him of his error and bring him back to the Catholic Church. I knew that I had to study the Bible for myself in order to disarm my brother and prove that the doctrines of the Catholic Church are found in the Bible. And study I did! I read the Catholic Bible, both in English and Maltese. I also asked questions to my religious instruction teacher so that I would be better prepared.

The Bible Reaches My Heart

The reading of the Bible had an unexpected and unforeseen effect. Initially, I used the Bible merely as an argumentative tool. Gradually, however, the words of Scripture began to penetrate the very depths of my soul. Because my brother always seemed to be able to quote Scripture to prove his point, I was determined that I would do the same. However, as I read the Bible, there was a gradual shift in my concern. I was no longer merely interested in a religious argument, but I had a pressing concern about my personal salvation and relationship with the Lord.

The Sermon on the Mount particularly impressed me, and I determined to make it the standard of my life. I tried to follow the teaching of the Lord; I thought that this would gain me much merit. Yet, the harder I tried, the more evident it became that I could never reach the high moral and spiritual standard demanded by Christ. His standards were beyond my reach. An overwhelming sense of frustration and defeat forced me to reconsider my religious beliefs about good works. How could I be as perfect as our heavenly Father is perfect—as Jesus demands? I would have to attain this standard if I wanted to reach Heaven. I began to see that I was failing miserably to be right with God by my own obedience and goodness.

What the Bible Actually Says

When I discovered what the apostle Paul had to say about this matter, it was as if he were speaking directly to me:

> *For by grace are ye saved through faith, and that not of yourselves; it is the gift of God, not of works, lest any man should boast ...Therefore by the deeds of the law there shall no flesh be justified in his sight: for by the law is the knowledge of sin...Wherefore the law was our schoolmaster to bring us unto Christ, that we might be justified by faith.*
> (EPHESIANS 2:8, 9; ROMANS 3:20 AND GALATIANS 3:24)

I must have read these passages a hundred times. Why does the apostle Paul say that works do not save us? As a Catholic, I believed that I was supposed to do good works in order to merit eternal life, and I was trying to be right with God by obeying His law. Instead, the law was revealing my failures and weaknesses. God was breaking my pride and preparing me to believe in Jesus Christ.

Christ, the Sin-bearer

As a Roman Catholic, I knew that salvation had to do with the sacrifice of Christ on the cross. We used to repeat this prayer, especially during Lent, "We adore You, O Christ, and we praise You. Because by Your Holy Cross, You have redeemed the world." We were taught that Jesus opened the gate of heaven that had been closed by Adam's sin, and that now it was up to us to enter that open door by doing good and participating in the sacraments. With further reading of the Bible, I discovered that the Lord Jesus accomplished something much greater than that. It says:

Who his own self bare our sins in his own body on the tree, that we, being dead to sins, should live unto righteousness: by whose stripes ye were healed...For Christ also hath once suffered for sins, the just for the unjust, that he might bring us to God." (1 PETER 2:24; 3:18)

The work of Jesus was much, much greater than opening the door of heaven for hard working Catholics. The Bible was saying that Jesus paid the debt for all my sins. Instead of me working all my life and doing penance and good works to pay for my sins, Jesus did this for me.

He bore my sins on the cross. How different this was to what I had been taught to believe. The punishment for sin is not repeating a few prayers or suffering in the fires of purgatory. The penalty for sin is death; yet, Jesus died in the place of sinners. The Lord Jesus did not just make salvation possible by opening the door of Heaven. No, on the cross Jesus became the substitute for sinners by dying in their place. Therefore, we cannot possibly make satisfaction for our sin or merit eternal life by anything we do; rather, we must entrust our salvation into the hands of the Lord Jesus Christ. He is able to save completely; His blood cleanses from all sin.

His Work, or Mine?

God brought me to this crossroad. On one hand, I could continue to live according to the religion that promised me eternal life on the merits of my works. On the other hand, I could abandon that teaching and completely trust in the Lord Jesus Christ alone for my salvation. I was alone at home one evening when I knelt down and prayed. I acknowledged my sin and guilt and expressed my faith in Lord Jesus Christ. I admitted that I could not pay my debt by doing good, and I asked God to receive me for the sake of Jesus Christ His Son. He did. The joy in my heart was unspeakable!

God illustrated to me the wonderful truth of Jesus' substitutionary death on my fifteenth birthday. I was supposed to be helping my father in the fields. Instead, I was driving the tractor up and down a busy road without my father's permission and without a driving license. I was involved in a traffic accident, causing hundreds of dollars worth of damages to the brand new van involved in the collision. It was entirely my fault. My father was not guilty. Yet, my father paid all the damages for me. I did not pay a single penny. I will always be grateful for my father's goodness. That is exactly what the Son of God did on my behalf. He died for me, freed me from sin that I may live for Him who loves me with such amazing love.

—JOE MIZZI

If you have any comments or questions kindly
email me at: josephmizzi@onvol.net

Joe Mizzi is the founder and director of Just for Catholics:
http://www.justforcatholics.org/index.htm

MATTHEW CSERHATI

Grace in Christ in Hungary

I WAS BORN IN THE UNITED STATES, AND UPON THE BEHEST OF MY Catholic father, I attended a Catholic private elementary school in Maryland. Later, after I had moved there with my twin brother, I attended a Franciscan high school in the city of Szentendre, Hungary. My uncle, a Franciscan priest, was working in Switzerland.

I would describe myself as a person who used to be a typical Catholic, although my Catholic faith had been tainted by modern thoughts. However, I tried to be a good Catholic before I was seventeen years of age. My Catholic faith meant keeping the traditions and orders of the Catholic church. I read one or two books about Catholicism. When I was a bit older, I read Dante's Divine Comedy. My basic train of thought was to be a good person and to work as many good deeds as possible in order to enter the kingdom of heaven. I thought that I would be so good that it would be a breeze to get in.

A Deep Impression

I was really fascinated by the Catholic faith—the pomp of it all. I even read a few parts of the Bible. At that time, though Catholic, I believed that the Bible was the ultimate source of truth. Still, I believed that the priests and the pope in Rome were so clever that they would always be able to infallibly interpret it in the right way. I

Matthew is on the left with his brother.
Below is his uncle, a Franciscan priest

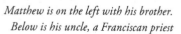

did not know that the Catholic Bible, which I read, had some parts added to it, for example, as when compared to the true canon of the Old Testament! In fact, there were things in my life in conflict with what the Bible said. For example, I thought that I would be good enough to "allow myself a few little sins now and then," because my "good deeds' economy" allowed it. I thought that, even in the worst case, I would be able to scratch myself out a place in lower purgatory and then make my way back to heaven.

Little I knew, that in my spiritual condition, I would have to stand before God's perfect standard on Judgment Day. *"As it is written, 'There is none righteous, no, not one: There is none that understandeth, there is none that seeketh after God. They are all gone out of the way, they are together become unprofitable; there is none that doeth good, no, not one.'"* (ROMANS 3:10-12)

The Old Nature at Work

There were times when I did quite horrendous things, such as beating the cat, being mean to the neighbor's kids, or sometimes fighting with my own brother, which made our mother quite sad. In Catholic school, we read the story of the prodigal son. He was the son who went and sinned his life away in decadence, but later came back to his father in repentance. We often overlook this parable. (LUKE 15:11-32) It is written that the older son had a hardened heart towards his younger brother and was far from God: After the younger brother returns, we read, *"And he [a servant] said unto him, 'Thy brother is come; and thy father hath killed the fatted calf, because he hath received him safe and sound.' And he was angry, and would not go in."* (LUKE 15:27, 28) Not unlike the older son, I was simply trying to bargain with God and give Him my good deeds instead of searching out His will for my life. The following verses from John tell something about this. The Bible speaks of the Samaritan woman who "ritually" worshipped on the mountain, but still did not know God. *"But the hour cometh, and now is, when the true worshippers shall worship the Father in spirit and in truth: for the Father seeketh such to worship him. God is a Spirit: and they that worship him must worship him in spirit and in truth."* (JOHN 4:23, 24)

Besides these sins, which I had previously overlooked, I was filled with a false sense of smugness and superiority towards those who were not Catholic or Christian, and who, therefore, were sinners. I would feel sort of a just anger at sinful people who seemed to have it good. Little did I know (that God desires to have all men saved and to come to the knowledge of the truth. (1 TIMOTHY 2:3-5) Many of my Catholic friends are in this situation. Because of this, I believe many Catholics fall prey to hypocrisy.

Seeing Things the Way They Were

As a Catholic, I would have been outraged if any negative critique or slander would befall the Roman church or the Pope—which itself is quite a source of judgmentalism—even my wishing people into hell. What I did not understand at that time was why one of my teachers said that Good Friday was a good day for humanity; a day one should be happy for Jesus' death. I did not understand why we should have been happy for the death of the Son of God, since we had to earn our way into heaven anyway. While reading Dante's works, another thing that I did not understand was why pagans were also included in the "nine circles"(The orbits of the nine planets of the solar system) of heaven.

A major shift happened in my life when I was in high school, and, by this time, I was even more prepared to commit my life to Catholicism. As I saw it, the high school I attended was an institution meant to "catholicize" the students; a plan to spread Catholicism all over the country. Before entering high school, I learned by rote memory answers to questions regarding the Catholic faith with the assistance of a Father Theodosius. My baptism was celebrated at the Church of Pasarét in the capital city of Budapest. At the beginning of high school, I pretty much revered our priestly teachers. I thought that they were good people who would lovingly help my brother and me because we had just recently come from America and were still having difficulties with the Hungarian language. The problem was that I underestimated the sinfulness of human nature. I would describe the four years in high school as one of the worst periods in my life. Because we came from another country, all the other students and even some of the teachers took advantage of us. Since my brother and I were sensitive, their abuse was very hard on us. It was no type of ordinary abuse, however. Kicking, punching, and insulting us was quite common. So much so, that the torment was so great for my brother that he had to go to a sanitarium for three months. During this dark period, I realized that I had to help my brother if I wanted to say that I was a good person. However, the sad fact was that at this time my understanding of human nature had to crumble, because I did not help him. It was very much like *"For they loved the praise of men more than the praise of God."* (JOHN 12:43) This was a heavy burden, which I had to carry for two years. Yes, as everybody else, I was a sinful person. Indeed, I needed forgiveness.

Discovering the Real Jesus

God had not abandoned me; one day I went home after the history teacher had given me a failing grade on a test because of who I was. At home, I found a Bible lying on the table. I opened it and read, *"Better is a dinner of herbs where love is, than a stalled ox and hatred therewith."* (PROVERBS 15:17) This was to later help me in not trying to find favor with the people at high school who loathed me, but to try to find the will of God. After high school, another great turning point occurred in my life. It was at this time that I went to a Christian camp to the north of Szentendre. Real Christians were spending their summer there. I sensed that these people were quite different than those people I had met at high school. They talked to Jesus Christ in a very personal way, as though they knew him like they knew any other person. They trusted in Jesus, instead of trusting in something by which (if they would repeat prayers by rote) they could reach some desired result. The Bible talks about this: *"And by their prayer for you, which long after you for the exceeding grace of God in you."* (2 CORINTHIANS 9:14) Their prayers differed from my Catholic prayers in that they were based on Scripture and not just some repeated memorized prayers. They emptied their hearts out to Jesus Christ in a very personal way. This was strange for me as a Catholic, because even though at times I felt God close to me, I still felt awkward when coming before Him. They told me about how one can get to know Jesus as Lord, Savior, and Redeemer. I was happy that by the end of the camp I was able to go to my brother for forgiveness.

My Conversion

Later on, as I attended Christian church services and Bible studies, I understood how one becomes a Christian. This was the grace of God, as I see it. I was convicted of sin; I realized my lost condition before the All Holy God, and I was ready, by God's grace, to believe on the Lord Christ Jesus. I realized that I was spiritually dead in trespasses and sins and therefore without any hope of salvation. My receiving from Christ, and in Christ, is all summed up in one word—grace. *"And of his fulness have all we received, and grace for grace."* (JOHN 1:16)

Now I can proclaim that I am a child of God who has received forgiveness, once and for all time, totally free from the bondage of sin. I can now stand in front of Him, thankfully not to my own merit, but to the merit of the true and perfect Jesus Christ. Soon afterwards, prayer took on a new meaning when I asked for, and gave thanks for, personal things. I am thankful that now I can personally rely on God and the Holy Spirit.

Now I know that I have eternal life, not because of what I did—not counting on my own dubious righteousness, but on the righteousness of Jesus Christ, through whom we have everything God wishes to give as a gift, which does not have to be earned through toil—but received by faith alone.

Answered Prayers

A verse from the Bible, which I had often heard after becoming a Christian, is *"But seek ye first the kingdom of God, and his righteousness; and all these things shall be added unto you."* (MATTHEW 6:33) As a concrete example, I could tell you how I was able to get what should have been a doctoral position at the Biological Research Center in Szeged after not being able to find a position anywhere around Budapest. Many places were filled up, and I was studying to be a bioinformatician,* which is quite a new science within biology, meaning even less places to secure employment. Yet, I was able to get a position at Szeged through the help of Christian friends. All my thanks for this goes to the God of grace. As I can see now, God has led me on a wonderful path to a deeper knowledge of Him from the Bible.

Sharing the True Gospel

What is most important to me was that after I was born again I felt free to do good deeds. God had set me free to do them, but not to placate his anger. I am free in His love to do them, and I know that I am able to do them; I do not have to fear punishment if I do not have them. For the love and mercy of God, I felt free to hate sin and turn away from it. Compared to my prior life as a Catholic, I found it surprising that I was able to speak with people about God. I was even able to talk to a few of my biology teachers at the university about my belief in a literal six-day

---

* Bioinformatics or computational biology is the use of techniques from applied mathematics, informatics, statistics, and computer science to solve biological problems.

creation and the importance of the Gospel. I can also say with Paul as he states in his letter to the Romans: *"I beseech you therefore, brethren, by the mercies of God, that ye present your bodies a living sacrifice, holy, acceptable unto God, which is your reasonable service. And be not conformed to this world: but be ye transformed by the renewing of your mind, that ye may prove what is that good, and acceptable, and perfect, will of God."* (ROMANS 12:1, 2)

The message of the Gospel, of all that the Lord Christ did or suffered, is that the Lord Jesus Christ is ready to receive all sinners that come to Him. Know that He is able to make us right with the Father; He is ready and willing to receive us. The testimony that He has given us concerning His goodness and love cannot be called into question and none dare question or deny His power. It is rightly taken for granted that Christ is able to touch us with His grace although we may have lived many years of our lives in rites and rituals that proved to be empty. Believe He can, and He will! Christ Jesus is able to save all those, and only those, who come to God by Him. All things in heaven and earth are committed unto Him. All power is His, and He will use it for the assured salvation of all that come to Him in faith. Believe on Him alone. You will be secure, accepted in the Beloved, that you may behold His Glory, knowing that such will be for all eternity. *"Therefore if any man be in Christ, he is a new creature: old things are passed away; behold, all things are become new."* (2 CORINTHIANS 5:17)

In His name,
MATTHEW CSERHATI

If you wish to contact me, please email me at: cs_matyi@yahoo.com

MARY MCGUIGAN

A Training Ground for Discernment

MOM WAS A "DEVOUT" METHODIST IN 1913 WHEN SHE "DARED" TO MARRY a "devout" Catholic man. As a result, her family disowned her. This was later negated when the loving sisters of Mom chose to renew relationships in their golden years. Into this union were born eighteen children: eleven boys and seven girls. Three of these died in infancy. Mom and dad knelt by their bedside each evening and prayed. They attended Mass every Sunday. During the Second World War, they attended Mass almost every day and lit the red vigil lights in the front of the church, paying $.25 each for five lights in honor of their five sons who served in the U.S. military. All of them came home alive, although two or three of them had been injured. Each received the Purple Heart. A grand celebration was held beginning with a Mass of Thanksgiving, a great meal, photographs taken, and a dance to which the neighborhood was invited.

A few months before the war broke out, my oldest sister entered the Franciscan Sisters of the Holy Family. This group of nuns came two weeks each summer to teach "vacation school" in our home parish. One of my sisters always admired them and their work, and she decided she wanted to live this life. She was seventeen when she and another sister who was sixteen also decided to join the convent to become Franciscan Sisters of the Holy Family. The sixteen-year-old stayed only six weeks and returned home due to being home sick. My third sister made the remark that no matter how long she had to wait she was also going to become a Sister. This statement came because of a mandate by our dad that before we could go away to school we had to learn to cook and keep house. After eighth grade, we all stayed home for this express purpose. For some reason, this third sister was allowed to go into the convent immediately after eighth grade. Two years later, sister number two returned to the convent to stay. I was the next girl in line. My parents had made several remarks that they were so glad that the girls were in the convent because they were "safe." They were not getting into trouble, as were some of the other girls in our community their age. These remarks influenced me to also consider becoming a nun. I considered myself unloved by my father and I do not remember one single conversation with him. I asked my mom to ask Dad if he wanted me to join the convent. Mom would not say whether they wanted me to become a Sister. She said that it was up to me. When I decided to go, I asked her to tell Dad. She said that he did not say much, but she said he was surprised. I believe he considered me too much of a 'wild' teenager to think of such a vocation.

I worked during the summer of 1950 at candling eggs in the local produce company. It was my first job away from home. With the money I earned, I purchased the necessary items for the convent and had $34 left over. This money I gave to my dad while on our trip to the convent where I entered as a postulant—wanting to seek admission into a religious order.

There were three years in training to become a nun. The first year as a postulant, we wore mid-calf length black dresses with a small cape over the shoulders and a white collar similar to a priest's collar. Long black stockings and black shoes completed our outfits. We studied the rule of the order (a set of guidelines formulated by the founders of the community) and Church history (according to the Catholic Church's view). After completion of this year, we were examined by some official designated by the authorities at the Motherhouse, to see whether we were ready to become Sisters. We then participated in a ceremony where we dressed as brides and received our nun habits. This took place in the chapel, and we were allowed to invite our immediate families.

The following year was called "Canonical Year" because we studied Canon Law or "Law of the Catholic Church." It was considered a very important year and we were more restricted from contact with family and friends.

After our third year, we took temporary vows. That meant they were for one year only and would be renewed each year for the following two years before we would be allowed to take final, perpetual vows. During that three-year period, we were to pursue our duties in whatever the convent decided for us. These duties could be housekeeping, teaching, nursing, etc.; whatever the community of sisters had decided was appropriate for each member to do.

A few incidents occurred during my training years. One of them was when I mentioned to the Postulant Mistress that I could not make up my mind whether I wanted to become a housekeeper or a teacher. Her remark was "You will become a teacher." That ended the discussion. Another time, I got up the courage to approach the Novice Mistress and tell her that I was afraid to speak with her. Since I had three older sisters who were also in the convent, I had a reputation to live up to. My sisters were well respected, so I was to follow suit. Even though we had been taught that our family heritage was not to be pursued, it now seemed important that I follow their pattern and not be an individual! This affected me.

We were also told to have blind obedience, i.e., do as we were told and not to ask questions. In those three years of training, we were given specific cleaning duties, which we were to do each day. I tried to perform mine as quickly as possible and then go to study hall. One morning the Novice Mistress came into the study hall and asked me why I had not done my cleaning. I said that I had done it. She said that I had not done it. When I insisted, she became visibly angry and stormed out of the room. I could not understand why she would insist that I had not done my work when I knew that I had. Perhaps it was part of the blind obedience training, and I was to humbly acknowledge my mistake and go do the work over.

My first assignment after convent was to a "mission" in the Chicago area. When I left the convent, one of my brothers thought that if I had not been sent to Chicago I would not have left the convent. He and another member of my family thought the "Big City" was my undoing. I was to teach third grade. At the time, I had no training in teaching. The Chicago area did not require teachers to have Bachelor of Arts degrees. I had not completed my high school, so I was sent to that area. My high school education and teacher training was completed during my first year of teaching. I sometimes think of those poor students that I had that first year of teaching. I was very strict and unyielding, and I am sure some of them suffered mental anguish from my methods. There were fifty-three students in my classroom.

After our first year on mission, the other Sisters and I would travel back to the Motherhouse during the summer months to study. That was when college courses were completed. An older Sister was assigned to counsel and/or supervise the younger Sisters who were still under temporary

vows. After my first year, this Sister called me into her office and told me that one of the older Sisters who was living with me during my first year of teaching was concerned about me because I was a bit "giddy" at the convent. I was admonished to become more serious. This caused me much anxiety and I "clammed up" during the next year. I cried myself to sleep nearly every night, and there was no one in whom I could confide. As a result, I ended up in the hospital with a side ache. It definitely was imagined, as the doctors could find nothing physically wrong with me. I recall sitting in the middle of the hospital bed joking and laughing with another patient in the room. I was making no sense at all. Another Sister, who was living with me at that time, was given a leave of absence and received services as a mental patient. She later left the community. At any rate, I continued this "clamming up" for the next two or three years.

One great cause of anxiety for me was during the closing of a school year and the ensuing summer months. Each Sister had one trunk in which she could place her personal belongings. Before leaving to attend school or other summer assignments, she was to pack all her belongings into this trunk. This was so that if she were re-assigned during the summer, she would not have to travel back to her last mission but could proceed to her new assignment and then the former mission would have her trunk shipped to her at her new position. This process each summer caused a loss of sleep and other anxieties for me. Toward the end of July, after the evening meal, all the Sisters in the convent would line up according to age. Those who entered the earliest were first, and in silence, they would proceed to the chapel. As they came to the chapel door, the Mother Superior would hand each one a small slip of paper with the next year's assignments. Numerous Sisters shed many tears at this time. This was part of our vow of obedience.

Poverty was never a problem for me, probably due to the poverty in which our family lived. However, it is difficult to see any sense of poverty within the confines of convent life now. My Sisters and their fellow companions have all the material comforts that would qualify them as middle and upper class citizens. They travel and live where they wish, either alone in apartments or wherever they choose. They may also receive monetary gifts from their lay friends.

Superiors at the various missions were assigned for three periods and then they could serve another term of three years, but no more. My second mission was in another part of the Chicago area. The Sister who was the Superior was also the principal of the school. Her second term as Superior ended and she remained on as principal. An older Sister was assigned the Superior position. She was from a small community in Iowa and certainly was not used to the Big City. She came with a determination to bridle the wild happenings she had heard were going on at this particular mission. There was friction big time! She lasted only one year and both she and the principal were transferred the following year. The next year a new Superior/Principal was assigned to our convent. She did not want the position but, naturally, she was to take the position anyway. By mid-year, I was doing the work of the principal because she was not able physically, mentally, nor emotionally to do what was expected of her.

As stated above, in the novitiate we were encouraged to blind obedience. Do not ask questions because we were doing what God wanted us to do. During this year, when I was "acting principal," we received directives from the authorities at the Motherhouse that if we saw things that we felt were not as they should be we could make them known to these authorities. Five or six of us who were on this mission during that year decided to write our concerns to the Motherhouse. We stated what was and was not going on at this particular mission and what we thought should be done. As a result, all of those who wrote concerns were reassigned to other missions.

My next place of work was in a suburb of Chicago. During this time, the "community" began changing the design of our "habits." They were modified to shorter lengths with veils that were shorter and placed back on the head so that there was hair showing. This particular mission had a principal who was also from small town USA. She began to rely on the "in group" of mothers at the school. They influenced her as to which students were from good families and which were from questionable families. I was accustomed to being drawn to those students who were considered the "outcasts." We got along fine and I was able to help them deal with some of their problems. Principals were to begin rating their teachers that year. I received unsatisfactory ratings.

These 'questionable' students would drop in at the convent in the evenings to just sit and talk. They had nothing in particular to say but just wanted to get some attention and to be heard. This was suburbia and they lived in houses instead of "homes." One day, the Superior questioned me about this turn of events. She thought that since this was the time when the Sisters were to be gathered together for their "recreation" period for the day, I should be with them instead of being with these students. She asked if I would be interested in seeing a psychiatrist. The Diocese of Chicago had recently set up a mental health program and Sisters were now allowed to see any of the assigned doctors of various professions to get the help they needed. I agreed to see this psychiatrist and began going to him once a week. I was a little hesitant because I knew that he was not a Catholic and probably would not understand my situation. After the third or fourth visit, he said to me, "Perhaps you had a vocation to be a nun at one time but that is changing, and you no longer have a vocation to be a nun." This remark frightened me and I refused to go back to him again. My reason for being frightened was that it was stressed upon us while we were in training that once we passed our sixth year in the convent and had taken our solemn vows, we were to stay and were not to leave the convent. This was our vocation. The Lord must have had other plans for me. I do not remember telling anyone why I would not go back, but my Superior found a priest who was considered a great counselor for Sisters. Most of his clients were women: Sisters and laywomen.

Another practice that was suggested to us was to renew our vows each day after Holy Communion. I did this daily until the last few months that I was a nun, so I was sincere in doing what I had been taught was right. These events were "the beginning of the end" for me in the convent. During the summer of 1969, I graduated from college, having done all of my schoolwork during the summer sessions provided by the convent. A fellow sister that had been at the same mission with me during the previous year had heard that I had planned to marry a former student. She made this rumor known to the Motherhouse. I was summoned there and told that if that were my intention I should leave immediately. The only alternative was that they would reassign me to a mission in Iowa because the sister who sent in the rumor could not live with me any longer knowing what she knew about me. I said that I had planned to consult with the area representative in the fall about a leave of absence anyway. When I was told of being reassigned, I made up my mind right then that I would take a leave of absence that fall. I went back to the mission in the Chicago suburbs to pack my belongings and leave. I said that I did not wish to speak with the authorities in Iowa at the time. They did not honor my wishes. They had a lower authority phone me and then talked to the Mother Superior to try to persuade me to stay. She also reminded me that my mother might be quite upset if one of her six daughters were to leave the convent!

I chose as my date of departure September 1, 1969. This was to be a year of leave of absence. The local Superior loaned me $400. The Motherhouse loaned me $900, which I was to pay back with five percent interest. The priest counselor "gave" me a couple of hundred dollars. I repaid the $900 within five to six months and the local Superior was paid within another few months. I found a studio apartment on Chicago's North Side and a teaching position with the Chicago Board of Education. The priest helped me look for and buy my first car. I purchased furniture and other things from secondhand stores and thrift shops.

During that year, I consulted with the Diocese's representative overseeing the nuns who were leaving at that time. There were many. He helped me to formulate my reasons for becoming a Sister. These included the influence brought on because of my older sisters and my parents' satisfaction with them; the fact that I thought I was "safe" in a convent—it was a sure ticket to heaven. I would not have to care for my hair any longer, which had always been a source of concern for me. He also assisted me in obtaining the necessary dispensation from Rome so that I was 'legally' relieved of any further obligations to the convent. This he did after I had made it clear in my own mind that there was no future in my returning to the convent to live as a Sister.

Some of the reactions from my family were supposed to convince me to return to the convent. One of my sisters said that I could do much good in the convent. I also told her that I could do much good outside the convent. Another said that if I was going to leave, do it now before I get too old! One had no comment. Another tried putting a guilt trip on me for leaving. The fifth one was a little hurt and wondered whether she had done anything to make me want to leave. I also had a brother who had been a Trappist monk* for eight or nine years and he left and married. He felt so guilty after leaving the monastery that he spent many agonizing days of whether he should return or not. He even drove part way there only to turn around and return home. He had not taken solemn vows so was free to go (according to the church). My brother who was a priest asked, "Why leave? You have three meals a day, a roof over your head." To which I replied, "I believe there is more to life than that." So, after nineteen years as a nun, I was back "in the world"—free.

A year and a half after I left the convent, I decided to attend a dance for Catholic singles. It was held at St. Peter's Church in downtown Chicago on a Saturday night. That night, I met my future husband, John. I had always dreamed of marrying a "curly black haired Irishman." His hair was not black, but it was curly and he was Irish. We married January 8, 1972. Most of my family drove from Iowa to Chicago for the wedding, which was held at the Catholic Church. I was marrying a Catholic, so I was still Catholic. At the time, that did not bother me. John used to be proud to say he had married an ex-nun. He stopped that when he thought people believed he was the reason that I had left the convent.

The fall before we married, John had an experience at a church on Chicago's West Side. Somehow, he seemed to have trusted on Christ Jesus alone for his salvation, but did not understand what that entailed. After being married a few months, he began watching TV evangelists on Sunday mornings. He would watch them and then we would go to Mass. One Sunday, one evangelist offered a free New Testament. John sent for it and began reading it with much eagerness. Sometimes he would cry and sometimes he would laugh. I started to get a bit jealous because he was spending too much time with the New Testament. A few Sundays later, he decided to leave the TV on and heard another preacher. This one offered viewers a free weekend at his organization's headquarters. All we had to pay was

---

* A Trappist is member of a branch of the Cistercian order of monks noted for an austere rule including a vow of silence. The name comes from La Trappe in Normandy, where the order was founded.

the airfare; we decided to go. As we were packing, John packed handkerchiefs. I did not know why he would be doing this because we usually
used tissue, but I said nothing. When we arrived at our destination and
were seated—waiting for the speaker, I began to weep. I cried and cried,
not knowing why. That is when John's handkerchiefs came in handy. I
had seen that I needed faith and repentance. I came to realize that I was a
sinner. As a Catholic, and as a nun, I had only looked to the sacraments.
However, these rituals had not changed my heart. Somehow I had seen
I needed conviction of sin as I had wanted to be born again as Jesus had
said, *"Except a man be born of water and of the Spirit, he cannot enter into the
kingdom of God. That which is born of the flesh is flesh; and that which is born
of the Spirit is spirit."* (JOHN 3:5, 6) The Lord indeed convicted me, and after
the speaker left, I went into a room where counselors prayed for me. That
day, I trusted in Jesus Christ alone for my salvation, and I was born again.

Nothing spectacular happened in my life that I took notice of at that
time. One Sunday morning, John watched his usual TV programs and
then we went to Mass. After we came home, he said that he could not stand
going to Mass any more. They were not teaching the Bible. I told him not
to go if he could not stand it. He was surprised at my response. A few
weeks later, I was speaking with a former nun with whom I had lived. She
had believed on Jesus Christ for her salvation while still in the convent.
While speaking to her on the phone one day, she mentioned that God does
not live in houses made by man. (ACTS 17:24) That was a new revelation to
me. It was a direct reference to the Holy Eucharist for me and was influ-
ential in my being able to break from the Catholic tradition of the Holy
Eucharist being the real body and blood of Christ.

Visits with my family members have been different. We live far from
any of them, so it is not too difficult to continue being Christian without
going to a Catholic Church to satisfy them. There have been times when I
was forbidden to take part in some of their important ceremonies because
they knew I was no longer a "practicing" Catholic. I do understand Satan's wily ways, but I will not be persuaded by him to deny my Jesus. I
explained to some of my family that the laws of the Church were made by
man and therefore, they can be changed by man. A dispensation from my
vows was not breaking any of God's laws, only man's.

Another evangelist that we watched on TV was a director of a retreat in
southern Florida. When we decided to leave Chicago for warmer climate,

we arranged to stay at this retreat for a week or two. We had glorious days of Christian teaching and fellowship. We then felt led to travel to north Florida where we purchased a small farm. We now know that the main reason for moving to that area was to be taught the Word of God. Shortly after arriving at our new home, the Lord inspired a young man from Tallahassee to "teach John." Since our born-again experiences, we left Chicago, had some teaching at the retreat, but we were in need of Bible teaching. This young man visited our home on a weekly basis and taught us the Scriptures. In early spring of 1981, the Lord told him not to come to our home any longer. We were equipped and were to further mature without him. Within two to three months of his leaving us on our own, we moved to Hawaii for more adventures with the Lord. The young man and his wife have continued to be our friends for the past 25 years. The Lord continues to work in our lives. One favorite Scripture is, *"in all thy ways acknowledge him and he shall direct thy paths."* (PROVERBS 3:6)

John and I are convinced that we are saved and secure in Jesus Christ. What is at stake is God's incorruptible truth in the words, *"That I might make thee know the certainty of the words of truth."* (PROVERB 22:21) Certainty is needed in the salvation of our immortal souls. We have the wonder and praise in the Apostle Paul's words, *"For ye have not received the spirit of bondage again to fear; but ye have received the Spirit of adoption, whereby we cry, Abba, Father. The Spirit itself beareth witness with our spirit, that we are the children of God."* (ROMANS 8:15, 16) The Holy Spirit was the sole and wonderful Cause of our being "born again." In the words of Jesus, *"It is the spirit that quickeneth; the flesh profiteth nothing...."* (JOHN 6:63) The Lord God gloriously saved us sinners, *"...according to his mercy he saved us, by the washing of regeneration, and renewing of the Holy Ghost."* (TITUS 3:5)

Here we now live in Lihue Hawaii; we continue in the grace of God. God is All Holy. This is the reason why we need to be in right standing before Him on the terms He prescribes. Turn to Him in faith alone for the salvation that He alone gives: by the conviction of the Holy Spirit, so, like John and I, you may experience the words of Scripture personally, *"For by grace are ye saved through faith; and that not of yourselves: it is the gift of God: Not of works, lest any man should boast."* (EPHESIANS 2:8, 9)

—Mary McGuigan

STAN P. WEBER

Falling In Love with the Biblical Jesus

WHAT COULD CHANGE THE FAITH OF A CATHOLIC FROM BIRTH (AND FORMER altar boy) in his 38th year? The answer is the grace and power of God and His Word, the Holy Scriptures! Once a fiercely independent electrical engineer, successful businessman, married fifteen years with two children, I had gotten myself into financial and marital trouble. I had always prided myself in having my life in control. I was the "middle child" of five boys, and I felt I was the most secure in life. I had always tried to balance life's priorities, including religion, but things slowly got away from me. I never truly drifted from going to Mass, or practicing my Catholic faith, but I did go through periods where other things became more important.

Shirking My Home Responsibilities

We always tried to go to Saturday evening Mass so we would not "mess up" our Sundays. This left me free to do whatever I desired on that day—which was often devoted to "me." With the pressures of our second child, lots of business travel, and a slowly building line of credit card debt, I would often retreat to my hobbies on the weekend. This was my way of escaping my responsibilities of child rearing and the load was being unfairly dumped on my wife. This probably went on for a few years. However, it finally reached the "melting point" and

My first Holy Communion (age 6) with my grandmother and two aunts behind me, and my mother in the background, April 1961.

she erupted. After having my wife give me an ultimatum, I agreed to go to marriage counseling.

This went on for a few months. Since I agreed to go to marriage counseling and drop my hobbies, things were going a lot better between my wife and me. She told me that an upcoming "Christian Women's Conference" was being held and she wanted to go with a friend from her work place. I said, "Sure, go and have a good time, you deserve a night away," and then seriously added, "but don't you come back a Jesus freak or anything like that. OK?" My wife came back from the conference, and she never spoke a word about it other than she had enjoyed the time away. However, I did notice a change in her behavior, and it was for the better. She began to be more pleasant and agreeable, and I certainly was not going to argue about that. She also began bringing children's Bible stories into the home and started reading them to the kids at night. She changed the radio from playing my "heavy metal" station to a "Christian" station with songs about Jesus. The whole home atmosphere began to change to a more serene and calm one, which was much different than the previous cold silence and quiet anger that had been hanging so heavily there. This just convicted me even more. It was as if my wife was getting her life in order, but I was still lagging behind. She gave me a six cassette tape series entitled "The Man Who Would Be Christ" from a Christian pastor and teacher by the name of John MacArthur. I was fascinated by this series, as I had never before heard someone actually "teach" Bible passages. The topic was about the antichrist; I had never known what the Bible had to say about this fellow. What I knew about him was from Hollywood and movies like "The Omen." Daily, my wife had been going to Mass, and after we returned from Church one Sunday, she confessed that she just was not "getting anything out of it." I countered with, "Well, that's because we probably haven't been putting enough into it."

My wife was actually becoming the spiritual leader of our family and I knew that was not right; that was supposed to be my role! And with that, I endeavored to become as spiritual as I could be. In typical "engineer" fashion, I dove headfirst into being as devout a Catholic as I knew how, even to the point of copying my mother and saying a rosary before bedtime each night. I then figured that the best way would be to follow the example of my godfather. He had just recently become a deacon in a Catholic church in my hometown, New Orleans. I sought out my local priest and a deacon and inquired of them as to what was required for me to become a Catholic deacon. However, I was gently persuaded by the deacon to, "Wait until your two boys get a little older." I can honestly say that I was disappointed, but I went to a local bookstore anyway and bought several books on Catholic Church history along with the Catholic Catechism. I then began to study Catholic Church history and Catholic teachings while seriously reading the Bible. To my amazement, I finally began to understand the New Testament, as the Lord's word urges us, *"Seek the Lord, and his strength: seek his face evermore. Remember his marvellous works that he hath done; his wonders, and the judgments of his mouth."* (PSALM 105:4-5) Now, I had read portions of the New Testament and liked them. While in Catholic high school religion classes all had been dry and hard, not making much sense to me at the time.

A New Understanding

I found myself really enjoying this picture of Jesus that I had not "seen" before. Every time the self-righteous religious leaders of His day tried to pin Him down, He came back with amazing answers and replies. I did not realize it at the time, but I was slowly starting to love this biblical Jesus. Moreover, this I would have to attribute to God's work in my heart. For John said, *"We love him, because he first loved us."* He spoke with compassion to sinners like me, and He had a very simple message. He was telling people that He had come to save sinners, and they needed to repent and believe in Him, otherwise, they were going to suffer eternal punishment. I was amazed that the message was twofold and straightforward. He did not leave any room for other choices. It was either Jesus Christ or nothing! Why had I never seen that message before?

I also saw the Apostles in a new light. The Catholic Church taught me that they were 'godlike' saints, and I had always prayed to marble statues of them as I grew up. However, in the New Testament, I saw simple men, bumbling and blundering along as they followed Jesus. They were actually funny, and I would often catch myself yelling at the pages of Scripture, "Hey guys, don't you see what Jesus meant by that? How come you guys don't get it? Yet, I see what He is saying—so clearly!"

Meanwhile, as I continued reading Catholic Church history and the New Testament at the same time, I began to grow very uneasy. I did not see certain Catholic teachings in the New Testament, i.e., a continuing Levitical priesthood, worshiping Mary, purgatory, saying the Rosary, praying to the saints, etc., and my uneasiness began to increase. What was going on here? I did not expect my feelings to be going in this direction. I was just trying to find Jesus and get my life straightened out; I was not looking for problems with my religious background. My continued reading of the Bible showed me that an individual is made right before God by the grace of God through faith alone in His Son, Jesus Christ. (EPHESIANS 2:8, 9) Jesus said He was the only way that a person could ever get into heaven. I could not find any mention of being a Catholic, Evangelical, or any other faith anywhere in the New Testament. I simply saw that the first believers were called "Christians" and they believed what Jesus Christ taught them.

The Catholic Church against the Bible

I began to seriously pray and call out to God to help me sort out what was happening here. Continued prayer and study showed me that the Catholic Church taught a different way to be saved than what Scripture boldly declared. The Catholic Church taught that it started at baptism, which made you "clean" from original sin, and then you continued to co-operate with God by continuously receiving the Sacraments for the rest of your life. At no time in your life could you ever be certain of going to heaven, as that was called the "sin of presumption." Committing a mortal sin at any time put you in grave danger of directly going to hell when you died—unless you hurried to the confessional and received the sacramental absolution from a priest. Missing Mass or a Holy Day of Obligation was a mortal sin, and I could not even tell you what the Holy Days of Obligation during the year were, even if my life depended on it. The Bible, on the other hand, stated that we are saved as soon as we repent of our sins and believe in Jesus Christ. (ROMANS 10:9, 10, 13; 2 PETER 3:9) It was an immediate thing, and once the transaction occurred, it was irreversible.

The Bible states that you can absolutely know you have eternal life, no doubt whatsoever! (ROMANS 8:30, 35-39) How could the Catholic Church's teachings be completely opposite of what the Bible taught? Of these two, one had to be wrong, because they both could not be right. They are di-ametrically opposed to one another. I finally began to share these things with my wife and she confessed that she had always felt something "wasn't quite right with the Catholic teachings" with which she had been raised. I was shocked! I had never questioned Rome and her teachings. She was the

Church, the only one true Church. She taught that there was no salvation outside of her. If you were not a Catholic, you were going to hell; it was just that simple. Did we dare to keep talking about these things? We had both been raised Catholic in New Orleans. All of our extended family was Catholic. We had two priests at our wedding; our sons were both baptized at the church where she and I had attended while growing up. We were actually questioning the Church we had loved, respected, and believed since childhood. Could all those Sisters, Brothers, and priests that had taught us been wrong? Did they see what we were seeing? Did they even read their Bibles? Surely, they had taken the time to compare what the teachings of the Church were as compared to the Holy Scripture, or had they?

Then my wife told me the details of her night at the Christian Women's Conference. She had heard the Gospel message for the first time, and she had repented of her sins and believed in the promises Jesus stated in the Bible. She was "saved!" She had done exactly what I had just been reading in the Book of Romans. She called upon the Lord and the transaction had occurred! I thought, "Good grief!" What in the world was happening? I thrust myself even deeper into reading the Scripture and the Catholic Church's teachings. I had to be sure. I had to be absolutely certain. After a few days, I finally realized that as the spiritual leader of my family, I had a decision to make. Would I lead my family based on Rome's teachings, and traditions, or would I stand on God's Word alone? Whom would I trust? With their eternal destiny at stake, I could not afford to be wrong. In the home we were living in at that time, my bathroom faced east. Early in the morning, it would be flooded with a beautiful yellow sunlight so that I did not have to switch on the electric light. This specific morning, I talked to God in a way I had never done before. I begged forgiveness for my sins that had caused Him to send Jesus Christ to die in my place on the cross of Calvary. I told Him that I was going to totally trust Him and the promises that I had read in His Word. He would be my Lord and Savior, and I would forever be His servant from that time forward. My whole trust for this life, the next life, and my family's would be in His hands. I promised I would never fall for the teachings of men ever again, only what His Word, the Scriptures taught. I rejected Roman Catholicism forever. I felt my sins and guilt being washed away.

I know that my testimony is not the norm. All of what I described above happened over about an eight-week period. God healed our marriage. We horrified the marriage counselor by telling her that God had intervened, He had forgiven us, we had both forgiven each other, and our sessions were going to be abruptly ending. She was not a happy camper about that! She was convinced that I had found a new "scam" and was worried I would hide behind the Bible instead of facing my "real" problems. We recovered unscathed from the financial problems; having learned from those painful lessons, we have remained practically debt-free since then. In the years following, our two children have professed Christ as their Savior. We began immediately fellowshipping at a small Baptist church in July 1993; we were both baptized the following month. I became a deacon in 1994. I realized that God had answered my prayer to become a deacon, but it was in the time and place He had planned for me all along.

What an awesome God! I would later be astounded to read in First Peter 3:1-2 what had happened to me. It states, *"Wives, likewise be submissive to your own husbands, that even if some do not obey the Word, they, without a word, may be won by the conduct of their wives, when they observe your chaste conduct accompanied by fear* (reverence for the Lord)." That is exactly what happened! My wife was saved first, and then through her chaste conduct and her newfound reverence for Jesus Christ, I was won over to the Lord. Amazing! We would go on to assist in the planting of a new church in October of 1998. My wife was the church secretary, and I became a teaching elder, where I presently teach the Scripture and preach whenever the pastor is on vacation. My wife and I belong to a group called "Ex-Catholics for Christ." Our love and concern for those still unknowingly "trapped" in the false gospel of Roman Catholicism is great. My seventy-year-old parents, once lifelong Catholics, left the Catholic Church in 1995, and now attend a Bible teaching/preaching church in New Orleans.

My oldest brother and his wife also left the Catholic Church, only leaving my three remaining brothers to be saved by the Lord at the appointed time. That is our prayer. I now know, firsthand, how the Apostle Paul must have felt. After many years in Judaism, with its rules and rituals and becoming a Pharisee, the Lord instantly "saved" him while traveling on the road to Damascus. After learning the truth, his greatest burden was to share what the Lord had revealed to him with his lost, Jewish kinsmen. Just as those Jews who were zealous for the traditions of men rejected Paul, so have those who follow the Roman Catholic traditions of men rejected me at times. However, that does not stop me from following the direct command of the Lord found in the book of Matthew. (MATTHEW 28:18-20) We are to witness to all that will listen; my heart especially beats stronger for my former fellow Roman Catholics. I now know God was calling me to Himself; all the while I thought "I" was calling out to Him. Praise His Holy name; He is so faithful—just as He promises. *"All that the Father gives me will come to me, and whoever comes to me I will never drive away."* (JOHN 6:37) I ask that this testimony of God's amazing grace be used for His glory and honor.

Autumn 2014 Update: My father went home to be with the Lord in December 2003 at age 80, and my mother followed him into Heaven at age 88 in 2011. They both remained believers to the end. Praise God! One of my three remaining brothers accepted Christ, left the Roman Catholic Church, and is now obediently serving God outside of Houston, Texas. That leaves two remaining brothers, whom we pray for continuously.

One thing that I left out of my testimony details was that, when my Dad and Mom were at the "asking questions" stage, they reached a point that they REALLY wanted to know the answers.

Stan and Jeanine Weber

So, I offered to fly to New Orleans, LA from Denver, CO to join them for a joint meeting with their local priest—a meeting where they could ask him all the questions they now had. They agreed, but were too afraid to ask the priest themselves, so they wanted me to do all the talking. I did, and it turned out to be a pivotal point for the two of them! When the priest asked my dad, "Has this discussion affected your faith?" he responded, "Yes, it has. For every question Stan asked you, you began with 'the Catholic Church teaches...' whereas he was able to show us the answers directly from the Bible. So yes indeed, it has!" I was never so proud of my dad in my entire life! For seventy-plus-year-old "lifelong" Catholics to interact with a priest in that manner was nothing short of miraculous.

I pray that my dad and mom's willingness to seek the Lord, to overcome their fear of asking the priest about their faith, what the Church teaches, and where it is found in the Bible, will give you, the reader who is questioning these things, a God-given confidence to do the same.

Over the past 20 years, as people have read my testimony and felt compelled to email me, their responses fall into two distinct categories:

1. First are those who are argumentative and combative—saying such things as, "You don't know what the Roman Catholic Church teaches," or "I was born a Catholic and I will die a Catholic." When I feel prompted by the Holy Spirit to engage those folks—showing them the CLEAR teachings of the Roman Catholic Church in the Catholic Catechism—they almost always refuse to accept that the teachings are DIFFERENT from what the Bible teaches. While this breaks my heart, the Bible also tells me that this is spiritual blindness, and no amount of coaxing on my part will make any headway. I must totally turn this over to the Lord, although my heart cries out for them to stop looking to man-made religious rules and traditions, but instead put their faith and trust in Jesus Christ alone.

2. But, second, there are those who read my testimony and who email me with encouraging words such as, "I, too, have been thinking about these things. The Roman Catholic Church just isn't satisfying my desire to seek the Lord", or "I thought I was alone in thinking these things! I am so glad that I came across your website, as you have articulated what I was feeling."

In October 1998, my wife and I were privileged to help plant a new church in the Denver area. From October 1998 through October 2012 I was privileged to serve there as a teaching elder (Adult Sunday school) and my wife led women's ministry. But, in October 2012, due to an unexpected resignation of our senior pastor, the church leaders prayed for an interim pastor and they contacted me and requested that I serve in this capacity, in spite of the responsibilities associated with my executive management consulting firm. Feeling God's clear call on my heart, I placed my consulting practice on hold and stepped into full time ministry, became ordained by the Rocky Mountain Conservative Baptist Association, and took on the day-to-day duties of the interim senior pastorate at Castle Pines Community Church.[1] After serving nearly one year, and being asked to seriously consider staying on permanently in the position—something I

1 http://www.castlepineschurch.org/

did not feel called to do—our pastoral search committee hired a gifted and experienced new senior pastor, and I was blessed to "hand the baton" over to him.

In October of 2013, my wife and I sold our home in Colorado after nearly 28 years and moved outside of Houston, TX. Crossroads Baptist Church of The Woodlands has become our new church home, and we are serving in various capacities as God has given us opportunity.[2]

Our God is an awesome God, and He is so faithful! Praise His holy name, forever and ever.

An obedient servant of Jesus Christ,
STAN WEBER

Please feel free to email me at: stan@stanweber.com

JOHANNA ALEXANDER

The Holy Bible, the Word of God, Guides Me

In January of 1949, not long after the Second World War, I was born in Holland. My father was a Roman Catholic, but my mother had no religious preference though she had attended an Evangelical Sunday school in her younger years. Mother's father was an atheist, and her moth-

er was possibly a Methodist. Before my mother married my father, she was required to become a Roman Catholic. So, she studied the doctrines of the faith and was baptized as a member into the Roman Catholic Church. However, mother never embraced the religion; she attended church, but her heart was not in it.

Shortly after I was born, my parents saw to it that I was baptized. Baptism, according to the Roman Catholic Church, means that one is cleansed from original sin and becomes a member of the Church. From then on, until I was into my teens, my parents took me to church with them. At age seven, I received the Sacrament of the Eucharist, and at the age of ten, I received the Sacrament of Confirmation.

I believed in the miraculous appearances of the Roman Catholic Mary, the Mother of God, and prayed to the Lady of Fatima. I studied the history of the Roman Catholic Church and the lives of the saints. I was fascinated with the mysticism of the saints who were canonized within the church. I read many stories about them. Moreover, I wanted to be as holy as they were.

180

Trying to Please God

In those years, I believed God's love for me was on a conditional basis and that I could never be good enough or holy enough to please Him. Therefore, I went to confession regularly and eagerly practiced the indulgences to pay for my sins. I received communion quite often to become, or at least feel, more sanctified. I prayed the rosary to Mary, and I prayed to the saints. I made indulgences for the souls of the dead who may be in purgatory so that God would have mercy on them and bring them into heaven.

I zealously practiced Catholicism for many years; a priest married my fiancé and me. Later, we saw to it that our children were baptized into the Church. I belonged to the Legion of Mary, the Catholic Women's League, and taught Catechism. We attended church as a family until my husband quit going. After that, our children attended church with me.

On the Road Toward True Liberty

In the winter of 1973, some dear Christian ladies invited me to a Bible study. I went out of sheer boredom from being cooped up with my two babies in the house. It was in the middle of a long winter when my husband was out working in the oil fields for sixteen to twenty hours a day. These ladies offered babysitting for the children, and the coffee pot was always on.

I felt love from these women, and I started reading the Bible with them and while at home. I was more than excited at the wonderful things I was learning. I had only known the Bible as a storybook up until then. I was told that the Bible is a true and living Word. Furthermore, I was told that biblical prophecies have come true and about the "hope" of seeing Christ one day soon. This study went on for some time; I was seeing discrepancies with what the Roman Catholic Church taught. However, we moved away and I continued in the Catholic Church with my children. I became involved with the Charismatic Movement with meetings held in the Catholic Church's basement. I continued to search because I was not satisfied with what I was hearing from the priests and the bishop at this Church. The Mass became a boring ritual. *"But if from thence thou shalt seek the LORD thy God, thou shalt find him, if thou seek him with all thy heart and with all thy soul."* (DEUTERONOMY 4:29)

Since I loved reading, I frequented the public library with my children. I was searching in the religion section of the library and came across the

book called, "The Hiding Place" by Corrie ten Boom. The following is copied from
Corrie ten Boom's history site. Her story had me riveted to the end, and it spoke to
my heart. Here is an excerpt from her book
about her life during the war.

Casper and his daughters, Corrie and
Betsie, risked their lives. This non-violent
resistance against the Nazi-oppressors was
the Ten Booms' way of living out their
Christian faith. This faith led them to
hide Jews, students who refused to coop-
erate with the Nazis, and members of the
Dutch underground resistance movement.
During 1943 and into 1944, there were
usually 6-7 people illegally living in this
home: 4 Jews and 2 or 3 members of the Dutch underground. Corrie and
Betsie spent 10 months in three different prisons, the last was the infamous
Ravensbruck Concentration Camp located near Germany.

Her sister, Betsie, died in camp, but Corrie was released because of a
clerical mistake. All the time Corrie was in the prison, she witnessed for
Jesus Christ to the guards, and she was a support to the fellow prisoners.
Corrie was a woman who was faithful to God. I have read about her work
since she immigrated to the United States shortly after the war. She died
on her 91st birthday, April 15, 1983.

I continued to read the Bible, pray, and search for answers. It was not
until the year 1979 that God opened the eyes of my heart to accept the
truth in His Word. In 1949, I was born of flesh and blood from my mother's womb, and in 1979, I was born of the Spirit and became a child of
God, as the following Bible texts teach,

> "But as many as received him, to them gave he power to become the sons of
> God, even to them that believe on his name: Which were born, not of
> blood, nor of the will of the flesh, nor of the will of man, but of God."
> (JOHN 1:12-13)

> "He that believeth on the Son hath everlasting life: and he that believeth
> not the Son shall not see life; but the wrath of God abideth on him."
> (JOHN 3:36)

"These things have I written unto you that believe on the name of the Son of God; that ye may know that ye have eternal life, and that ye may believe on the name of the Son of God." (1JOHN 5:13)

True Liberty Arrives!

I finally had to admit there were stark differences between what the Roman Catholic Church taught in the Baltimore Catechism and the Council of Trent, from the truth taught in the Bible. I could not believe that I was so enmeshed in such heresy as taught in the Roman Catholic Church. I was overcome with sorrow for not having worshipped God in spirit and in truth. I prayed to God, repented of my sins, and trusted in Jesus Christ, the Son of God. I finally realized that baptism, or membership in a church, is not the way of salvation. It is only through Jesus Christ we are saved and only through His drawing influence we even come to Him and His Word.

"And I, if I be lifted up from the earth, will draw all men unto me." (JOHN 12:32) *"No man can come to me, except the Father which hath sent me draw him: and I will raise him up at the last day."* (JOHN 6:44)

The accounts in the Bible were no longer just stories, they were true, and they became alive and made sense to me. The Word became relevant to my everyday life, and God spoke to my heart. I could not put the Bible down as I hungered for the truth written between the two covers of the Holy Bible. *"For the word of God is quick, and powerful, and sharper than any two-edged sword, piercing even to the dividing asunder of soul and spirit, and of the joints and marrow, and is a discerner of the thoughts and intents of the heart."* (HEBREWS 4:12)

I felt God's overwhelming love for those around me and I knew that my sins had been fully forgiven. I finally understood why God sent His Son, Jesus Christ, to die such a brutal death on the Cross—for me. You see, God demands justice, purity, and holiness, and there was no way that I could measure up to His standards, no matter how hard I worked at it or how many indulgences I paid. God offered Jesus, His only Son, the pure and holy sacrifice, in my stead. By His death on the cross, Jesus took my place to pay the penalty for my sin, once and for all. By His Holy Spirit and grace, I put off my old selfish spirit and put on the new Spirit in Christ.

Today, though I am still a sinful human being, I can stand before God as though without sin because Jesus Christ redeemed and justified me through His shed blood on the Cross. He took all my sin on Himself; He took what I deserved. God sent me His Holy Spirit to indwell, to direct, and to empower me, as the following Bible texts explain,

> *"And hope maketh not ashamed; because the love of God is shed abroad in our hearts by the Holy Ghost which is given unto us."* (ROMAN 5:5)

> *"Howbeit when he, the Spirit of Truth, is come, he will guide you into all truth: for he shall not speak of himself; but whatsoever he shall hear, that shall he speak: and he will show you things to come."* (JOHN 16:13)

> *"Then said Jesus to those Jews which believed on him, 'If ye continue in my word, then are ye my disciples indeed.'"* (JOHN 8:31)

As Charles Spurgeon said, "Real conversion by the Holy Spirit is as distinct and radical a change as though an old man were placed in a mill and ground young again."

In the year 1982, I finally left the Roman Catholic Church for good. It had been a terrible struggle for me; I was so indoctrinated by Roman Catholicism. Today, through His Word, Jesus Christ, the Son of God, motivates me to serve God in love and in truth. I am not motivated by fear of guilt or punishment. As I stay close to Jesus Christ and abide in Him, I am able to live a life pleasing to the Father. God is not finished with me yet, for I am still a sinful being! The difference is I am forgiven, and I am His child forever. Instead of going to a Catholic priest, I can now go directly to Jesus, my Redeemer, my Mediator, and my only Advocate to God the Father, for the forgiveness of my sins as the following Bible texts explain,

> *"My little children, these things write I unto you, that ye sin not. And if any man sin, we have an advocate with the Father, Jesus Christ the righteous:"* (1 JOHN 2:1)

> *"If we say that we have no sin, we deceive ourselves, and the truth is not in us. If we confess our sins, he is faithful and just to forgive us our sins, and to cleanse us from all unrighteousness. If we say that we have not sinned, we make him a liar, and his word is not in us."* (1 JOHN 1:8-10)

True Liberty is Forever!

The moment I was born from above, I received the gift of eternal life through God's Son, Jesus. I am now a child of the King—forever. I now know there is a better place waiting for me. And, I am now assured that I will see Jesus in heaven, whether it is when the body of Christ meets Him in the air (1 THESSALONIANS 4:17) or when I die and go to the grave and my soul will rise up to be with Him. (2 CORINTHIANS 5:8) What a blessed day that will be!

I attend a small group Bible study and the Word of God is alive to me. I found it very important to fellowship with other believers that are part of the body of Christ as we are commanded to do in the Bible. It is good to attend a Bible believing church where the pastor preaches repentance and interprets the Bible by using other verses of the Bible. God was so gracious to give me the opportunity to witness the gospel to my parents. My mother later embraced Christ as her Savior and my father and I had great conversations. I had the privilege to be with them when they were dying, mom in 1991, and dad in 1994. I had a chance to pray with each of them at the end of their lives. God be praised!

As being a part of the body of Christ, we can be a godly support to our fellow believers while in return they can spur us on to good works in Christ. In God's power and grace, I witness the gospel to those in my circle of influence and pray that God will open the understanding of their hearts. I love to study and meditate daily on God's Word and try to take time to pray and praise Him throughout the day. To the glory of God, my life is full as wife, mother, grandmother, friend, and hospice worker, as the following Bible texts explain,

> *"This is the covenant that I will make with them after those days, saith the Lord, I will put my laws into their hearts, and in their minds will I write them; And their sins and iniquities will I remember no more."* (HEBREWS 10:16, 17)

> *"Stand fast therefore in the liberty wherewith Christ hath made us free, and be not entangled again with the yoke of bondage."* (GALATIANS 5:1)

—JOHANNA ALEXANDER

Anthony "Tony" Carosi

From Darkness to Light: The Testimony of a Philly Altar Boy

Learning to be a Good Catholic Boy

On March 7, 1960, I was born to Guido Luigi Carosi, and Mary Louise (Ruffo) Carosi at 49th and Lancaster Sts. in the city of Philadelphia, Pennsylvania. My family was Italian-American and devoutly Roman Catholic. Soon after my birth, I was baptized into the Church. Our church, Our Lady of the Angels was the pride of the neighborhood. Our community built their lives around that church, and my early years were to be no exception.

Roman Catholicism became a way of life for me. The Archdiocese had allowed the Italian immigrants to finance the establishment of Our Lady of the Angels. along with all its extensions of ministry, on their own. One of those ministries was a Catholic grade school that admitted only those of Italian descent, and in 1966 I enrolled as a first-grader. The nuns called, the sisters of the Immaculate Heart of Mary, served as the faculty. The nuns strictly enforced firm discipline and we learned to live by a well-worn saying: "They are always right and you are always wrong." In second grade, I took the traditional Catholic sacrament of First Holy Communion. I received Confirmation as a fourth-grader, and soon after, Penance—the confession of personal sins to the priest.

The school nuns were not by any means my only source of Catholic education. My father taught us to faithfully attend church every Sunday morning and every Holy Day of Obligation. With the Catholic Church playing such a prominent role in my family, it quickly became an object of fascination for me. My older brother, Frank, and I loved to play church, and we could often be found setting up an altar in our bedroom and inviting the rest of the family to our Mass. My Aunt Dorothy Adalgisa, helped me start a collection of Funeral Holy Cards, medals, and statues of the Roman Catholic Saints. I also collected Mass Cards. A Mass Card, essentially a modern day indulgence, was given to any person who paid money to have a Mass performed for a deceased loved one suffering in purgatory. The church taught that some of the sins of that departed loved one would be pardoned through the Mass, inching that tormented soul closer to heaven.

Like every good Catholic, I believed that the church could sacramentally absolve people, dead or alive, of the guilt and punishment due for their sins. The forgiveness of sins that was necessary to be in God's favor came only through the Catholic Church.

In sixth grade, I became an altar boy at Our Lady of the Angels. I took great pride in my new position, and dutifully executed my responsibilities to prepare the church altar, help the priest change into his ceremonial garments, and assist him in the Mass and other special services. I vividly recall Via Crucis, the Way of the Cross, a ritual commemorating Jesus' route to the crucifixion and ending with His resurrection. During the ceremony, I would stand facing the priest, steadily holding a long-stemmed candle to illuminate his text. As the priest's chanting and the people's responses droned on for what seemed to be an eternity, the hot, melting wax would run down the candlestick and drip onto my clenched hands. Terrified of the possible consequences of complaining or even flinching at the pain, I would silently repeat over and over, "I want to be a good Catholic."

The Feast of St. Gabriel

Although I devoutly revered the Roman Catholic Church, I distinctly remember glaring inconsistencies that betrayed all the ceremonial piety of the church. Every year, early in June, Our Lady of the Angles celebrated the Feast of St. Gabriel as a fundraising festival. The festival always started in the morning with the Italian Verdi Band playing music and marching around the streets of the neighborhood. People would come out of their homes to join the festivities and would begin following the band, forming a long line. Four life-size statues were propped high up on pedestals for all to see: the Virgin Mary, Saint Emedio, Saint Nicolas, and Saint Gabriel—patron saint of the parish. As the men marched the statues down the streets, the elderly would pin five, ten, and twenty-dollar bills onto the silk scarves that draped each statue's neck. Back at home that day, I would proudly display my entire statue collection on the porch wall of my row home for passers-by to admire.

Notwithstanding all the official pomp and circumstance surrounding the Feast of St. Gabriel, the very concept underlying the entire event was unbiblical. The one command that the Roman Catholic Church conveniently eliminates from the Ten Commandments declares, *"Thou shalt not make unto thee any graven image or any likeness of any thing that is in the heaven above...Thou shalt not bow down thyself to them, nor serve them: For I the LORD thy God am a jealous God."* (Exodus 20:4, 5) But the inconsistencies did not stop with the idolatry of the festival. The afternoon always took on a raucous party atmosphere generated by food, alcohol, dancing, gambling, carnival rides, and the grease pole. In reality, it was hardly holy, religious fervor that motivated the events of that day. As I look back, I can hardly believe I had a part in all of that. If Christ was righteously angry with the temple money changers for greedily making God's house a place of merchandise—*"It is written, My house shall be called the house of prayer, but ye have made it a den of thieves"* (Matthew 21:13)—certainly I and my church were just as guilty as those evil men that Christ drove out of the temple.

Difficulty and Turmoil

Living in the city of Philadelphia was not easy. The constant racial tension between whites and blacks set boundary lines on all sides around my neighborhood. Most of our community was lower, middle class, and could never have afforded to move away from the hostility. Besides, Our Lady of the Angels was our source of unity and pride, and to move away from the church we had established was nearly unthinkable.

Notwithstanding the influence of Our Lady of the Angels, our community was sporadically transformed into a war zone, especially during the summer months. Hurled bottles, fist fights, bat clubbings, stabbings, and even shootings were not unheard of, and caused public uneasiness and general unrest. The Pagans, a motorcycle gang, made inroads into our neighborhood and only increased the frequency and severity of the riots. Drug dealers openly hung out on our streets, making easy sales to teenagers.

The constant, in-your-face blatancy of it all, made a life of sin nearly impossible to escape. All my early Catholic upbringing and education proved powerless to stem the rising tide of wickedness in my own heart. When I reached my teenage years and started high school at St. Thomas Moore, I was quickly entrapped by the sins that were so prevalent in my environment and so appealing to my own lusts. The Scriptures clearly explain exactly what I was experiencing, and even more sobering, where I was headed: *"But every man is tempted when he is drawn away of his own lust, and enticed. Then when lust hath conceived, it bringeth forth sin, and sin, when it is finished, bringeth forth death."* (JAMES 1:14, 15)

From Years of Pride to Years of Guilt

Like most teenagers, I wanted my independence. While I was in high school, my cousin, George, gave me a great price on a 1966 black, four-door Caddy that was big as a boat and rode as smooth as anything. With the keys to a ride like that in my pocket, I really thought I was something. But as the Bible says, *"Pride goeth before destruction, and an haughty spirit before a fall,"* (PROVERBS 16:18) and my pride was just asking for destruction.

That pride-driven fall came my senior year, as my grades dropped to an all-time low, and I was unsure if I was even going to graduate. There was no chance of my going to college, not only because I disliked school, but also because we simply could never have afforded it. Dad expected me to work and to help pay the bills. I knew things would be different for me after high school and I was scared of the uncertain future that lay ahead of me.

I did graduate, and shortly after graduation, I started my first full-time job—a job I hated, feeling I did not belong. I began to lose confidence and any remnant of self-esteem. My slavery to sinful habits only served to further magnify my weakness, and I became very introverted. I remember so many times sitting on my bed through the middle of the night crying, and telling myself how I hated this world and hated the way I was living my life. I felt the profound weight of the awful burden of my sins and I wanted to change. My inner turmoil became so obvious that my parents urged me to see a doctor, but I refused. I wanted to work it out myself.

With nowhere else to turn, I started to go back to church at Our Lady of the Angels, but not just on Sundays. Every day of the week, at 6:30 in the morning, I would go to Mass before making my way to work. I wanted to get close to God and this was the only way I knew how. Once again, I became a very devout Catholic, but to my great frustration, I still keenly felt the unrelenting weight of my sins.

God's Word Brings Hope

Soon my trips to church became conscious acts of penance for the sins I had committed the night before. There was a constant sense of emptiness in my soul, a void that needed to be filled. I just wanted peace in my heart, and I knew there had to be more to life than the way I was living. I was searching, yet not really knowing what I was looking for.

I found what I was looking for in an unlikely place. I remember one day visiting my Aunt Adalgisa, who lived across the street. It was May, which in the Roman Catholic calendar was the month of the Blessed Mother Mary. Aunt Adalgisa was just ending a time of worship with the church ladies who gathered in her home to pray the rosaries. I noticed a book under her Catholic statue of *The Infant of Prague*. When I picked it up, I saw it was the Holy Bible. Immediately I was curious, but my Aunt told me to put it back because it was not for me to read. When I got home, I asked my mom if we had a Bible, to which she said, "Yes," and gave it to me. I looked up a familiar passage, Psalm 23. How those beautiful words touched my heart. I kept the Bible by my bed and continued to read the Psalms each night.

When I reached Psalm 38, I was unprepared for what I read, *"O LORD rebuke me not in Thy wrath: Neither chasten me in Thy hot displeasure. For Thine arrows stick fast in me, and Thy hand presseth me sore. There is no soundness in my flesh because of Thine anger, neither is there any rest in my bones because of my sin. For mine iniquities are gone over mine head as an heavy burden, they are too heavy for me."* (PSALM 38:1-4) These words cut into my soul like a knife. My eyes began to fill up with tears as my heart became overwhelmed with "joy." I could not believe what I was reading—I was not alone! It hit me that David had experienced exactly what I was experiencing and he had felt exactly how I felt. I started to believe and trust that the Bible really was the Word of God, and what I read, I kept in my heart.

Soon, the thought began to torment me, "All these years growing up as a Catholic, and not once have I ever been encouraged to read the Bible—why?" As that question plagued me, I started to drift away from the Church. I began to realize that the Mass actually kept me from drawing closer to God with all its vain repetition. The Bible, in contrast, gave me real hope and direction. Paul's message to the Romans was being worked out in my own heart: *"Faith cometh by hearing, and hearing by the Word of God."* (ROMANS 10:17)

At the Cross

The Lord had shown me that I was the greatest sinner I knew; the Lord had planted the seed and I was ripe for salvation. One day, months after my encounter with David in Psalm 38, I was playing basketball at the neighborhood playground. While I was playing, I noticed my cousin, George, and Joe Duffy (who would become a close friend in Christ) on the sidelines, both trying to get my attention. They were so distracting that I left playing the game before it was over. As soon as I walked over to them, they confronted me, right there, with my need of salvation. They told me that I needed to be born again. They said that if I did not repent of my sins I would perish and go to hell, but that if I would believe that Jesus Christ died on the cross for my sins, I would have eternal life. What they said about believing in Christ and admitting to being a sinner was nothing new to me, but I had never thought about where I would spend eternity. Stung by their words, I arrogantly responded, "No one knows where they are going after this life, so what gives you the right to say otherwise?" They shared two Scripture verses with me, *"For God so loved the world, that he gave his only begotten Son, that whosoever believeth in him should not perish, but have everlasting life,"* (JOHN 3:16) and, *"That ye may know that ye have eternal life."* (1 JOHN 5:13) When they had finished, they invited me out to their church.

A week or two later, I visited Berean Baptist Church with them and heard the Gospel preached for the first time, and how I loved it! After the service, I rushed home knowing that I had to get before the Lord to pray. When I got into my bedroom, immediately I dropped down to my knees and I began to cry out to the Lord for his help just as a son would cry to his father. I confessed to Him how sinful I had been and how unworthy I was of Him even considering me. I believed what the Scripture said, *"without shedding of blood is no remission."* (HEBREWS 9:22) I asked God to forgive me of my sin and to save my soul from the torments of hell. I continued to pray for about an hour, expressing as best as I could my faith in Christ as my Savior, and when I finished, I felt physically and mentally drained.

A New Morning, A New Life

The next morning when I awoke, there was a change. I was different and I saw the world as different. Everything clicked—like a light switch had been turned on in my darkened mind. The eyes of my understanding were opened, and I knew Jesus Christ was my personal Savior—I was born again. Once again, the Bible was proving itself in my own experience: *"For God, who commanded the light to shine out of darkness, hath shined in*

Tony Carosi, after his conversion

our hearts, to give the light of the knowledge of the glory of God in the face of Jesus Christ;"* (2 CORINTHIANS 4:6) *"And ye shall know the truth and the truth shall make you free."* (JOHN 8:32) My heart was overwhelmed with joy because the burden of my sins was lifted. I had finally found peace with God, a peace that truly passes all understanding, and a peace that I still know today. Jesus Christ is the answer to life, as He said, *"I am the way, the truth, and the life."* (JOHN 14:6)

The Bible declares, *"Therefore if any man be in Christ, he is a new creature: old things are passed away; behold, all things are become new."* (2 CORINTHIANS 5:17) My life did indeed become new. The Lord blessed in the days ahead. He progressively purged many of the worldly things out of my life, and continues that work in me—only to make me a vessel fit to serve Him. In the years that have followed, He has blessed me with a beautiful wife, Veronica, and two boys whom I love very much. He has placed me in a Bible-believing, Christ-preaching church where my family and I have been able to grow. Truly, the Lord is good and merciful. Like the Psalmist, all I can end with is, *"Praise ye the Lord!"* (PSALM 150:6)

—TONY CAROSI

Jennifer Irvine

The Lord in Whom I Have Redemption

I was born in Broken Hill, New South Wales, Australia, during the Second World War. My parents were from several generations of Roman Catholics. I am the third of four daughters. This is a brief outline of my life and later conversion to the knowledge of salvation and the Lord Jesus Christ. When I was a few weeks old, a priest baptized me by sprinkling, and, thus, I became a Roman Catholic, a daughter of what I was told was the One True Church. Much of my very early years are sketchy, but I do have recollection of some things; a few of which are very clear in my mind. There are things I will endeavour to share with you, and may the Lord be glorified.

As a very small child, my dear father encouraged his children to say by heart the Hail Mary and the Our Father. He often rewarded us for our achievements. When I learned the Hail Mary he gave me threepence, and for learning the Our Father, I received sixpence!

I commenced school at the Convent, in Broken Hill, when I was four and a half years old. I am naturally left-handed, but I remember the nun trying very hard to make me write with my right hand. However, that effort was not successful! Fox was the name of the bishop of Broken Hill. As I remember, the community did not speak well of Bishop Fox. He was a large, stern, rotund man, and looked formidable in his lavish bishop's attire. At school one day, the children were told to line up to meet the bishop on one of his visits to the school. We were to address him as "My Lord" and kiss the ring on his finger, supposedly embedded with martyr's bones.

From this early age, I trained in what I would later learn to be Rome's doctrines, idolatries, and superstitions. Above all, I believed that the Roman church was the One True Church. I always wore my Brown Scapular and a Miraculous Medal as did my sisters. The Brown Scapular consisted of a piece of brown cord made as a long necklace with little pieces of cloth at opposite ends, (one worn at the back and one at the front) which were imprinted with religious icons of "saints." This I wore under my clothing. The story goes that "Saint" Simon Stock long ago received an apparition that if this piece of cloth were faithfully worn, the wearer would never go to the fires of hell! The "Miraculous Medal" was a little oval shaped piece of metal with a graven image of Mary, and this was worn to ward off evil happenings to the wearer. There were many medals and paraphernalia that "good" Catholics pinned, draped, or hung on their selves.

In later years, my favorite medal was the St. Christopher medal. He was the patron saint of safety when travelling. This I wore at all times on a chain around my neck. No Catholic would be without his St. Christopher medal in his car. Sadly, in later years, St. Christopher mysteriously disappeared from Rome's list of "saints." Our travel "protector" had vanished!

I made my First Confession when I was seven years old. The priest would come to the school; we usually did not go into the Confessional Box but would kneel down at the priest's feet, telling him our sins and from him receive absolution. The priest would then give me my penance, which was sometimes three Hail Mary's and three Our Father's. The penance was for reparation (or to repay God) and help share in Christ's sacrifice. I remember the way I would cringe when I had to kneel down at the feet of a "holy priest" and tell him just how naughty and wicked I had been! My first Holy Communion soon followed my first Confession, and the nun told all the children that we had received Jesus into our hearts. I recall the words of the second commandment in the Bible, which Rome removed and changed to accommodate her idolatry, *"Thou shalt not make unto thee any graven image, or any likeness of any thing that is in heaven above, or that is in the earth beneath, or that is in the water under the earth. Thou shalt not bow down thyself to them, or serve them…."* (EXODUS 20:4, 5A)

In 1953, Elizabeth II was crowned Queen of England and the Commonwealth. As a coronation gift, the children of the Commonwealth received a lovely little white Bible, that is, except the children who attended Roman Catholic schools. We were not permitted to have a Bible by orders of the Vatican and the bishops. Instead, we received an ordinary looking "Four Gospels." At school, Bible lessons were taken from a book called "Bible History." This, in fact, consisted of selected stories rather than the true and living words of God, which alone can save. We had the Bible stories, but NO BIBLE!

Secondary school became more concentrated with religious instruction. For one hour, it was given as the first lesson of the day; before lunch for half an hour and immediately following lunch for half an hour, perhaps for one hour. On special "saints' days," there were Masses and other religious duties, including confessions to the priest.

The words of the priests and nuns were sacrosanct—regarded as sacred and inviolable—and therefore never questioned. Every classroom at Catholic schools had a graven image of Mary in a prominent place. Each year on May 1, this image was crowned with flowers, and there would be special hymns and prayers offered to this idol. Religious instruction consisted of stories from saints' lives, learning hymns—sometimes in Latin. Hymns were sung to all, including Mary, St. Joseph, the Sacred Heart, the Guardian Angel, St. Patrick, the Blessed Sacrament, and only occasionally to Jesus. I learned the Gregorian chants for High Mass in Latin, and prayers by rote in Latin and English.

A Friend Named Connie

At school, I was a friend with a little girl named Connie. Connie was one of those bubbly, friendly children, and even though she was a couple of years younger than I, we enjoyed each other's company. In the large complex, along with the school, there was a church, a convent, and the priests' priory* to which new priests were assigned when they had arrived from another country.

As an eleven year old, my mind began reeling at the story Connie began to relate to me one day after school. A new priest had lured her to the priory on the previous day and sexually assaulted her in a most debauched

---

* A monastery or nunnery governed by a prior or prioress; prior: the head of a house of friars (or nuns).

way. I was so horrified! Unknown to us, a senior nun was listening to us talking from inside the building. The following day the nun summoned me to her office, and she told (or rather warned) me not to repeat what Connie had told me. She said that the priest was sick and we needed to pray for him! I did not even tell my parents, as I was silenced and afraid. Who would believe me anyway? I still think of Connie from time to time, and wonder if she ever did get to tell her story. That same priest moved to a parish in another suburb. When I saw him many years later, I remembered him.

The Missionary

During my early and mid-teen years, my family often invited visiting missionary priests and friends to our home for meals. One priest in particular was a favorite among many of us, whom I will only call G.P., as he was affectionately known. He would visit the schools and the churches around Australia, and he was very popular and charismatic. His mission in the area would last for a week, and he would then move on to another area. Sometimes a group of young people would go to other districts to hear him. He would hear confessions, and because he knew me, he would always chat with me after absolution and say how nice it was to re-acquaint. Looking back, I remember feeling uncomfortable around him. At times, he was too touchy-feely, and over-complimentary for a "holy" priest.

In the neighbourhood where I lived was a girl named Ruth. She lived with her mother and older half sister. Ruth played classical and modern piano, and we all enjoyed the entertainment of her skillful playing. Ruth, and her sister, would often join us when the priest, "G.P.," came to visit. There was an "incident" with the priest and this young woman when he took her for a ride in his car one night. I never heard what happened, I was too young, but I was aware of the whisperings around me, and the silence, when I asked questions. Of course, it was, as always, the "flirtations" of a young woman blamed!

Sometime after I was married, this priest contacted me when he was in town, and asked if he could visit. Because of him being a long time friend of my family, I arranged a time when my husband and children were present, and we all had a meal together. A couple of days later, he telephoned me at home to thank me for the meal. Then he added, "I would like to have seen you alone!" I made sure he did not!

In 1970, my dear father died, and in the years following, I was aware of a strange emptiness and an ache somewhere in my being, but I knew by then the sacraments and Mass of Rome had no comfort for me. There is so very much more I could write about, but for the sake of brevity, I will end here with my journey in Rome.

One night I had a dream about a friend whom I had not seen for many years. This friend was married to a Pentecostal pastor. I told my husband, and he said I should contact her. She and I had a happy night of fellowship and a meal together, and not long after that, we began attending the same Pentecostal church. This was such an exciting time for me, as never before had I heard the Bible preached. Several weeks later, I committed my life to the Lord Jesus Christ. In retrospect, there was no real foundational teaching, no sound doctrine, Antinomianism* and much confusion. I began hearing things like, "You're a King's kid," and "God wants you to have the best!" The teaching was that we were no longer under any of the Old Testament Law, but rather we were "in Christ" and God's Holiness, His Law and His Justice were never preached. It was "peace, love, and let's get together!"

The Charismatic "renewal" was in full swing and, to my amazement, the Christian churches were getting together with priests and charismatic Roman Catholics who were still attending the Mass, praying to Mary and the saints, and continuing business as usual. "All is well," the shepherds

* Antinomianism, is believing that Christians are released by grace, from obeying moral laws.

told me. "This is a 'New Thing' the Lord is doing." The Roman Catholics were also speaking in tongues. They had the baptism of the Holy Spirit, too! Who was I to question what God was doing? Some pastors were involved in the local ministers' fraternal and even took members of their congregations to visit the Catholic Church with their singing groups. Priests were invited to speak at conferences, and paintings of Jesus began appearing for sale in Christian bookshops.

Down in my being there was a feeling of deep foreboding. Sometimes on returning home, I got to feeling quite ill from some of the large meetings with "superstar" names. Kathryn Kuhlman and her protégés were extolled as super spiritual beings with gifts of healing and prophecy, and the local pastors were coveting and practicing the same deceitful "gifts." A spectacle we often witnessed was "leg growing." I later discovered it was actually "leg pulling!" A person with one leg supposedly shorter than the other would be seated in a chair, and the preacher would gather others around and they would stretch their hands toward the person seated. With much noise and clapping, the leg would "grow." Things were going from the ridiculous to the bizarre. Through all these trying times, I was aware of the Lord's hand on my life, and I prayed He would lead me (us) in the truth. Jesus said, *"...thy Word is Truth."* (JOHN 17:17)

During my years in the Pentecostal/Charismatic movement there were many times when alarm bells would ring in my head, but by not having the appropriate biblical or doctrinal knowledge, it was difficult to "put one's finger on the error" pushed by religious deceivers. However, there was no way that I was going back to, or even having fellowship with—Papal Rome.

"My people are destroyed for lack of knowledge" (HOSEA 4:6)

The Word of God was my mainstay, and though not being a scholar or theologically trained, I would read texts in the Bible that were at variance with what I had been taught, leaving me with more questions than answers. I knew that things in the Pentecostal/Charismatic arena were deteriorating at breakneck speed; I was becoming a "spiritual leper" by not being in step with the rest, and I was always asking the "wrong" questions. My protests fell on deaf ears. When I raised my concerns and protests, one man said to me, "Stop putting out fires!" He did not seem to see that his house was ablaze! Condemnation set in, and I began to feel that I was wrong. I soon became despondent.

But thou, O Lord, art a shield for me; my glory and the lifter up of mine head. I cried unto the Lord with my voice, and He heard me out of His holy hill."…I will not be afraid of ten thousands of people, that have set themselves against me round about. …Salvation belongeth unto the Lord: thy blessing is upon Thy people. (PSALM 3:3-4, 6, 8) *YES, SALVATION BELONGETH UNTO THE LORD!*

The Book Shop

All the "Christian" bookstores I knew about were full of what I would call junk: versions and perversions of the Bible; charismatic books with the Word-Faith/Prosperity preachers like Benny Hinn, Kenneth Hagin, the Copelands, Kathryn Kuhlman, along with Contemporary Christian Music, and all manner of trinkets similar to what Roman Catholic shops had in them. A lady who had heard about me through an acquaintance, and whom I had never met, would phone me occasionally. We were, as one would say, "on the same wavelength." She had been a Roman Catholic, and we had many good chats on the phone about past things. This lady would go to the large libraries and investigate Rome's history. I began to hear about things like the Reformation, the Inquisition, and the way "martyrs' bones" were sometimes obtained, and so on. She, too, had reservations about Pentecostalism. Then one day, she told me about a little bookshop called the Reformation Bookshop, which was located in the city. This shop is now called, "Faith and Freedom Ministries."

I began making trips into the city to buy books bought by money saved from my precious housekeeping allowance. Somehow, the Lord seemed to multiply my pennies, and the kind minister who owned the bookstore would sometimes give me a book free of charge. I loved reading and studying the books, and I would read at every opportunity. Slowly, things were making sense and Scriptures were coming alive. I began sharing these books with my husband, and the Lord began to open our eyes to the truth. I soon learned that the Pentecostal/Charismatic movement had grabbed the shadow and left the substance.

Later that year, I began to pray that the Lord would find us a "way out" of the Pentecostal church. He did, but not in the way I would have liked. It proved to be a very painful and rather devastating experience, and yet His grace sustained us. *"For my thoughts are not your thoughts, neither are your ways my ways, saith the Lord."* (ISAIAH 55:8) I found myself in spiritual turmoil and in a vacuum, not knowing which way to turn. After all, the "Spirit-filled" church was supposed to be "the one." What were the others? Although I knew I had begun a journey as a Christian—my own rebellious heart, a lack of biblical teaching, a worldly church, wrong doctrine, bad experiences, and now mistrust—all made for a "bitter pill to swallow."

The Pentecostal/Charismatic mindset told us that churches without the baptism of the Holy Spirit do not have the Holy Spirit at all! "Ordered" services were considered dead "churchianity," and the old hymns were not "new songs." (PSALMS 96:1) In our Pentecostal/Charismatic mind, obeying God's laws and His precepts were tantamount to legalism. Therefore, settling into the "old paths" of Christianity was very difficult and, in fact, took us many years. The reading of Puritan books and some of the teachers from bygone days of true revivals became a great help. I began to read about the doctrines of grace, in God's eternal plan of redemption and His everlasting love toward His own. *"Yea, I have loved thee with an everlasting love: therefore with loving kindness have I drawn thee."* (JEREMIAH 31:3)

"New Evangelicalism" and "Modernism" were definitely not for us! Charismatic leanings were creeping into most churches. After several years of "going nowhere" to church on a regular basis, and just visiting wherever we could, I knew I was slipping backward. We lived in a small country town for a few years, and by God's merciful providence we came across a house church in a neighbouring farming community. The preaching was so different, and so challenging! This was a blessing and a turning point. The doctrines of grace were so clearly taught, and the elder taught the holiness of God from the Old and New Testaments. The uplifting and beautiful hymns of the faith sung in the services were "from the heart."

A verse from an old hymn really spoke to my heart one day. I had sung it many times before, but this time was different.

> Nothing in my hand I bring,
> Simply to Thy cross I cling.
> Naked, come to Thee for dress;
> Helpless look to Thee for grace;
> Foul, I to the fountain fly;
> Wash me Saviour, or I die.

We will never come to the end of our trials in this world, but like Job of old I can say, *"I have heard of Thee by the hearing of the ear, but now mine eye seeth Thee. Wherefore I abhor myself, and repent in dust and ashes."* (JOB 42:5-6)

I am not a "King's kid," but I am His child. I have been washed in the precious blood of our Lord and Saviour, Jesus Christ. With the help of God's grace through His Holy Spirit, there is much still to learn and a long way to go in this earthly journey. I deserve nothing but His judgment, but I found grace—undeserved, precious grace.

We moved back to the city some years ago, and we found many (formerly sound) city and suburban churches awash with: entertainment, *Alpha*, Rick Warren's *40 Days of Purpose*, the *Seeker-Sensitive Church*, the *Emergent Church*, and all kinds of weird and cunning allurements to bring unchurched "Harry and Sally" in. Mega-churches with "another gospel" and "another Jesus" (2 CORINTHIANS 11:4) were popping up all over the country. Contemporary Christian Music has played a leading role in these false movements, along with the exploding number of Bible versions and their perversions. Most so-called churches have been influenced by the Charismatics; basically it amounts to "anything goes." Sound churches in our city, and probably in most of this country of Australia, are now few and far between. Many young people are drawn to the crowds and the "good times" these churches offer them. They give the people what they want, but sadly, not what they need.

May the Lord, by His truth and grace, preserve the few faithful men who have not relinquished true biblical faith, and may the Lord give us the strength and courage to stand with them.

—JENNIFER IRVINE

If you wish to share your thoughts with my husband, or me, please email us at:
wesnjenn@iprimus.com.au

Joseph Bergamini

In Maximum Security Prison Yet Free in Christ

As I write this, I am in a prison cell. I write this for the glory of God, for it is He alone that is worthy. I write this with a heavy heart for Catholics. There are many Catholics in this prison. Many of my friends are Catholic. I write this to sincere Catholics to show that Catholicism cannot save you. Only Jesus alone can save a sinner from his sins. I write this to Catholics to show that God is faithful and that by His grace He can save the worst of sinners, even those such as me.

I can remember being excited as I was about to receive the "body and blood of Christ" for the very first time. I was seven years old and was about to receive my first "holy" communion. I attended religious instructions for about one year, which was taught by a very sweet old nun. After six months of practicing the ceremony, I was about to receive my first communion. My parents had me dressed in a new suit and carrying a new black Bible. I had shiny rosary beads to match my shiny new shoes. This was a very special occasion. I was told that the Holy Communion was very important and that I would be receiving Jesus into my body when I digested the Eucharist. I would be receiving Jesus' literal body and blood!

My First Communion

As I walked down the center aisle towards the altar, my heart was beating fast. The priest was adorned in ornate robes. "The body of Christ," said the priest. "Amen," I replied. The priest placed the Eucharist on my tongue. An altar boy standing on the side held a golden plate attached to a rod. This plate was positioned under my chin. This was in case the Eucharist fell out of my mouth; the plate would catch the Eucharist before it would fall to the floor. After receiving the Eucharist, I closed my eyes and waited for something to happen. I did not feel any different after receiving the body of Christ. I did not even like the taste of the Eucharist—it tasted like cardboard. I had waited a year to partake of the sacrament and nothing happened. I thought that something was wrong with me. I was expecting some magical, life transformation to transpire. I remember feeling guilty for not feeling different. My family made a big fuss over this and there was nothing to it. Maybe I was bad or maybe I did not do something right. Even after that first communion, I still hoped for a "miracle" to happen every time that I received another communion. I thought that there was some special "power" in the Eucharist. That is because the Catholic Church taught me to believe this as a child.

My First Penance

When I was in the third grade, I made my first penance. I was very nervous the first time. Over the years, it seemed that the priests always set the same penance; say some "Hail Marys" and an "Act of Contrition." This would assure me that my sins were forgiven. The priest had power to forgive my sins and to set my penance. These were a few of my early experiences growing up Catholic.

Truth over Fiction

By the time that I was thirteen, I had many questions about God and the Church. It was at that time that I made my confirmation. I really wanted to learn about my faith. I also asked many questions about the pope and Mary. They seemed to be the most prominent aspects of Catholicism. Every garden in my neighborhood had a statue of Mary in it. This was to assure a healthy garden. Pope John Paul II was the new pope at this time; he was seen on many television stations, and written about in many magazines.

I began reading the gospels and I did not see much about Mary and found nothing about the pope. I inquired about this and the priests told me that Mary was the mother of God and that she hears our prayers. The priests also told me that the pope was the head of the Church. The gospels emphasized Jesus Christ, yet my Catholic upbringing emphasized Mary and the pope.

Teenage Years

In my teenage years, I began to use drugs and got heavily involved in rock 'n' roll music. Occasionally, I would go to confession and attend the Mass. My Irish/Italian heritage was steeped in Catholicism, so, although

I did not attend church much, the Catholic influence still had an impact on my life.

At the age of eighteen, I had my first experience with Christ Jesus the Lord. Prior to that I knew about Him, but after this experience, I knew His real presence. I had been using many drugs, and I was in very bad shape. I, nonetheless, cried out to the Lord as I was sitting on that cold basement floor crying, and then something happened. It was the first time that I actually felt the peace and love of God. This was a profound experience in my life and a real turning point. I knew Christ Jesus in some real way, not through the sacraments of the Catholic Church, but by direct contact whereby He had graciously reached down to me. I immediately stopped using drugs and I stopped looking at pornography. However, I did not surrender my life completely to Jesus. There was still sin in my life with which I did not fully repent. I did not deal with my Catholicism because I did not know the Word of God in the Scriptures. However, I began to see clearly. This I will explain as we go along. I am thankful for that experience on that basement floor because it was the first major experience in my life where God revealed to me that He was real and that He loved me. This He did, not with any rites or sacraments, but directly. This he did on that basement floor, not in a church building.

Early Adult and Tragedy

When I was twenty-three, a severe tragedy occurred in my life. Words cannot adequately describe the severity of this incident. While under the influence of drugs and alcohol, I took the life of my beloved mother! This was the most horrible thing that could ever happen. Only God knows the pain and devastation that I inflicted on my family and loved ones. I was taken to a criminal hospital. The grace of God kept my mind from snapping completely. God also kept me away from any tranquilizers. My mother was my best friend. She was the first person to tell me about God. She had wanted me to become a priest after I told her about my experience on the basement floor.

After this incident, I still sought solace in the Catholic Church. After all, this was the only "church" I knew. A few priests, deacons, and nuns helped me a great deal at this time. However, they could not offer me the spiritual help that I really needed. I needed the "sincere milk" of the Word of God. (I PETER 2:2)

While in the county jail, I met a Christian who worked with prisoners. God used this man mightily to reach me with the true gospel. This Christian man very patiently began to show me verses in the Bible that were contrary to the teachings of the Catholic Church. He pointed out what Jesus said to the Pharisees in calling anyone on earth "Father." (MATTHEW 23:9) Every Catholic priest is called "Father." This man showed me from the Scriptures that Jesus was the only Mediator. (1TIMOTHY 2:5) Yet, the Catholic Catechism states that Mary and all the saints can mediate for us before a Holy God. Although I saw this clearly in the Bible, I still attended Catholic services. My parents and grandparents were all Catholic. I thought that being Catholic was a family thing. I agreed that the Catholic Church was wrong in many areas, but I still considered myself a Catholic.

The Law has its Day

I was sentenced to 25 years to life in prison. After leaving the county jail, I began serving my time in a maximum-security state prison. I was frightened, but God comforted me. God placed me in a cell next to a Christian man who ministered to me in a mighty way. He shared the Scriptures with some Christians and me and began giving me the gospel with love and patience. One dear Christian man gave me a book to read. This book revealed many errors in the Catholic Church by referring to the Scriptures. After reading this book and listening to the counsel of these men, I forsook Catholicism and repented before God.

Trusting in Christ Alone

It was at this stage of my life that I looked unto Christ Jesus alone for my salvation that I might receive from Him His perfect life and the perfect remission of my sin, *"Being justified freely by His grace, through the redemption that is in Christ Jesus."* (ROMANS 3:24) It was God's grace and the payment He gave that made me right before God—wholly accepted in Christ Jesus the Lord—complete in Him. (COLOSSIANS 2:10) It was at this stage that I fully repented of my sin, remembering the words of Christ Jesus, *"… repent ye, and believe the gospel."* (MARK 1:15) I repented of all religion and of personal sin so that my eyes—and trust—were totally on Christ Jesus and what He had done in my place. I remembered that Christ Jesus came in the words of Matthew's gospel, *"…for He shall save His people from their sins."* (MATTHEW 1:21)

My aunt was furious with me when I told her that I was no longer a Catholic. I must admit that I was a bit puffed up as well as angry at the fact that I had been following a religion and not following Jesus. I took my frustration out on many Catholics, including members of my own family. I then came across where Paul writes that the servant of the Lord must not quarrel, but be gentle and humble. (2 TIMOTHY 2:22-26) We must "speak the truth in love," not in anger. (EPHESIANS 4:15) Around this time, I was introduced to the Berean Beacon ministry. I began writing to brother Richard Bennett, a former Catholic priest. He gave me advice in how to witness to Catholics. He showed me clearly—using the Scriptures—that God's grace is in Christ Jesus. The wonder of God's grace is always in Christ from beginning to end, starting with His divine call to the glory of His name. As true believers, we adhere to God only and to His written Word, as did the Lord and the apostles after Him. We are saved before the All Holy God by grace alone, through faith alone, and in Christ Jesus alone, and all glory and praise is to God alone.

Re-baptized

I had been baptized as an infant into the Catholic Church, but now that I was reading the entire Bible, I realized that I should be baptized again as a new believer. So, I was baptized in the prison baptistry on March 25, 1995. I was immersed into a portable tank that was set up in the chapel. I was convinced by the Scriptures that I now had to live totally for Christ.

The Bible Reveals the Truth about Salvation

At this time, I was really studying and meditating on the Scriptures. It was then that I realized that many Evangelicals have departed from the truth of the Gospel. I encountered a lot of legalism and elitism within the prison walls. I also witnessed that many Evangelicals have no problem with Roman Catholic doctrines and traditions. Throughout the centuries, Evangelicals had maintained that justification was by faith alone and that a sinful being was declared justified before the All Holy God by His grace alone. I see that many Evangelicals of every denomination have become quite confused on this subject, and other subjects, and some of them have begun even working together in a relationship with the Catholic Church, not being aware that the Church of Rome is preaching another Gospel. (GALATIANS 1:6-10) Here in prison, I see the same thing that is happening in the world outside, that chaplains and others are working together with the Roman Catholics and no one is quite sure of the doctrine of salvation. The Church has come to be in a very sad condition. Much of the work that I have done during my time in prison is trying to show what salvation really is, not only to the Catholics, but also to people who call themselves Evangelicals.

A New Friend

I have corresponded with a brother (a pastor) who has been imprisoned in Zambia, Africa for many years. His name is Stanley Kunda. He had found in Zambia the same thing that we find here in the United States, that many people have no understanding of what it is to be saved by grace alone, through faith alone, and in Christ Jesus alone. Brother Kunda and I have encouraged one another by sending letters through the Berean Beacon ministry of Richard Bennett. It is amazing what the Lord has done in giving the true gospel. There in Zambia, many have come to see the true light of the gospel. As I write this testimony, Stanley Kunda has been released from a maximum-security prison; my prayers and thoughts go with him.

The Gospel: The Power of God unto Salvation

As I grow in the grace and knowledge of Jesus Christ, I see that the gospel is a simple, yet profound truth. The gospel is also the *"...power of God unto salvation...."* (ROMANS 1:16) No man can add to what Jesus has done. The sacraments of Catholicism cannot contribute to anyone's salvation. Water baptism does not save. Christ alone paid the price for our redemption. Prayers, church attendance, positions, and good works—none of these can declare us righteous before an All Holy God. Jesus alone was well pleasing to His father. (MATTHEW 3:17) *"For He hath made Him to be sin for us, who knew no sin, that we might be made the righteousness of God in Him."* (2 CORINTHIANS 5:21) Jesus took the penalty that we deserved. Christ alone is our righteousness. Christ became for us *wisdom, righteousness, sanctification, and redemption.* (1 CORINTHIANS 1:30) To God be the glory!

The Blessings of God

Now that I have been incarcerated for 12 years, I find that I am still learning and unlearning. I have had to let go of certain beliefs that I have held to because they were not based upon God's Word. God has been faithful to me. He has kept me safe all these years. He touched my father's heart, and we have a relationship today. God has brought a beautiful Christian woman into my life, and we are engaged to be married. God has bestowed His grace upon me by bringing me into a wonderful family of believers. He has made me a new man. I am in a relationship with Almighty God. I remember these words: *"Unto Him that loved us and washed us from our sins in His own blood, and hath made us kings and priests unto God and His father, to Him be glory and dominion forever and ever. Amen."* (REVELATION 1:5-6) The world may see me as a murderer and convict, yet God sees me as royalty! God has set me free from the bondage of sin and darkness, from the chains of drug dependency, and from the bondage of religion. The Son has made me free, indeed. (JOHN 8:36) I now stand fast in the liberty that Jesus has granted me. (GALATIANS 5:1) *Blessing, honor, glory, and power be unto Him that sitteth upon on the throne, and unto the Lamb forever and ever, Amen!* (REVELATION 5:13)

—JOSEPH BERGAMINI

ROBERT EMMET HOLMES

From Catholic to the Truth

BEING A CARNAL CATHOLIC IS HAVING THE BEST OF BOTH WORLDS, OR SO I thought. However, my carnality and my religion were both taking me to hell. The Catholic Church is like *"...the way of an adulterous woman; she eateth, and wipeth her mouth, and saith, I have done no wickedness."* (PROVERBS 30:20) My lot was like the man Lot, a picture of a carnal Laodicean—an unfaithful saint.

To me, the Catholic Church was to be feared and respected—in that order. I remember at a carnival at Saint Adain's, the church I grew up in until the age of fifteen, a priest was greeting everyone, but I feared to greet him.

I grew up in an Irish Catholic family; my father was a New York City cop with an attitude. I was number three in the family. I went to Catholic Church until I was fifteen years old, when I started drinking. As far back as I can remember, my family was Catholic. But I was named after a "Black Bloody Protestant, bold Robert Emmet the Darain of Ireland." The following is my personal testimony of salvation.

Born Catholic

My parents thought a Catholic education was important, so for two years I attended first and second grade at Saint Mel's in Queens, New York. We moved out to Long Island sometime around 1967 when I was seven, and when I went to public school in the middle of the school year, I got left back. I went to CCD (Confraternity of Christian Doctrine) at Saint Aidan's on Wednesday afternoon, but I do not remember much, except for riding on a bus and seeing lines of kids going from the bus into the school. The nuns would hand out religious books, but I could not read, so it did not matter much to me. I remember getting a paperback of the Good News for Modern Man and looking at the stick figures in the book. I had no idea that it was a Bible. Actually, it is a paraphrase of the Bible.

I did graduate with modified English and modified Social Studies and Phys. Ed. from Herrick's High. In the afternoon, I went to Boces, a trade school to learn how to be an auto mechanic. I remember filling out an employment application and not being able to spell mechanic, so I would write auto mech. As far as indoctrination into the Catholic faith, I was born into it. I was baptized as an infant, confirmed as a young boy, and received my first Holy Communion. I started lying and confessing my sins to priests at an early age.

When I was young, I went on Saturday to the confessional booth in the back of the church and would wait in line maybe ten to fifteen feet away, so as not to hear. When I was in the booth it was dark; the little door would open and a priest would say something I did not understand, and I would say, "Bless me father, for I have sinned. It has been two weeks since my last confession." My fear was getting my line wrong. It never lasted long; I was never specific, always vague. I think once or twice the priest would try to get more information from me, but I never told him much. Then he would say something and tell me to say five "Hail Mary's," and two "Our Father's." I would then go to the altar and pray the vain repetitious prayers. *"The way of the wicked is as darkness,"* (PROVERBS 4:19) I had no clue as to what I was doing, but I knew it was not right.

I remember my younger bother, Dan, about a year younger than I, becoming an altar boy. To this day I have no idea why I was never asked to become one. I would go to the Mass he was serving as an assistant. He would place a metal tray under a person's chin just in case the wafer fell. Dan would put it close to my neck, but I thought it was a big joke. I remember going back where he would dress and he showed me where the alcohol was kept. Thoughts of dedicating my life to God in this way never entered my mind. Serving God was the last thing on my mind, serving sin was.

I had another brother, Chris, who went to see Pope Pius II on Long Island in order to become a priest. I thought of my brother as square, and that he was a social misfit. I thought this of anyone who was interested in becoming more Catholic.

My Loyalty to the Flesh

As a Catholic, I never knew that the Catholic Church taught the Eucharist was the actual body and blood of our Lord Jesus Christ. I found that out when I became a Christian. I remember witnessing to a Catholic and asking him if he was a Christian, and he said, "No I'm a Catholic." Most Catholics have no idea what their church teaches.

After I received my first Holy Communion, the only thing I was interested in was getting my picture taken so it would be on the wall in my home. There were eight pictures of everyone in their new clothes. We were poor, so new clothes were nice to have.

Nanny's House, Holy Water, and the Rosary

As a child, I remember holy water. My grandparents were the only ones that used it on a regular basis. When our family would visit them, grandmother would make us stick our fingers into the water and bless ourselves. Kathleen White was her name. She was a rather large woman, and she loved candy and cookies. Of all the people in my world at that age, I could say I loved her. There were not many of whom I could say that. Well, she loved to pray the rosary on her knees. How I hated that boring prayer. I was still a boy—ten years old. I wanted to watch TV and eat sweets. She used to have big statues of the Virgin Mary in her room. They frightened me. I would sometimes spend the night, but I never liked looking at them in the dark.

Others and "The Way"

My first thought of *"the way and the truth"* (JOHN 14:6) was at the age of fifteen. A friend from high school, Robbie Williamson, invited me to a person's house where they were having a religious meeting to hear about God. I was not against God, and if someone had truth, I was interested in hearing what he or she had to say. This shocked my friend because of the way I lived my life. I remember being hurt because I "was" looking; I just had never heard the truth before.

It is strange what your mind remembers. The only thing I remember about this meeting was the impression I got from the person running the meeting. He was in his basement, sitting in a high-back, stuffed chair with a 3'x3' picture on the wall behind him of what was supposed to represent Jesus. I remember asking many questions, but I did not get much response, except: "You are a confused boy." He might have been a Christian, but he did not know much about the Bible.

There was a Friday night RAP thing the Catholic Church had going for teens that I went to when I was about sixteen. A Tony Bellise was in

212 ON THE WINGS OF GRACE ALONE

charge of these meetings. I went to his meeting because I liked him as a person. He was a nice guy, but he was not a Christian. His message was on how we treat each other, rather than on how we treat God; it was more on humanist love than love for God.

The Navy, a Way Out

After living a life to the satisfying of the flesh, I decided my only way out was by joining the military. I wanted to be clean in body, soul, and spirit. My military years changed my life. October 31, 1980, on Halloween day, was my first day in the US Navy. From Fort Hamilton, Brooklyn, NY, I went to Orlando, Florida for boot camp. It was hard on me, but I needed the discipline. I knew that I needed help, so I went to church on Sunday while I was in boot camp. At the base chapel there were seven different kinds of Christian services that I attended. This, I could say, was the first time in my life that I really was looking for God. In one of the services on the base there was a small group that was trying to speak in an unknown language. This was my first exposure to "speaking in tongues" in the flesh. I wanted it because I thought it was of God. Well, after seven weeks of this, it was my turn to speak in tongues; everyone put their hands on me but nothing happened. I remember being a little disappointed, but it was not for me. During my time in boot camp there was a Bible study at night. I do not think the person running the study really believed what he was reading. But for the first time in my life I realized that God had a "Book" and I wanted to know about it, even though I could only read on a sixth grade level. In the Bible study, we read out of the book of Revelation. I asked the person running the study if he really believed what he was reading. He said it was all symbolic. I did not believe him, but I kept my opinions to myself. Well, I got out of boot camp and the pressure was off. I got to my duty station and started back toward the life style that I was trying to get away from.

The U-turn That Made the Difference

Three months after I got out of boot camp in Orlando, Florida, I was back to my old ways again. I was stationed at the Naval Air Station at Jacksonville, Florida for schooling on airplanes. I stopped looking for God and did not think there was much more I could do. I knew I could not live a holy life in the flesh, you know—outwardly appearing righteous unto men as many Catholics do. On Friday, March 13, 1981, I was planning to go to the Gatornationals, a drag race in Gainesville, Florida. It was about three hours from the base by car on Interstate 10. I remember a Navy friend, Kevin Knoll, was suppose to drive me, but he left without me. I thought I would be able to get there. The week before, I hitched-hiked to Bike Week at Daytona, Florida and had a great time. Being left behind was not going to stop me from going, so I put my thumb out and started on my own once again. I got a few small rides right away. One of the last rides on my way to the races was from a person who just wanted to get out and drive because of some personal problems. I think his child was sick in the hospital, and he was very depressed about the problem. I wanted to help him but had nothing to offer him.

I was standing for three hours on Interstate 10, out of Jacksonville, without one ride. In the distance, I saw a rest area on the other side of the Interstate. So, I decided to make a "U-turn." Once I got to the rest area, I sat down in the parking lot for about a minute and a car pulled in and parked in front of where I was sitting. I asked him if he was going back to the Navy base. He said he was and gave me a ride. As we started back to the base, about twenty miles away, he asked me a few questions that God used to change my life forever.

Ten o'clock at Night on Friday the Thirteenth, May 1981

May 13, 1981, is a day I will never forget—the day of my salvation. Well, I was on my way back to the base when the driver started to ask me these questions. The first question he asked me was. "Do you mind if I ask you a personal question?" My first thought about this guy was not good. I did not know what he wanted, but I said, "No." He asked me, "If you were to die today, do you know where you would go?" I told him I was Catholic. He said, "I did not ask if you were Catholic, but if you know where you are going when you die." That moment in time was the first time I felt conviction of my sins. I had never felt that before. I told him I would probably go to hell because as every good Catholic knows, if you do not go to Mass every Sunday, it is a mortal sin.

We finally got back to the base, and in the parking lot he asked me if I wanted to ask the Lord Jesus Christ to save me from my sins. I could not believe it was that simple. The hard part was that he wanted me to get out of the car and kneel down, in the parking lot of the barracks, and call upon the name of the Lord. Taking the free gift for salvation was the easy part, humbling myself was the hard part. Thus by God's grace I turned to Jesus Christ and in faith, and believed solely on Him, as I knew the Bible verses, *"For by grace are you saved through faith; and that not of yourselves: it is the gift of God: Not of works, lest any man should boast."* (EPHESIANS 2:8-9)

Spiritually Minded is Life and Peace

Now my affections are mostly set on things above and not on things of the flesh, because to be carnally minded is death. I try to be spiritually minded and think on things that are good and holy, because as a man thinks in his heart so is he. (PROVERBS 23:7) So I keep my heart with all diligence and hide His Word in my heart that I might not sin against Him. So: *"Let us hear the conclusion of the whole matter: Fear God, and keep his commandments: for this is the whole duty of man. For God shall bring every work into judgment, with every secret thing, whether it be good, or whether it be evil."* (ECCLESIASTES 12:13) The great thing to be then judged of concerning every work is whether it be good or evil, conformable to the will of the Lord God or a violation of it.

—BOB HOLMES

If you would like to contact me I would welcome your message, just email me at:
avkjv1611ad@juno.com

GREG JAMES

From Ritual To Regeneration

ONE OF THE MOST GUT-WRENCHING AND PAINFUL THINGS I HAVE HAD to face in my life has been the confrontation between the doctrines and claims of my Catholic faith and the Word of God as found in the Holy Scriptures.

While far from perfect, I tried my best to be a good Catholic so that my name would be found in the "Book of Life" on the Judgment Day. After almost 50 years of unyielding loyalty to the Catholic Church and Catholic teachings, the grace of God broke the stranglehold of sin in my life.

Born and raised in a Roman Catholic family, I have vivid memories of a childhood dominated by the mysteries and the rituals of "The Faith" as I received them from my parents, grandparents, aunts, and uncles. I remember the crucifix that hung in each bedroom in our home, the holy water font on each doorpost, the statues of Jesus, Mary-and-Joseph, and the Sacred Heart in Grandma's room. I remember the Sunday Missal that each adult carried to Mass on Sundays and Holy Days. I could not wait until I could have one for my own, so that I might be able to understand the solemn language that the priest spoke as he stood in front of the altar and prayed. I thought it must be the special language spoken between God and the priest during the Mass. Then there was the ever-present Rosary that both the ladies and the men carried at all times.

A Child of God

All of these things, and more, were reinforced by virtue of my Catholic school education, and they were indelibly etched into my character by repetition, memorization, and practice. The stern Sisters of Notre Dame, robed in their foreboding black garb, appeared to me as the very agents of God Himself as they drilled us on the Baltimore Catechism and the proper behavior to display while in church or in the presence of a priest. The infrequent classroom visits by the parish priest, or even the Monsignor, were special occasions for which the Sisters carefully prepared us—rehearsing catechism answers and formula prayers over and over so that we could impress "Father" with our religious skills. I also learned that I was a "child of God"—because I was baptized a Catholic and was now special in His eyes compared to other kids who had not been baptized a Catholic. I had no recollection of my baptism because it happened when I was about three weeks old, but I still have the pictures taken of my baptism in my family album. Nevertheless, I learned on that day that I had been made a child of God and an heir of heaven and would now move on to greater things.

The first important event that I remember from those early days is my First Holy Communion. For months in advance, the Sisters rehearsed the class on every detail attending the ritual pomp of the "big" day. Over and over, we were marched up the center aisle of the church—two by two, boys on the right and girls on the left, short to tall from front to back—hands folded in pious respect and as silent as a breeze as we peeled off to our places in the church pews. The "clicker" in Sister's hand governed every move. As a group, we repeated the answers to questions we were to be asked by the priest and prayers we were required to say as part of the ceremony. What precision!

In the Dark

However, there were two aspects of this coming event that struck fear into my heart and some of my classmate's hearts as well. Before we made our First Communion, we had to go to our First Confession. I remember the dread that accompanied me in the days leading up to the fateful moment when I pulled aside the curtain and entered the darkness of the confessional box. Although we had been taught that the priest was there to forgive our sins and would not be scolding or angry, I could not imagine why I had to enter this dark, cramped place and recite the things I was taught to say to him. I was not even sure that I had committed the sins that I had picked from the list we were given to help us make a "good" confession. Fortunately, my training once again saved the day as I recited the formulas that were repeated during the prior months. The dread stayed with me for many years—every time I approached the confessional box. Even as an adult, I felt like a child as I knelt before the priest and recited my sins and the same prayers that I learned so long ago. From the very first, I recall the relief I felt when I had finished confessing and the priest gave me absolution and penance. In later years I could not help but wonder, if Jesus died for my sins, as I was taught, what good was it going to do saying five Our Father's and five Hail Mary's as my penance?

It was not until many years later that the truth of God's Word in the Holy Scriptures finally sunk in. I remember reading in the Bible, *"But he was wounded for our transgressions, he was bruised for our iniquities: the chastisement of our peace was upon him; and with his stripes we are healed. All we like sheep have gone astray; we have turned every one to his own way; and the LORD hath laid on him the iniquity of us all."* (ISAIAH 53:5, 6)

Jesus had already died in my place for "all" my sins. There was nothing I could do—or had to do—that He had not done for me already. Jesus paid the full price for all my sins. God the Father sent Him to earth specifically for that purpose, and before He took His last breath as he hung dying on the Cross He said, *"It is finished."* (JOHN 19:30)

Body and Blood

Nevertheless, I managed to go through my First Confession, and First Communion day finally arrived. All the boys were decked out in blue "communion" suits and the girls in their white "communion" dresses. As Sister's clicker moved us up the church aisle in perfect unison, our parents and family members looked on with big smiles and cameras flashing. When the time came to kneel at the communion rail, all of the instruction I had received took over and my thoughts went to the great care I must take to kneel quietly as the priest approached, and stick out my tongue far enough that the communion wafer could be safely inserted into my mouth. I then had to return to my seat and wait until the host melted, being careful that nothing else touched it. I could not use my finger to scrape it off the roof of my mouth where it was stuck, nor, heaven forbid, try to chew it. We were taught that the priest changed the wafer into the body and blood, soul and divinity of Jesus himself. He had to be treated with the utmost respect and piety. I was convinced that I actually carried Jesus inside my stomach.

A highlight of that day came after Mass when Sister presented us with our first Missal and Rosary. Almost everyone in my family had a gift of a medal or cross on a chain; some gave cards with money. However, the Missal held the deepest mysteries for me. On one page was printed the "special" Latin language that the priest spoke, and on the facing page I could read the meaning in English! Now, maybe I could learn to talk with God too—as the priest did. It was, unfortunately, many years before I learned that God did not speak a special, mysterious language, but hears and answers every prayer that a believer utters, regardless of our language. He even sends the Holy Spirit to every believer, to pray for us when our words fail us.

At any rate, the "big" day was over. I expected to feel different, holier, and closer to God; but I did not. As time passed, and we advanced, the Sisters explained more of what was expected of us if we were to remain a child of God. Keeping the Ten Commandments of God, and the Six Commandments of the Church, was basic, as was receiving as many of the Sacraments as possible. We were taken to Confession every two weeks and were told to receive communion every Sunday. Sunday Mass was an absolute "must." If we missed Sunday Mass, except for a very good reason, like sickness, we committed a Mortal Sin. Mortal Sin cut us off from God, and if we died without going to Confession, we would go straight to Hell. Venial Sins were not as bad. We had to tell them to the priest in confession, but they did not cause us to go straight to Hell if we died without Confession.

We were also required to go to Mass and communion before school on every First Friday during the school year and were encouraged to make the Five First Saturdays because the promise of a happy death was attached to everyone who completed all five in a row. I remember doing them repeatedly; just to be certain I would be safe.

Soldier of Christ

In seventh grade, we began the preparation for receiving the Sacrament of Confirmation. Once again, rehearsals, practice of prayers, and studies on the meaning of the Sacrament were repeated time after time to insure our clear understanding and perfect performance. I still can recite the answer of the Baltimore Catechism as it asked the question:

Q. What is a Sacrament?

A. A Sacrament is a Sign, instituted by Christ to give Grace.

However, this time was to be far different from First Communion Day. This time, at Confirmation, we were going to receive the Holy Spirit. We would no longer be only children of God, but now we would become Soldiers of Christ. This power of the Holy Spirit was to be conferred on us by the Bishop himself who we had never seen before, but who, we were told, was a very important priest with great powers. He, or someone special appointed by him, was the only one who could perform this deed. As he spoke the words of the sacrament, he anointed me with "holy" oil and gently slapped my face to show that I had now received the Holy Spirit; this was a serious matter. What a shock it was when, later in life, I learned that the Holy Spirit is not "conferred" on us by a Bishop. God's word teaches us that Jesus and the Father sent the Holy Spirit when Jesus returned to Heaven after His resurrection.

From that day on there were many appeals to "give my life to Christ" by considering the possibility of becoming a priest. The girls in class were encouraged to consider becoming a nun, a "bride of Christ." We were often told that this vocation was the highest and most important to which we could aspire. My family reinforced the idea, as many Catholic families do; almost taking for granted that at least one child would enter the religious

life. A scholarship to Catholic High School followed graduation. The Christian Brothers had a reputation for being demanding and strict. The reputation was well deserved. From the beginning, religion was the major subject of study with a requirement to study Latin and another foreign language. English, math, and science also set us in good stead for the academic demands of college to follow. There was, however, a constant drumbeat for religious vocations and many of my classmates left during junior and senior years or immediately after graduation to attend minor seminary. Although I knew my parents would be happy if I made that decision, I was grateful that there was no pressure from home to do so. I was not ready. I knew that I was not "good" enough for such an exalted position.

Second Best

In my senior year, I met a beautiful redheaded Irish girl from our "sister" Catholic High School and it was as though I had known her all my life. She, too, struggled with the decision to pursue a religious vocation as a nun and I almost lost her to the Sisters of Mercy. Four years later she became my wife and to this day remains my precious and beautiful spouse. We were married at Mass in her parish. Her "favorite" priest, who presented us with the gift of a Papal Blessing, performed the Sacrament of Matrimony. As part of the ceremony, my wife laid flowers at the feet of the statue of the Virgin Mary, appealing to Mary for her special grace to be a good wife and mother. Three children, a house in the suburbs, a good job, and a wonderful wife at home to raise the children—it was a wonderful life! Friends and neighbors saw us as the "perfect couple," and we prided ourselves on our reputation. Nevertheless, one particular couple returned home from a "Marriage Encounter" weekend, hosted by the Jesuits, and would not rest until we agreed to sign for a weekend ourselves. They explained that it was designed to make good marriages even better! So we went, not knowing what to expect, and wound up being asked to train as a "presenting team" couple for future weekends. We would work side-by-side with a priest and two other couples sharing our own stories and especially our love for our Sacrament. The appeal was irresistible to me. The first morning of the weekend was spent examining our feelings with the appeal to see us as "good" since "God does not make junk." This appeal spoke to my view of myself that I "wasn't good enough" and hooked me from the beginning. Here was the perfect opportunity to have my marriage and to have "special" work to do for the Catholic Church. For the very first time outside of the readings at Mass, I heard the presenting priest quote biblical "things." He paraphrased the words of Jesus to encourage us to join the team, *"You have not chosen me, but I have chosen you..."* (John 15:16) and words about pouring *"new wine into new wineskins, not old wineskins."* (Mark 2:22) I did not fully understand, but who could resist being chosen by Jesus Himself? Vatican Council II had raised the "vocation" of Catholic Sacramental Marriage to new heights. Although still second best, I now considered myself to be a lot closer to being "good enough" because of our Sacrament.

As with the entirety of my Catholic training up to that point, I simply accepted what was presented without examining it closely. Other friends who were part of the "team" drifted toward the rapidly growing Catholic Charismatic Movement. They urged us to come to Charismatic Masses and prayer meetings where we would learn how to pray and worship with exuberance as well as learn all about the Bible. It was here that I began to read and seriously study the Word of God. For the most part, the Bible seemed to be clearly understandable. I had been taught, however, that it was not permitted for me to try to understand the Bible by myself since the Church Magisterium alone had been given the authority to interpret Holy

Scripture. So, I thought it might be helpful to get closer to priests who must surely be able to understand and teach me the mysteries of the Bible. I joined the Third Order of St. Francis and eventually became the founding Prefect of the New Pentecost Community of the Third Order on Long Island, NY. The spiritual director, a Franciscan priest, and I were to work together to grow the community and direct its spiritual life and works. During that time, I was shocked to learn that he had very little understanding and practically no interest in the Bible. His worldview was formed and controlled by the Rule of St. Francis. God's Word was filtered through that rule. That did not seem to me to be what Jesus had in mind when He said to Satan, *"... It is written, That man shall not live by bread alone, but by every word of God."* (LUKE 4:4) It seemed very strange to me that a priest would choose to live by a "Rule" rather than simply obey the words of Jesus.

Searching the Scriptures

As I studied the New Testament, I struggled more and more with the discrepancies I found between what the Bible says and what I had learned from my Catechism. I decided to stop read-ing the Bible because I thought I had misin-terpreted what I read. It was safer to concen-trate on the catechism because everything in it was simple and easy to understand. Howev-er, I continued to struggle with many Roman Catholic doctrines that so clearly denied the teachings I had found in Scripture—as well as others that were nowhere to be found in the Bible. I could not stay away from the Bible for long. I knew it was the very word of God—the word of eternal life. I resumed my Bible studies.

It became eminently clear to me that the Catholic doctrine of salvation and the scriptural doctrine of salvation disagree significantly. That is, without a doubt, the most important difference of all because our eternal destiny depends on our trust in the saving death and resurrection of Jesus as our Substitute. We will be lost if we place our trust in anyone, or anything else, but Jesus. No sacra-ment, no Mass, no pope, no lifetime of good works can save us...only the once for all sacrifice of Jesus at Calvary...*"For by grace are ye saved through faith;, and that not of yourselves: it is the gift of God: not of works, lest any man should boast.*

For we are his workmanship, created in Christ Jesus unto good works, which God hath before ordained that we should walk in them." (EPHESIANS 2:8-10)

I knew I had to make a choice; I knew I could not reconcile my lifelong efforts to "save" myself with the clear Word of God. Christ saves us when we trust Him alone for our salvation. I could not continue the "Roman Catholic" things I was doing and maintain my integrity. Truly, this would be taking the Lord's name in vain.

I resigned from the Third Order of St. Francis and left the Roman Catholic Church. I found a good, solid, Bible believing, Bible teaching church where Jesus is exalted. His grace has brought me unspeakable joy and gratitude. Nevertheless, as you can well imagine, my decision to distance myself from Catholicism resulted in anger, grief, and resentment from many of my family members and friends. This estrangement has been most hurtful. It was an almost insurmountable obstacle to me as I struggled with making my decision. However, Jesus Christ's words, recorded in the Gospel of Mark, spoke volumes to me. Jesus said, *"For whosoever will save his life shall lose it; but whosoever shall lose his life for my sake and the gospel's, the same shall save it." (MARK 8:35)*

It is not that I did something heroic; it is definitely not that I wanted to do something to "save" myself; that is simply impossible because it is only total trust in Jesus Christ that can save us. My decision rests on the gift of faith and the grace of salvation freely given by the all-Holy God. Now I know the true meaning of Jesus Christ's words that I heard so long ago, *"Ye have not chosen me, but I have chosen you." (JOHN 15:16)* Indeed it is stated that, *"According as he hath chosen us in him before the foundation of the world, that we should be holy and without blame before him in love." (EPHESIANS 1:4)* Thus I can now say from my heart, *"Blessed be the God and Father of our Lord Jesus Christ, who hath blessed us with all spiritual blessings in heavenly places in Christ." (EPHESIANS 1: 3)* I believe that it is the honor and glory of Jesus Christ, and the truth of the Gospel that are at stake because, *"Neither is there salvation in any other: for there is none other name under heaven given among men, whereby we must be saved." (ACTS 4:12)*

—GREG JAMES

It would be an encouragement to me to hear from you,
My email address is: jamznjamz@yahoo.com

PAUL SMITH

From Confusion to Understanding

My name is Paul; I am the eleventh child of a large Roman Catholic Family, which totaled fourteen children—seven boys and seven girls. Some of my earliest memories include my parents walking us up to Saint Mary's Church, which was one block up the street from our house. We would file into the church, my father and mother first, then us children from smallest to largest behind them. We then sat on a pew close to the front. At that time in the early 1960's, there were many big families. However, we were the largest in the parish, and my father was quite proud of his brood.

From a very young age, we were taught right from wrong, but it was not explained to us why. Any questions were always answered, "Because I said so," or "Mom said so." The Roman Church was always referred to as "the one, true, holy Roman Apostolic Church." It was the final authority. We were taught that the decisions it made were guaranteed to be infallible. The Pope was always correct, because he was Christ's vicar on earth. I remember being taught that any church other than the "one true holy Roman Apostolic Church" was a false church, and consequently, its members would go to hell.

I felt proud and fortunate to be so "lucky" to grow up in this church, yet at the same time it seemed to me very unfair of God to send people from other churches to hell if they were "good." After all, there were others I liked, and some seemed to love God, but they did not belong to the Roman Catholic Church. These were the very beginnings of mental conflicts over spiritual matters that in latter years would nearly drive me insane.

I was also taught that man had a free will. If I chose what was right and participated in the Roman Catholic Church's sacraments, this would merit grace from God. Yet, as hard as I tried I was unable to stop sinning. I was taught that sin was bad and it made God (and my dad) very angry with me. I was also taught in communion the Eucharist wafer was the actual physical body of Jesus, and it could not be consumed in a state of sin. To leave the state of sin and be able to have communion, I would have to go to a priest and confess my sins, then he gave me my penance. It was only after doing the penance would the priest forgive my sins. In my young mind, I accepted all of this as a way of making God happy with me.

In our large family, we constantly fought with our brothers and sisters over things such as toys and food. The temptation of stealing cookies out of the pantry overwhelmed me many times. The consequences of doing this were cookies, then guilt, and shame. I tried to put my sins out of my mind. I tried to hide them. I tried to hide from God. Try that sometime! Of course, my mother would get angry, "Who stole the cookies?" In my fear of punishment from my angry father, I would lie to her and then feel even worse about myself. To go to confession scared me to death. I would feel my heart pounding even thinking about it. The guilt and shame would trap me. I thought at that time, the only way to rid myself of this guilt was to go to confession and do penance. The penance was always something such as saying ten "Hail Marys" and four "our Fathers." It was never to go to your mother and tell her you lied and replace what you stole. I distinctly remember walking away from confession one day with a lightened heart when suddenly a dark realization struck me, the only way I would ever get to heaven was if I died in a state of grace. The only way I would die in a state of grace would be if I were killed immediately after leaving the confessional! I knew that I could not be sin free for any length of time! This thought greatly disturbed me. I was about eight years old at the time.

In our house, my parents had many statues and crucifixes with the dead body of Christ hanging on them. The biggest, a statue of the Virgin Mary, was on top of the television in our large dining room. It was mandatory to pray the rosary every night at nine p.m., and then we kids had to go to bed. After years of praying the rosary, and as my leg bones began to grow faster, I developed large bumps on my knees that would hurt intensely as I knelt to pray. I could not understand why we had to repeat the same prayers over and over again; did not God hear us the first time? It was so monotonous

that I could barely maintain my posture; I would try to put these things out of my mind as I mumbled the words. In my mind, God and the devil were fighting each other, the devil was very powerful, and God needed all the help He could get from us by doing our penance. My father also had a small statue of Saint Michael the archangel fighting the devil. It depicted Saint Michael with his sword outstretched standing on the devil. One day, my next oldest brother, Joe, showed me that if you turned it upside down it looked like the devil was winning over Saint Michael. I remember that this frightened us.

My older brothers eventually quit going to Mass, praying the rosary, and generally being a part of the family. Sometimes my older brothers would sneak out the window at night and smoke cigarettes. If my father found out, he would beat them in anger. I could never figure out why it was okay for my mother and father to smoke, but not my older brothers. To me smoking was obviously bad for you and therefore wrong. It seemed to me that there was a double standard. If you drank, smoked, or swore, all you would need to do was go to church and do penance, and everything would be all right again.

My older teenage brothers grew up in the late 1960s. We lived in southern California, and going to the beach was a big part of our lives. My older brothers were experienced surfers. While we were children, we idolized them. We thought they were "cool." The rock & roll drug culture and the Vietnam War were going full blast by this time. My older brothers, knowing they would probably be drafted, took us under their wings as they realized they might never see us again. They started taking us places with them, buying us hamburgers and going surfing. This was a big treat to us younger brothers and for the first time in my life, I felt a real camaraderie, and it felt good.

My father always seemed distant from us boys. He rarely showed affection to us. Running his large machine shop to provide for his fourteen children, not to mention his employees' and their families, he was too busy to have time or energy to spend elsewhere. Besides, he never explained things or answered my deep questions about life. Perhaps he did not know the answers.

As we younger boys began surfing with our older brothers, the "generation gap" between our parents and us seemed to grow into the size of a canyon. As my body matured, my sins now included those of a sexual nature. I was taught that sex was for making babies and nothing else. The guilt and shame resulting from my sin was unbearable. In short, about the age of sixteen, a connection was made in my mind. I found that by changing the way I felt, I could alleviate some of the pain from guilt and shame. I learned that by drinking and smoking pot I could make myself feel "good."

By the time I was twenty years old, I had progressed to a hardcore drug addict. My mind was a seething cauldron of deep mental and spiritual conflicts most of which I could not even articulate. If I had free will, why did I always choose what was evil? Obviously, I was evil or possibly even possessed. In the midst of all this, I noticed a profound change in some of my friends; they quit partying (drinking and smoking pot) and seemed genuinely happy. They invited me to hear some bands play on a Saturday night. That sounded like fun to me, so I went with them. After the music, a man got up and started preaching the Bible from the Gospels. I was familiar with the Gospels, yet in the Catholic Church Christ seemed to be still hanging on the cross. This was much different; here Christ seemed to be alive and risen! The man talked about sin and the need to repent; to turn from sin. He spoke of receiving Christ and confessing Him before men. This was a huge Evangelical church; there were thousands of people there. My mind and heart were so focused on what the preacher was saying, I felt like I was the only person there, and God Himself was speaking through His word directly to me! The Spirit of God cut right into my heart and convicted me of my sin. I broke down in tears sobbing; it was as if scales fell from my eyes. Deep in my heart, it was revealed to me that the Bible was God's Word and Christ was risen and alive. The preacher said that we should come forward knowing that we are sinners and believe on Jesus Christ for salvation as the Scripture states, *"For by grace are you saved through faith; and that not of yourselves: it is the gift of God: not of works, lest any man should boast."* (EPHESIANS 2:8-9) Feeling as if it were God's grace within me, I believed on Jesus Christ for salvation. People prayed with me, and got my address.

After that evening, I noticed a profound change in myself. I felt clean; I did not want to do the sinful things that I used to do. God gave me a thirst to learn his Word. I read the Bible and prayed diligently three times a day. The church followed up with me and sent Bible studies in the mail. I participated in a correspondence course for about a year. I memorized many verses from the Bible at that time. I remember, *"If we say that we have no sin, we deceive ourselves, and the truth is not in us. If we confess our sins, he is faithful and just to forgive us our sins, and to cleanse us from all un-righteousness. If we say that we have not sinned, we make him a liar, and his word is not in us."* (1 JOHN 1:8-10) Some of these verses would literally change my life in later years.

Shortly after being "born again," I became increasingly aware that what the Bible taught and what the Roman Catholic Church taught were two entirely different things. Praying the rosary directly conflicted with what Christ taught, *"But when ye pray, use not vain repetitions, as the heathen do: for they think that they shall be heard for their much speaking."* (MATTHEW 6:7) As a child, I was taught that the Virgin Mary was more likely to hear our prayers because she was Christ's mother, and that she was a co-mediator with Christ, but my Bible unapologetically stated; *"For there is one God, and one mediator between God and men, the man Christ Jesus..."* (1 TIMOTHY 2:5) I believed as a child that the Roman Catholic priests were on a higher level of holiness than ordinary people, and I was taught to address them as "father" or "holy father." Again, this directly conflicted with Christ's teaching, *"And call no man your father upon the earth: for one is your Father, which is in heaven."* (MATTHEW 23:9) The whole notion of man's free will "meriting grace" was a contradiction in terms because the Bible says, *"And if by grace, then is it no more of works: otherwise grace is no more grace. But if it be of works, then is it no more grace: otherwise work is no more work."* (ROMANS 11:6) Meriting is a work and therefore nullifies grace! Besides,

God is indebted to no man. The Roman Catholic Church's use of statues and crucifixes with the dead body of Christ hanging on them appeared to me to be breaking the second commandment in Exodus 20:4-5. I then realized that a crucifix depicting the dead body of Christ on the cross was a false representation. He had risen from the dead! Besides, any attempt by man to depict God is a false image, because, being creatures we can never capture His transcendence. The Catholic Church's teachings about not eating meat on Fridays and not eating before communion, plus the fact that priests where not allowed to marry, directly contradicted the Bible. *"Now the Spirit speaketh expressly, that in the latter times some shall depart from the faith, giving heed to seducing spirits, and doctrines of devils; Speaking lies in hypocrisy; having their conscience seared with a hot iron; Forbidding to marry, and commanding to abstain from meats, which God hath created to be received with thanksgiving of them which believe and know the truth."* (1 TIMOTHY 4:1-3)

Then I could not find in the Bible anything about the Pope being Christ's successor, or "vicar." It appeared to me that people had a tendency to worship the Pope, by bowing to him and kissing his ring. Again, this completely contradicted the principles laid down in the Bible when Cornelius fell down at the apostle Peter's feet and worshipped him. *"But Peter took him up, saying, Stand up; I myself also am a man."* (ACTS 10:26) Also, *"That no flesh should glory in His presence."* (1 CORINTHIANSI:29) There are repeated warnings in the Bible of false prophets, false teachers, false christs, and the great apostasy, or falling away from the truth. (MATTHEW 7:15-20; 2 THESSALONIANS 2) Christ Himself says; *"Then if any man shall say unto you, Lo, here is the Christ, or there; believe it not. For there shall arise false Christs, and false prophets, and shall shew great signs and wonders; insomuch that, if it where possible, they shall deceive the very elect."* (MATTHEW 24:23, 24) Realizing all these things only left me with one possible frightful conclusion. Little did I realize, my studies where just beginning. Christ's teaching, that it was impossible for the elect to be deceived, simply mystified me.

As I said earlier, by the time I was twenty years old I had developed into a full-blown drug addict. This "saved experience" occurred when I was seventeen years old. I still lived at home and with much conflict. A year or so after this experience, I began giving into the temptations of my past. I was overcome by my own lust. I became an enigma of being saved and walking in the Lord, then falling from grace and into grievous sin. I doubted many times that I was saved. In my own body, it seemed as though there were two natures. On one hand, I had accepted Jesus Christ. I confessed Him with my mouth; I could not deny that He was Lord or that His Word was the absolute truth. However, on the other hand I was damned to hell, because when I fell into sin I knew what the Bible said: *"Know ye not that the unrighteous shall not inherit the kingdom of God? Be not deceived: neither fornicators, nor idolaters, nor adulterers, nor effeminate, nor abusers of themselves with mankind, nor thieves, nor covetous, nor drunkard, nor revilers, nor extortioners, shall inherit the kingdom of God."* (1 CORINTHIANS 6:9, 10)

It seemed I was saved or damned to hell depending upon what I did or did not do. I did not realize it at the time, but it was the same works-based righteousness of the Roman Church all over again. When I counseled with other Christians, they told me that we are saved based upon what Christ did, but it is up to us to believe and accept that. I accepted Jesus; therefore, I must be saved. These conflicts warred in my mind in various forms, yet they remained outside my awareness at the time. Nobody had the answers that would help me resolve the conflicts I felt I was between God's law and God's grace. Christians around me contradicted themselves as they told me we are saved by grace, but you have to do this, that, and the other thing. Drugs offered temporary relief from my torments. Yet the drugs created a bigger problem than the solution they offered. By the time I was twenty-seven years old my choices were to either die or go to prison. The church did not seem to be able to help me. My "help" came in the form of "self-help" programs. It seemed to me, at the time, that man had deeper problems, and that the Bible simply did not deal with them. I thought that I needed psychotherapy and "self-help," along with Christianity to help me. I quit using drugs out of sheer necessity and most of my serious problems left. I slowly and painfully became a responsible citizen and within two years I got married, for it is better to marry than to burn with passion. I married a wonderful Christian woman. It was a great struggle for me to provide for my family. Although we had severe marital difficulties right from the beginning, we never saw divorce as an option. We knew in our heart of hearts that the Lord promised to lead us in all truth, and that these trials were for our sanctification. We planned to stick it out, even if it meant hardship.

Home schooling appealed to us greatly, for a few reasons. We believed that it was wrong to separate a young child from his mother. It seemed to us that public schools were, put simply, institutions of humanistic indoctrination. To give our children to the state in order that they may teach them their values, morals, and beliefs, was clearly wrong to us. Our only other option, private school, was not affordable at the time. Besides, we firmly believed that children are a gift from God and their training was the parents' responsibility.

Since my wife grew up in an Evangelical background, church going was very important to her. In my case, going to church had a tendency to bring out my deepest conflicts: the requirements of God's law and holy living against the grace in Christ—in spite of my sinfulness. Church had a tendency to "rub me the wrong way." I resented going. At the time, I thought that church was optional. On many Sundays I would have rather gone surfing, yet my wife knew in her heart that the husband was the spiritual leader of the family and it was our biblical responsibility to raise our children in the fear and admonition of the Lord. This caused conflicts in our marriage and fights would ensue. Resentments built up in my wife. Looking back, my wife realized that she was trying to fit me into the "church scene" thinking this would fix me, when all along it was a form of self-righteousness. She knew that the law was good, but her deep resentments against me were reminding her that not even she kept the law of God. During her turmoil, God began to press on her heart to pray for me, bringing me in love before the Father, earnestly, and expectantly, resting on the promises of God. God gave her the strength and courage to do this.

At first, our young family visited a large evangelical church where most of our extended family and peers went. This church from outer appearances had it all: programs for every age group, huge orchestra, drama team, various support groups, single groups, divorcee groups, and etcetera. Despite my lack of enthusiasm, I went. I thought I was very different from the people who attended the church. Everyone had a happy face; I would put a smiley face on, regardless of the way I felt. I knew for certain that these people did not have the raging conflicts and sins that I had. Being so different from the seemingly perfect people around me, I felt there was something seriously wrong with me. The people who attended there seemed to be in a completely different category than I was in. Yet, at the same time I remembered; *"If we say that we have no sin, we deceive ourselves, and the truth is not in us."* (1 JOHN 1:8) In addition, *"...they that be whole need not a physician but they that are sick. But go ye and learn what that meaneth, I will have mercy, and not sacrifice: for I am not come to call the righteous, but sinners to repentance."* (MATTHEW 9:12, 13) Well, I knew for certain that I was not righteous; I definitely qualified there. Looking back, I now realize that two things helped cause these conflicts. First, the humanism that I tried to mix with Christianity told me that I was different, my problems were because I was a "victim" of my environment and that I had a "disease", and not because of sin. Secondly, I believed the leaders of that church did not know, or could not/did not explain the true biblical doctrine of grace! Today I know that true Christianity does not mix with anything else! I have also come to realize that like myself, all Christians struggle at times, but even more, Christ is able to empathize with believers, *"For we have not an high priest which cannot be touched with the feelings of our infirmities; but was in all points tempted like as we are, yet without sin."* (HEBREWS 4:15)

Soon we felt that the church was "too large" and "impersonal" for our liking. We also desired teaching that was more substantial. We found that many people moved on to another nearby church. It was much smaller, averaging several hundred people on Sunday as opposed to several thousand people. A Bible club was offered to teach young children key Scripture verses and play together with other Christian children. We took our children to this program for several years. I tried to fit into this church, but I felt superficial. My problems at the previous church just followed me. I sensed something was terribly amiss; yet I could never quire put my finger on it. The teaching was always lightweight, usually consisting of a Bible verse followed by a short sermon of application. Though we could not see it at the time, the teachings were based upon some of the same false assumptions that the Roman Catholic Church had and not founded upon Biblical principles.

My conflicts were not resolved! The focus of Sunday worship services seemed to be the music. I remember many times the frustration that we (and other members) felt after the band and/or congregation sang out our fifth praise song! "Preach the Bible," I screamed inside my head. We were starving for the meat of God's Word and did not even know it! The following week seldom picked up the Bible verse we left off at; it was another section, another theme, another analogy, and another modern application with seemingly no sense of continuity or focus.

Meanwhile Back at Home

My wife diligently taught our young boys the Bible. After the third time reading the entire Bible to our boys, she again came to Revelation. My wife realized that she could not teach Revelation to our children because she herself did not fully understand it. There were so many divergent opinions concerning its interpretation, with many people contradicting each other! She began having doubts concerning whether she was teaching correct doctrine or not. Meanwhile I was so caught up in providing the daily needs of my family that I had become apathetic, and shied away from areas that brought out conflict. The Lord pressed on my wife's heart to diligently seek the truth that she may properly teach biblical doctrine to our children. In home schooling our children with a classical education, we understood the necessity of seeing all subjects through the light of Scripture. History (His-story) is very important, the history of the church of utmost importance.

Studying church history, she began with the early church fathers defending orthodoxy against heresy. One day when I came home from work, she asked me if I knew what had happened at the Council of Ephesus in 431. I did not, so she proceeded to tell me about how Pelagius, a British monk, denied that the human race had fallen in Adam. Pelagius denied original sin, the total depravity of man, and predestination. Against this, Augustine taught that every man is conceived in sin and can be saved only through the grace of God according to His good pleasure.[1] The questions began piling up and engaging my own curiosity. "Total depravity" sounded like a good description of me, and I thought that maybe I had read the word "predestination" in Romans or Ephesians. My wife then told me that Pelagius' teachings were condemned as heresy at Ephesus. She also told me that the Synod of Orange in 529 condemned Semi-Pelagianism, which taught that it is up to the individual to accept or refuse God's offer of grace. I found all of this very compelling. I began to suspect that somewhere in all this there might be answers to my conflicts. When my wife reached the time of the Reformation, questions concerning these things began to pile up. Why was there a split between Roman Catholicism and the Reformers? Does man have a "free will?" Who was Luther? Who was Calvin? The only thing I knew about them was that when I was a child my mother told me

---

1   Kuiper, *The Church in History,* p. 39

they where devils. As a little boy, I thought anyone with the name Luther probably was a devil. The time to discern between true biblical doctrine and error was at hand. The foremost questions in our minds were, "How did God redeem us?" "What exactly is grace?" Moreover, "Why did God save the very worst of sinners like us?" We could understand why God would redeem "good people," but not people like ourselves. On what basis were we saved? My wife and I both accepted and professed Christ. However, was this the very basis by which we are saved, our own accepting and receiving Him? If it is, was that not works? The Bible clearly stated: *"But if it be works, then it is no more grace."* (ROMANS 11 :6)

God's election of certain individuals to salvation is the opening doctrine of the nature of His grace. Without God's election there would be no salvation, because being dead in trespasses and sins, man is just a rotting corpse and is in enmity against God. None of the churches that we previously visited taught about predestination and election. They steered clear of it, yet, all throughout the gospels, Christ makes mention of the elect of God. Predestination and election are a major theme in the New Testament, being mentioned no less than forty-seven times. God's predestination and election are directly related to the prophecies given to the Lord's chosen servants, the prophets. The prophets prophesied the future because God declared it from the beginning! *"Remember the former things of old: for I am GOD, and there is none else: I am GOD, and there is none like me, Declaring the end from the beginning, and from ancient times the things that are not yet done, saying, My counsel shall stand, and I will do all my pleasure: Calling a ravenous bird from the east, the man that executeth my counsel from a far country: yea, I have spoken it, I will also bring it to pass; I have purposed it, I will also do it."* (ISAIAH 46:9-11) God, being God, has created all things for the purpose of bringing glory to Himself. If there were one molecule not in His control, then He would cease being God. Scripture tells us that; *"For by Him were all things created, that are in heaven, and that are in earth, visible and invisible, whether they be thrones, or dominions, or principalities, or powers; all things were created by Him, and for Him: And He is before all things, and by Him all things consist."* (COLOSSIANS 1:16-17) Being omniscient, He knows all things, and even further, has determined all things.

Today, I know predestination and election are God's "secret weapon" that are used to humble the sinful pride of man who thinks that salvation is within man's power. By this, He redeems a chosen people for Himself to worship Him in spirit and in truth. I challenge you, the reader, to read the entire first chapter of Ephesians. While you are doing this, take specific note of the action verbs, and take note of who is doing the action.

The realization that God chose us, that we did not choose him, and further, this was predestined before the foundation of the world caused an explosion in our minds. (EPHESIANS 1:4) As a family, we became voracious readers. Rather than make us proud, it humbled us to the dust. Why God would choose rebellious sinners such as us is beyond our comprehension. Knowing that God is sovereign in all things, including salvation, is a prerequisite for a proper biblical understanding of the doctrine of grace and redemption, not to mention the doctrines of propitiation, justification, and sanctification.

When God revealed these wonderful truths to us from His Word, our family experienced the most wonderful resolution. Questions and doubts that plagued us were answered. So elegant in its simplicity, Gods election resolved the problem caused by works against grace. It is God's election of grace unto salvation, or nothing at all! Because, anything man does to merit grace is a work of the flesh. Grace is completely unmerited; otherwise, it is not grace. We also understood why there are so many problems in so many mainstream "evangelical" churches. Because these same, having departed from orthodox, historical biblical doctrines, are relying upon man's carnal reasoning and methods rather than upon what the Bible teaches. Many exclaim, "We can't teach that, it's too controversial!" or, "People won't like that!"

It is strange that God does not have the same fears. His truths are set forth plainly in Scripture, which they either ignore or twist to their own destruction. (2 PETER 3:14-16) Sure, it hurts man's pride, but is not that pride the very root of sin itself? Many others also have declared, "If we taught that, our churches would be so small." To such, God's Word answers, *"Enter ye in at the strait gate: for wide is the gate, and broad is the way, that leadeth to destruction, and many there be which go in thereat: Because strait is the gate, and narrow is the way, which leadeth unto life, and few there be that find it."* (MATTHEW 7:13, 14) The apostle Paul declares; *"For I am not ashamed of the gospel of Christ: for it is the power of God unto salvation to every one that believeth..."* (ROMANS 1:16) This same apostle emphatically declared; *"But though we, or an angel from heaven, preach any other gospel unto you than that which we have preached unto you, let him be accursed. As we said before, so say I now again, If any man preach any other gospel unto you than that ye have received, let him be accursed."* (GALATIANS 1:8, 9) For those that still think that belief is within their own power, the Lord Jesus states; *"…this is the work of God, that ye believe on Him whom He hath sent"* (JOHN 6:29) and again, *"…Therefore said I unto you, that no man can come unto me, except it were given unto him of my Father."* (JOHN 6:65) Belief is the result of salvation, not the cause of it! Any gospel other than this is "another" gospel!

Today, I no longer take one verse from the Bible, here and there, and attempt to build my own theology. I read whole sections and books of Scripture and let the words plainly speak for themselves, comparing Scripture with Scripture. I reject all humanism and psychology based upon the false notions of people like Freud and Rogers. True biblical counseling is a good thing. Yet, those who have a biblical knowledge of the doctrines of grace, justification, and sanctification seem to be few and far between. Today I know that I cannot manufacture in myself the fruit of the Holy Spirit; love, joy, peace, longsuffering, gentleness, goodness, faith, meekness, temperance, apart from the Holy Spirit of God. Those are God's attributes, not my own, and He gives those qualities to those who humbly submit to Him.

Regarding our will: today I know that my will is within God's will and power and not outside of it. I realize that if His will had not overpowered mine and caused me to believe, repent, and seek Him, I would be among the lost, confused, and damned.

I have shared my personal story with you in the hope that this would encourage and exhort you to humble yourself before God, to read His Word, the Bible. Study to know what it teaches, and pray that God would lead you to find a Bible believing church that teaches the whole Word of God. If you are not familiar with the Bible and want to know more, please allow me to suggest starting with a gospel such as Matthew, or John, then (or in the same day) read the book of Romans. Try to read Romans in one sitting, then, go over it again more slowly.

Finally dear reader; know that *"…God resisteth the proud, and giveth grace to the humble. Humble yourselves therefore under the mighty hand of God, that He may exalt you in due time: Casting all your care upon Him; for He careth for you."* (1 PETER 5:5-8)

—PAUL SMITH

I welcome your comments or questions. You can email me at:
jptechnologiesmachining@gmail.com

Randy M. Bourgeois

The Truth Shall Make You Free

Born on the Bayou

What a blessing to be born and raised in the heart of Cajun country on Bayou Lafourche in south Louisiana USA. On the bayou, there is ample opportunity to grow and learn in one of the richest cultures of our blessed United States of America. Here in Cajun country, you will find some of the tastiest foods along with a culture of fun loving, warm, and caring people of French heritage. People will drive miles to tour the Cajun country of south Louisiana, learn its culture, and enjoy the fine foods.

As one travels across the vast expanse of our great country, each stop along the way presents a learning experience from the history and heritage of that area. In each location, one can learn about the people who first settled each community, along with the legacies of outstanding citizens and traditions they handed down. For the most part, the present residents of each community still carry traditions of language, work, recreational interest, styles of living, and religious beliefs and practices, which were handed down from previous generations. While the "Bible Belt" along with various religions are found throughout the USA, the predominate religion of south Louisiana is Roman Catholicism.

Born on the Bayou in 1955, I was raised in the traditions of the Cajun people of Louisiana. I grew up hunting the swamplands and fishing the wetlands with my family and relatives.

Along with the other traditions of my heritage, I also was raised in the tradition of the Catholic Church. From here my testimonial from childhood to the present will paint the picture of how I was transformed from a devoted Catholic boy to a Christ-centered, Christ-serving Christian.

Born in Roman Catholicism

Traditionally, my parents were Catholic, and naturally christened me Catholic soon following my birth. Being good Catholic parents, they were very adamant in following the traditions of the known religion of our heritage. Roman Catholicism teaches that it is at one's christening that "infused grace" is received from God. The Catholic Catechism states: "Born with a fallen human nature and tainted by original sin, children also have need of the new birth in Baptism to be freed from the power of darkness and brought into the realm of the freedom of the children of God, to which all men are called. The sheer gratuitousness of the grace of salvation is particularly manifest in infant Baptism. The Church and the parents would deny a child the priceless grace of becoming a child of God were they not to confer Baptism shortly after birth." (CATHOLIC CATECHISM, PARAGRAPH 1250)

If you were to ever question teachers of the Catholic Catechism about the term "born again," spoken by Jesus in John 3:3, you would probably be told that this happened at your christening. At infant christening, Catholics believe that "original sin" is washed away and you are born anew to enter God's heaven. This gives some understanding as to why throughout their entire lives Catholics believe they are secure for heaven.

However, while studying the Bible, I have never found any instructions on christening infants, or that they need to have "original sin" washed away. The apostle Paul wrote that we are born with the sin nature of Adam, but not Adam's sin. *"Wherefore, as by one man sin entered into the world, and death by sin; and so death passed upon all men, for that all have sinned."* (ROMANS 5:12)

Interestingly, we find christening to have its beginning with the Roman Emperor Constantine (A.D. 272–337); who decreed, in A.D. 313, full tolerance to all religions in the empire, especially with regard to Christians. Constantine, desiring to keep national peace, declared that Rome have one state religion. Therefore, he decreed that all Rome be Christian; thus had all citizens christened. Subsequently, each new citizen born into Roman citizenship was christened Christian upon birth. The practice of christening was performed by sprinkling water. By Constantine's decree, everyone touched by the water was therefore christened Christian. The Roman Catholic Church adopted this practice calling it a baptism. The Catholic Catechism states: "The practice of infant Baptism is an immemorial tradition of the Church. There is explicit testimony to this practice from the second century on..." (CATHOLIC CATECHISM, PARAGRAPH 1252)

Amazingly, different religions have taken on various practices or modes of baptism, each proclaiming that theirs is correct. The three most common modes are sprinkling, pouring, and immersing. However, the English word baptism is translated from the Greek word baptisma (βαπτισμα), which can only be defined as immersing.

I began my education in public schools and made my First Communion at the age of seven. After attending public school for three years, my parents felt that I would perform better academically and socially if I were

transferred to the Catholic school. The following year I resumed my elementary education in the local Catholic school. While in Catholic school, I experienced a whole new regiment of disciplinarians. Most of my teachers were Catholic nuns from Spain. They were very adamant about each student learning Spanish as a second language. I mention this to say that the obvious goal was not to teach us about God, but the language of Spain.

Almost daily, upon arriving at school, we were led in a march to the church to participate in a Mass of the day. At each daily Mass, each student was expected to take the Eucharist. If any student did not, he or she was questioned in private as to what disobedience caused them to abstain from the sacred Host. We were taught that upon receiving the Eucharist, Jesus would help us to behave well in school that day, and that He would help us with our schoolwork. Of course, this was when we were taught that we took the literal Jesus into our being to live in us. I remember never being able to comprehend why we needed to return each day for the Eucharist. I used to wonder if Jesus left at some time, or did He fade away? This was long before I ever heard the word "Transubstantiation" (the belief that the bread and the wine are literally transformed into the body and blood of Jesus, yet with no noticeable change in form.) Nevertheless, just as transubstantiation describes, we were taught that the bread and wine literally became the body and blood of Jesus. As a boy, I never could understand how this could take place, except that God was all-powerful.

Now, having an understanding of the Word of God, I know there is not any teaching in Scripture about transubstantiation. At the last supper, Jesus did not teach transubstantiation, but that we should observe the Lord's Supper in remembrance of Him. The apostle Paul stated, *"And when He had given thanks, He brake it, and said, Take, eat: this is my body, which is broken for you: this do in remembrance of me."* (1 CORINTHIANS 11:24)

During my first year in Catholic school, I had an interest in becoming an altar boy. Soon after applying, I was called in to speak with the priest. Following many questions about my devotion to the task, I assume I answered correctly, because I was added to the roster of altar boys. As an altar boy, I learned the routines and rituals of service, yet I never really understood what I was performing or why I was performing such tasks—but only that I was doing a noble, religious thing that made the adults very proud of me.

By tradition, I made my Confirmation when entering into sixth grade. I believe most young people in that group had no idea what Confirmation was all about. We simply did what was expected of us—no questions asked.

Understanding Confirmation now, it is truly staggering to know what this practice teaches about God's grace. Roman Catholic Confirmation is the believed practice that there is an extra boost of infused grace following Catholic baptism, which is given to those Catholics who are moving from childhood to adolescence. This extra amount of grace is believed to give the young person the grace to deal with adult temptations while going through drastic change in growth. It is believed to also give the young Catholic the Holy Spirit who enables one the ability to devote one's life more closely to the church and her teachings. The Catholic Catechism states, "Confirmation perfects Baptismal grace; it is the sacrament which gives the Holy Spirit in order to root us more deeply in the divine filiations, incorporate us more firmly into Christ, strengthen our bond with the Church, associate us more closely with her mission, and help us bear witness to the Christian faith in words accompanied by deeds." (CATHOLIC CATECHISM, PARAGRAPH 1316) However, the Bible teaches that God issues grace at His will to those in need at anytime regardless of age. Again, there is no teaching in the Bible about adolescent children needing a boost of infused grace.

The Desire for the Priesthood

While in the fifth grade, a couple of other boys, including myself, began to meet together during recess time and talk about our interest in growing up and becoming priests. Although I had a deep and sincere desire to become a priest, I never made my parents aware of those desires, nor did I discuss them with anyone outside my group of friends on the school playground. I believe these feelings were genuine feelings of just wanting to get close to God and serve Him. As time went by, my desire to be a priest slowly diminished from my everyday thinking, while my attention turned toward recreation.

Priesthood itself is another practice of Catholicism that should be questioned. With the exception of a few Old Testament Priests being around during the time of the New Testament church—following the death, burial, and resurrection of Jesus—there are no teachings by Paul, or any of the other apostles, concerning the continuation of the priestly order found in the Old Testament. To the contrary, the New Testament speaks of every "born again believer" being a priest.

The word "priest" means "bridge builder." In New Testament theology, a priest is one having access to God. The apostle Peter wrote of all believers, *"Ye also, as lively stones, are built up a spiritual house, an holy priesthood, to offer up spiritual sacrifices, acceptable to God by Jesus Christ."* (I PETER 2:5) Peter also wrote, *"...ye are a chosen generation, a royal priesthood, an holy nation, a peculiar people; that ye should shew forth the praises of Him who hath called you out of darkness into His marvelous light."* (I PETER 2:9) The priesthood taught in Scriptures is often referred to as the "priesthood of believers." Moreover, the leaders in local church congregations are scripturally called pastors, elders, or bishops. Nowhere in New Testament Scripture do you find church leaders called priests.

The Rituals of Home Life

Though I cannot say that my parents were the strictest of Catholics, I can say that they followed closely to the traditions of the Catholic Church when it came to the practice of certain rituals. Catholics are taught to traditionally perform certain rituals with the hope of certain results.

Prior to my birth, my mother gave birth to her second son who was named Tommy. Sadly, Tommy died only a few days after arriving home. His death occurred from "an enlarged heart." Eight years following the death of Tommy, my parents built a new house, which had much more needed space than our previous house. We were now five children under the watchful care of our parents.

Still having Tommy ever upon their hearts and minds, my parents had a special altar built into the new house's wall at the end of the hall. It was simply an indentation in the wall where statues of Jesus and Mary were placed in fixed positions, and a candle burned perpetually for Tommy's soul.

In Catholicism, it is believed that candles can be burned for the release of a loved one's soul from the place of purgatory, or, in Tommy's case, because he was an infant at death, candles were burned so that his soul would be released from the holding place called "limbo." Undisputedly, the words and terms "purgatory" and "limbo" do not exist anywhere in the Bible. In fact, the Bible states; *"And as it is appointed unto men once to die, but after this the judgment."* (Hebrews 9:27) It is astounding that religions teach their people certain rituals and practices that are not found in the Bible. Jesus said to the religious, *"For laying aside the commandment of God, ye hold the tradition of men..."* (Mark 7:8) The apostle Paul warned, *"Beware lest any man spoil you through philosophy and vain deceit, after the tradition of men, after the rudiments of the world, and not after Christ."* (Colossians 2:8)

In the new house were also places that contained holy water. You would dip the tip of your fingers in the water and make the sign of the cross. As a child, I never knew the significance of this. But, somehow, it made you feel good, or holy.

Growing up in a traditional Catholic home, my parents also brought us to the church for "confession time." I remember wondering why I should tell all my bad behaviors to the priest. My mom told me that once I confessed my sins to the priest, they would all be forgiven and I would have a new beginning. In other words, the slate would be wiped clean. However, the Bible teaches that only in Christ does one have a new beginning. *"Therefore, if any man be in Christ, he is a new creature: old things are passed away; behold, all things are become new."* (2 Corinthians 5:17)

Catholicism teaches the Catholic priest absolves your sins. This means that the priest has the power from God to forgive sins. Of course, this is an error in the interpretation of, *"Whose soever sins ye remit, they are remitted unto them; and whose soever sins ye retain, they are retained."* (John 20:23) God said through the prophet Isaiah, *"I, even I, am He that blotteth out thy transgressions..."* (Isaiah 43:25) The Bible speaks nowhere about God giving man the power to absolve sins.

During the years I served as an altar boy, I feared confessing my sins to the same priest I would serve on the altar. I hoped that he would not recognize my voice behind the stained glass as I pronounced my sins before him. I feared that he would not allow me to serve as an altar boy any longer. Nevertheless, he either never recognized my voice, or if he did, he never brought any attention to my confessed behaviors that may have been out of line with being an altar boy.

Growing Up

At the ages of eleven and twelve, I spent all my school holiday time and most of my summer vacations on my uncle and aunt's farm. On that farm I really began to have an awareness of God's presence. As a child reaching adolescence, I cherished times alone while feeding the animals or picking crops from the field. This was a good time in my life. I enjoyed raising animals and being in the outdoors. That farm was a sanctuary where I could think, dream, and imagine all sorts of things. I remember getting alone out in the corncrib or back in the woods to just talk with God.

Near my home, about a half-mile walk through the sugarcane field, was a bayou with a large hackberry tree leaning toward the water. At times when I was troubled, I would walk to that hackberry tree and just cry out to God. I can truly testify of the many times God answered those prayers. When I became a true, born-again Christian many years ago at the age of thirty-one, and having become knowledgeable of the Scriptures, I began to wonder why God would answer the prayers of a lost adolescent boy. It occurred to me that during the times on my uncle and aunt's farm, the warmth I felt in knowing God's presence, and the answered prayers I prayed while under that old hackberry tree, was God's way of revealing to me the reality of His existence. It would be later in my life that I would hear the truth of God's Word and respond by faith alone to God's saving grace through the blood of Jesus.

At the age of thirteen, I began to follow the peers of my youth. My parents were not taking us to church much anymore, and my life in Catholic school had ended, since the sixth grade was the school's highest grade level. It was at that time in my life that my attention turned to teen dances, hot-rod cars, and dating. Throughout my teens, I drifted deep into the world with hardly a thought about God. Oh, I would think about God from time to time—like on Easter or Christmas. However, I mostly had a one-track mind with self-desire in the center.

My teen years were godless years of self-indulgence and rebellion. During my junior year in high school however, I met the girl of my dreams. She was kind, sweet, and very pretty. After a couple of years of dating, and after both graduating, we entered into matrimony. In 1974, we were married in the Catholic Church where I grew up. However, neither of us knew the Lord, nor did we want God in our lives.

Lost, and Did Not Know It

Being raised in the Catholic Church, I was never told that I was lost and that I needed salvation. These things are never spoken of among Catholics. As a Catholic, I believed that I was automatically going to heaven because I was Catholic. Catholics are given the understanding while growing up that they are of the "One True Church," that all other denominations and churches are teaching false teachings, and that everyone that is not Catholic is going to hell.

In this present time, now in my seventeenth year serving as a full-time pastor, I reflect back to things I was taught while in the Catholic school. As children, we were taught that we should never set foot in any church that was not Catholic. One day, the teacher illustrated by pointing out a certain church in the community that was not Catholic. She said, "Never go into other churches that are not Catholic Churches. The Pope forbids this. For instance, that red brick Baptist church on the Houma road is the kind of church you are forbidden to go into, or you will go to hell." Well, as it turned out—that red brick Baptist Church on the Houma road is the church that I pastor today.

I am reminded that many religious teachings outside the authority of the Bible may profess things to be of God, and at the same time, be blindly neglecting God's truths. Scripture teaches of the time Nicodemus came to Jesus by night and said, *"...Rabbi, we know that Thou art a teacher come from God: for no man can do these miracles that Thou doest, except God be with him. Jesus answered and said unto him; Verily, verily, I say unto thee, 'Except a man be born again, he cannot see the kingdom of God.'"* (JOHN 3:2-3) Here was a very religious man, even noted by Jesus as, *"...a master [teacher] of Israel..."* (JOHN 3:10) Then Jesus asked, *"...and knowest not these things?"* (JOHN 3:10) Nicodemus was the teacher of Israel, yet could not understand that he must be "born again." Has anything really changed in the day in which we live? We still find highly educated religious teachers not realizing that one is lost until he or she is saved by faith alone in the Lord Jesus Christ; or that the Bible must be the true source of authority, by which we should measure all teachings about God.

Even though I certainly was not a religious leader of my day, I was nevertheless "lost." Early in my marriage, my wife, being Southern Baptist, had a King James Bible she displayed on the coffee table of our home. At times, I would be rained out at work; I would come home and attempt to read her Bible, which I referred to as a "Baptist Bible." As Catholics, we were told that we "should not read the Bible or it would make us crazy." While in Catholic school, I was taught by the nuns and priests that the priests were the only people that God gave the ability to truly understand the Bible. Upon attempting to read my wife's King James Bible at the age of twenty, the belief that was taught to me many years before was being reinforced by my lack of understanding what the Bible meant. I spent most of my time in the book of Matthew because I knew that the red letters were the words of Jesus, and I wanted to know what Jesus was saying. However, I would get very frustrated after reading and reading and still not understanding.

He Sought Me

Throughout my teen years, and into my adult years, I cannot recall anyone witnessing to me from God's Word, or giving a testimony of salvation. Oh, I remember one time I was in the hospital, and someone I went to Catholic school with, came into my hospital room telling me I needed the Holy Ghost. However, his preaching had no credibility since he was a member of a church in the next community that was practicing some very strange things—like keeping a dead infant baby in an ice chest of ice believing it would rise from the dead in forty days. Well, law officials found them out and that church died.

For the next ten years, life went on with hardly any thought of God. There was a time however, at the age of twenty-three, that I felt once again I needed God in my life. My wife and I were having marriage difficulties and I was very unsettled about what I wanted in life. As a result, I went to the shopping mall one day and bought a rather large gold crucifix on a chain. Being raised in the Catholic teachings that statues will provide power and guidance for life, the crucifix was my choice. Moreover, I determined not to be a hypocrite and hung it on the outside of my shirt. As the people I worked with saw the crucifix, they would exclaim, "You getting religious on us, Randy?" My answer was usually, "I am just trying to live better, that's all."

The religious revival did not last more than a month, and I resumed my same unchanged lifestyle. Looking back, I now realize it was God who was drawing me to Himself. Jesus said, *"No man can come to me, except the Father which hath sent me draw him..."* (JOHN 6:44) My problem at this time of drawing was that I did not have the truth in which to respond. Perhaps God would have led me to truth if I had given Him a chance.

Throughout my twenties, I had some outstanding jobs in the oilfield, which gave me good opportunities to increase my knowledge in several fields of work. The companies I worked for gave me all sorts of personal benefits and the liberty to do my work as I saw fit.

Being a mechanic by trade, I resigned from the oilfield companies and opened my own business. My business consisted of auto repair, diesel engine repair, generator and pump repair, and working back in the oilfield pipe yards on pipe testing units. This also was one of my specialties since I had designed and built pipe-testing units while working for other companies. At the time, I believed I was doing well, having others working for me and the prospect of getting wealthy just over the horizon. However, in the mid 1980s, the oilfield in south Louisiana went bankrupt. One at a time, I had to layoff employees. The oil companies I had such a good working relationship with were going bankrupt, and owed me a lot of money.

It was at that time I felt my world was crumbling around me. My wife and I had a nine-year-old daughter and a four-year-old son. Like many, I began to wonder what I did wrong. One night, I began to have conviction for never taking my children to church. For a while, I thought this was the problem, since I remembered that as a child my parents took me to church each Sunday. One day, I shared my feelings with my wife. I told her I was thinking that one of the problems was that we were not taking our children to church. She said she agreed that we should be taking our children to church. The problem however, was which church would we attend? She being raised Baptist, and I being raised Catholic, placed us in a dilemma.

The next morning, I arrived at my place of business very early—before anyone came in. In the quietness, I cried out to God. I remember saying, "God, I believe you exist; I just don't know who you are. God, I am sick of religions and all their rules. Is not there anywhere that is teaching the truth about who you are? Just show me, and I promise I will take my children to church—whatever church!"

For the next few days, I was really thinking about what I said to God. I just was not sure about what church we should attend. One evening, my wife asked me what church would we attend. I said that perhaps, since I was Catholic, and she was Baptist, that we would attend one of them one week and the other the next week, and then we would decide where we would continue to attend.

The next day, I drove to the Baptist church to find out what were the times of their church services. They had a little sign out front with the times posted. The following Sunday, we attended the Baptist church. That Sunday, quite interestingly, I began to hear things about God and Jesus that I had never heard before.

Instead of attending the Catholic Church the following week, I decided that I wanted to hear more of what was being spoken at the Baptist church. I asked my wife what was it that the preacher was reading from. She told me it was the Bible. I had never heard someone read the Bible and articulate its truth like that before.

The third Sunday, we returned to the same church. Following the service, the pastor stood before the people and asked if anyone wanted to receive Jesus. My wife immediately walked forward. However, I was a little apprehensive. I had never been confronted with a need to make such a personal choice before. I felt, I too wanted a relationship with God. However, still having my Catholic upbringing wrestling in my mind, I felt I needed to somehow straighten up my own life and then God would accept me. As a Catholic, I was taught my works would merit me a place with God. I thought, "I haven't kept God's Ten Commandments," and I felt dirty. All my thoughts were—"Once I clean my own life—get rid of some bad habits, etc., then Jesus will come into my life." My thoughts were, "Why would Jesus come into someone that is polluted?"

Looking back, I can see now what was happening. The Holy Spirit of God was drawing me once again. It is worth stating again that Jesus said, *"No man can come to me, except the Father which hath sent me draw him…"* (JOHN 6:44) The apostle Paul wrote, *"…and that no man can say that Jesus is the Lord, but by the Holy Spirit."* (1 CORINTHIANS 12:3) Nevertheless, I still was under the impression that I first needed to clean up my own life before asking Jesus in. The next Sunday, returning to the same church, I was very discouraged—wrestling with the fact that I was dirty in sin and that God would not want a relationship with me that way. As the pastor began to preach God's Word, God knew just what I needed to hear. The pastor said, "If you believe that you must somehow keep all God's commandments, or first fulfill sacraments before Jesus will come into your life, He will never come in, because you can never make yourself righteous. You must come just as you are. God will take you—dirty baggage and all. Let it all be washed under the blood of Jesus. Trust Him alone for your salvation."

Again, looking back, I can see how we as Catholics were no different from the Jews of the apostle Paul's day. We were taught we must keep the Commandments or be rejected by God. We also were taught that we must fulfill our own righteousness. The apostle Paul wrote to the Romans, *"For I bear them record that they have a zeal of God, but not according to knowledge. For they being ignorant of God's righteousness, and going about to establish their own righteousness, have not submitted themselves unto the righteousness of God. For Christ is the end of the law for righteousness to everyone that believeth."* (ROMANS 10:2-4) As Catholics, we were taught we must fulfill the sacraments of the church or be rejected by God. However, the Bible says, *"For by grace are ye saved through faith; and that not of yourselves: it is the gift of God: Not of works, lest any man should boast."* (EPHESIANS 2:8, 9) The apostle wrote to Titus, *"Not by works of righteousness which we have done, but according to His mercy he saved us..."* (TITUS 3:5) As Catholics, we are taught that salvation is by works. The apostle Paul wrote to the Romans, *"And if by grace, then is it no more of works: otherwise grace is no more grace."* (ROMANS 11:6)

That very day, I returned home with my family, went into my bedroom, shut the door, and cried out to God to save me. I took my ring of keys out of my pocket and lifted them up and said, "God my life is like my holding all the keys of control myself. I no longer take control of my life. Lord Jesus, I place the keys of my life in your hands. They are the keys to my adventures and life pursuits—but they are also the keys to my dirty baggage—my sin. Please come into my life and save me. I submit my total life to you. You are God—I have no desire to play games with you anymore. I give you my life and will never try to take it back. Amen."

My New Life in Christ

During the first month following my complete trust on Christ, I began to notice some dramatic changes in several areas of my life. Old habits began to fall away. Many words in my usual vocabulary were no longer used. I even felt deep hurt inside every time I heard some of these same foul words being used by someone else. Jesus Himself was certainly shaping my life.

Church became a natural part of my life. There was never any question to whether or not I would be in church on Sunday. The fellowship and growing relationships with other Christians was something to which I always looked forward. Now, instead of going to church on Sunday in fear of committing a "mortal sin" for neglecting to attend, I go because Jesus lives in me, and I am a living, vital part of the "Body of Christ," the church. My life in the church is not a mere obligation, but of desire, because Jesus is my Lord, worthy of worship. The writer of Hebrews put it plainly when he wrote, *"And let us consider one another to provoke unto love and to good works: Not forsaking the assembling of ourselves together, as the manner of some is; but exhorting one another, and so much the more, as ye see the day approaching."* (HEBREWS 10:24, 25)

It was not long before my involvement in church was more than attending. About six months following my salvation, I began to lead a young boys' group called "Royal Ambassadors." What joy even today to see some of these young boys, now young men, serving the Lord!

Within the first year of God's salvation coming to me, I felt an undeniable call in my life I could not quite identify at the time. Through much prayer and counseling with my pastor, I had no further doubt that the call from God was to preach His Word. What a privilege to receive such a high calling from God.

In my second year of salvation, I was called to training in seminary. Following my first year in seminary, I was called to pastor my first church while continuing my seminary education.

As a pastor, however, my heart is continually burdened for my friends and family still trying to follow the endless struggles of earning righteousness through the Catholic Church. In a similar way, I am reminded of the apostle Paul's heartfelt burden for the Jewish people when he wrote, *"I say the truth in Christ, I lie not, my conscience also bearing witness in the Holy Spirit, that I have great heaviness and continual sorrow in my heart. For I could wish that myself were accursed from Christ for my brethren, my kinsmen according to the flesh."* (ROMANS 9:1-3) In the next chapter Paul wrote, *"Brethren, my heart's desire and prayer to God for Israel is that they might be saved. For I bear them record that they have a zeal of God, but not according to knowledge. For they being ignorant of God's righteousness, and going about to establish their own righteousness, have not submitted themselves unto the righteousness of God. For Christ is the end of the law for righteousness to everyone that believeth."* (ROMANS 10:1-4)

Through the years, this burden has led me to study Roman Catholicism as never before. Through countless seminars, workshops, reading books, studying the Catholic "Code of Canon Law," and the depth of Roman Catholicism's Catechism, I am now certified as an instructor to teach seminars called "Understanding the Doctrines of Roman Catholicism." The goal of this endeavor is to help Christian's know how to witness God's truth to the dearly loved Catholic people.

Therefore, as a born Roman Catholic, yet saved many years ago by faith in Jesus Christ alone, and serving as a full time pastor now in my seventeenth year, I give thanks to the God of my salvation. He alone was merciful and gracious to the sinner I was many years ago. He alone went to the Cross as the propitiation for the sin penalty I could never pay. In His love, He drew me to Himself, saved me, and called me into the joy of serving Him. Thus, I will continue to live the remainder of my life in the joy of His salvation, preaching His unadulterated Word, and leading others who have not yet come to know Him; in the Truth that can make them free.

—RANDY BOURGEOIS

You can contact me at: cajun_pastor@yahoo.com

Henry Nowakowski

A Catholic Priest Born From Above

Hello, my name is Henry Nowakowski. Let me tell you my life story.* I was born two years before the outbreak of WW II. Mind you, like everyone else, I had no say whatsoever as to when I would be born, where I would be born, to whom I would be born. No, the Creator God decided those particulars for me. It was He who decided I would be born in mid August of 1937 to John and Nellie Nowakowski in Vermilion, Alberta, Canada and not in Australia, Africa, or Algeria. In fact, if my grandparents on either side of my family had not immigrated to Canada from Poland in the late 1800's, 1897 to be precise, I might have been born in Poland. However, it was the Creator God who chose John and Nellie Nowakowski, first generation Canadians of the Nowakowski clan, who were farmers by trade, to be my parents.

And so it was, my life commenced in rural Alberta with two older brothers, John and Peter, both now deceased; and then later, two younger sisters, Gloria and Agnes, both still living. That was my first birth; it would be many years later before I would experience my second birth, my birth from above—my spiritual birth. In fact, it was not until my 45th year before that would occur. Much would transpire before that decisive, glorious, and life-changing event. Let me fill in some of the major details.

I was born into a devout Roman Catholic family. My family was diligent in the practice of their Roman Catholic faith. My parents were very hard working but lacking in much formal education. My father, John Sr., received a fourth grade education whereas my mother advanced double that, completing the 8th grade. However, both my parents, to their credit, placed much emphasis on the education of their children.

As I recall, growing up, as far as the practice of our religion was concerned, the Bible was more or less nonexistent. We did have a family Bible

* I celebrated my 75th birthday on August 18, 2012

in our home, but it was rarely read. However, baptisms were duly recorded therein. No, our devotions by and large were centered around the recitation of rote prayers, morning offerings, prayers before and after meals, the act of contrition, and of course the recitation of the family rosary in the evening. We lived by the slogan, "The Family that prays together, stays together."

Mass on Sundays and holy days of obligation were our weekly custom unless heavy winter snows or blizzards prevented us from attending. Again, the religious exercise was routine, monotonous, and foreign, as Latin was still in vogue. However, the gospel was read in English and the homily was delivered in the common vernacular.

The key to my religious upbringing and formation was to never ever question authority, especially church authority; hence, our parish priest was God's man. He represented the Bishop, who in turn represented the Pope, the "Holy Father," the "Vicar of Christ"; and therefore, he was infallible and incapable of erring in faith or morals. When our priest spoke, it was like God Himself speaking. Later I was to learn in the study of God's infallible revelation—His Holy Word, that the true biblical Vicar of Christ was no mere man but God Himself, in the Person of the Holy Spirit—the Third Person of the Blessed Trinity.

So it was such a religious legacy I inherited from my ancestors who were the recipients of the same, never the chain to be broken by any Nowakowski. In this legacy, I was indoctrinated. Nothing wrong with indoctrination if it is in the truth, but it is deadly if in falsehood.

Seminary Days

While growing up, I was what you would consider a "good" boy, almost always obedient, loving and kind, somewhat withdrawn, only average intelligence, never an intellectual. I did study hard; yet, received average grades. My two older brothers and I attended a Catholic boarding school from the ninth through the twelfth grade. It was when I was beginning the tenth grade that my oldest brother, John Jr., entered the diocesan seminary, St. Joseph's in Edmonton. After being groomed by a parish priest, and the Sisters of St. Joseph teaching in our high school, another classmate, Phil Mueller, and I entered that same diocesan seminary. That was one year after completing high school. During that intervening year, I worked on the family farm helping my father.

My seminary experience was one of self-denial, routine, rote prayer, and practices, as I was being trained to become a functional cleric. In other words, I was being fashioned to be a dispenser of God's grace through the rites of the institutional Roman Church; mainly the sacraments, with the sacrifice of the Mass and the Eucharist being the loftiest. I was to baptize, to witness marriage, and to officiate at funerals for those under my charge.

During the first two of six years at the seminary, the emphasis was on the study of philosophy, mainly the study of Aristotle and "the boys." You might ask, "Why in a Catholic seminary would you be studying the philosophy of pagan Greek philosophers?" That would be a good question. You must remember that "the theologian" of the Roman Church was and still is Thomas Aquinas one of the most brilliant men who ever lived. However, being brilliant does not make you wise, biblically speaking. Living in the 1200's, and confronted with Islam, he undertook to produce a philosophy/theology that was rational rather than the emotional one employed by the institutional Church of the day. Therefore, he drew upon the rationalism of Aristotle as his basis. After all, from where does the doctrine of transubstantiation come if not from Aristotle? In our seminary training, there was very little focus or study during those two years that was given to God's Word. Nor did we study the original languages of the Scriptures: Greek and Hebrew.

The next four years were taken up with the study of Roman Catholic thought and theology, meaning church doctrine, dogma, canon law, ethics, the study of the encyclicals of popes—both past and present, and social justice. Again, the focus was not on Scripture; it took second and third place in the scheme of things. Oh, yes, we did also study church history, but, through the lens of Roman Church perspective. In other words, very biased, never transparent. However, I admit, some of our study was biblically based and sound, such as the study of the Trinity.

During my entire seminary career, if I were to ask any one of my professors the question of the Philippian jailor, *"What must I do to be saved?"* (ACTS 16:30) he would have parroted the Roman party line, rather than the answer given by the Apostle Paul, or as he reiterated in his letter to the Ephesians, *"For by grace are ye saved through faith; and that not of yourselves, it is the gift of God; not of works, lest any man should boast."* (EPHESIANS 2:8-9) Their answer would likely be, "You must do what 'Mother Church' requires. Basically, be baptized as an infant, as that removes all stain of original sin; receive the other appropriate sacraments of the church, do good, do no evil;

and if you are in the state of grace, as we define it, when you die you will earn heaven as a reward."

Catholicism Versus Christianity

It was "do, do, do" as all other false religions prescribe and preach. Plain and simple, it is and was a works' righteousness; whereas, true religion adds two letters to the word "do," making it "done." Jesus, the Messiah, the God-Man did it all. As Jesus was dying upon the cross of Calvary, He proclaimed, *"It is finished"* (JOHN 19:30B), meaning it is accomplished—paid in full. Salvation was fully achieved. Jesus Christ is the Perfect Savior, and to deny that is heretical. To say that He needs help, or that a co-redeemer is necessary, is not only heretical, but it is idolatrous and blasphemous.

With the bad theology with which I was inculcated from my earliest childhood to my formative years in the seminary, I was to live the first forty or so years frustrated, striving—striving—striving without having full assurance of my salvation. To prove my point (as an aside), some two years ago, six others and I from the Evangelical Christian Church to which my wife and I belong, went on a mission trip to the Republic of Ireland. We spent two weeks in County Mayo with missionaries, Larry and Kathy Dunn. Larry, a former fisherman who lost his right hand in a fishing accident, is now a fisher of men in his native land. He, as a former Catholic, accepted the Biblical Gospel through the preaching of a street evangelist in Dublin. Now, going door to door in this predominantly Catholic country, one of our leading questions was, "Do you have full assurance of your eternal salvation?" No one, but no one, responded with, "I know my eternal destiny to be with God in His heavens, because I placed my trust in Christ and in Him ALONE: through His perfect life and His death upon the cross, He has atoned for my sins and credited me with His own righteousness." No, most would answer, if at all, "I hope so." No ringing endorsement to be sure.

Ordained to the Priesthood

After six years, my seminary studies were completed. It was on June 1, 1962, that I, along with several of my classmates were ordained to the priesthood by Archbishop Anthony Jordan, O.M.I. at St. James Parish Church in Edmonton. At the time, the cathedral church of St. Joseph's was being renovated, giving reason for the change in venue. My first mass,

I celebrated the following day at my home church, St. Columba in Clandon-ald, Alberta, Canada. As its name would indicate my home community, was originally settled by the Scots, followed closely by Irish immigrants. Al-though I am of Polish heritage, I grew up in this community, which by this time was more diverse in its ethnic makeup. I must say, these were joyous, though solemn, occasions for all involved, especially for family members.

My active ministry began in a rocky fashion. Not long after being post-ed to the town of Vegreville as a curate, I came down with hepatitis. In and out of the hospital over the next six months, I was finally diagnosed by a specialist in Edmonton as having a liver condition known as Gilbert's Dis-ease, a condition of the liver, not life-threatening I was happy to discover.

During this first year of ministry, when I was able, I had charge of a mission church in the town of Mundare, some ten miles from Vegreville. This community had a heavy presence of Ukrainians and, of course, they had their own Greek Catholic Church. A much smaller group of Mundare inhabitants were of Polish origin, so, with a last name such as mine, the Archbishop thought this to be a natural fit, despite, unfortunately, the fact I knew little of the language. It came as a revelation to me as to how devot-ed these Polish people were to their relics, to their rosary, to their statues, and especially to their "Mary." In fact, within the parish boundaries, there was a grotto dedicated to Mary, with statues galore and the Stations of the Cross outlining the outdoor park-like field of green. Every year on August 15th, come rain or shine, during the Feast of the Assumption, hundreds from near and far thronged as pilgrims to honor Mary, to go to confes-sion, receive communion, and participate in other activities. Sermons were preached in the Polish language throughout the day and into the evening hours. All this occurred outdoors, so rain was always a threat. Many of these same people you would only see in church at Christmas and Easter, but you could count on them being at the Skaro Grotto on the Feast of the Assumption. They were much like the Catholic who frequented the church on only three occasions during his lifetime: when he was hatched, when he was matched, and when he was dispatched. In many ways, this all had the character of a carnival with its booths ringing the infield, people selling their wares, whether they be statues, rosaries, trinkets or other novelties. Bottles of Lourdes holy water were also on hand to be purchased.

During that brief first year, I officiated at several funerals in that Polish parish. I vividly recall, even so many years later, the weeping and wailing that took place at the gravesite by these poor, misguided, unenlightened folk, mourning as those that have no hope. And so they were ... without hope. These sheep were surely blind, but just as blind was their novice shepherd.

Within one year of my ordination, I received a second posting, this time to a city parish; namely, St. Anthony, an affluent parish on the south side of Edmonton. My status, curate, remained the same. However, this time the parish priest was Monsignor Foran, known to some as a frustrated bishop. He ran a tight ship and made it clear to the two curates connected with the parish, to Father Larry Bonner who served as chaplain to the University Hospital, and to the housekeeper, that "whatever happened in the rectory, stayed in the rectory." The Monsignor indulged in such cravings as overeating and watching television all hours of the day and night. His favorite pastime was playing the "ponies" with Mary the housekeeper being his accomplice, by her going down the street each morning and placing "Monsie's" bet on the afternoon races with his bookie. The month of January he spent in the South with his priest-friend, Bert O'Brien, frequenting the racetracks where no one would recognize him. He was setting quite an example for us younger priests. There is no wonder his admonition was, "Whatever happens in this rectory, stays in this rectory."

Vatican II's Affect on the Priesthood

Much was afoot during the time of the early 1960's, the assassination of an American president, as well as the Council known as Vatican Council II. That Council did much to awaken the Catholic world. Change was upon us: vernacular in the liturgy, priests' conferences, questioning of authority both inside and outside the church were operative and a trademark of the times. Celibacy became an issue within the church, at least in Western Canada. After all, the first so-called pope was married, so, why not allow a simple priest to do likewise? Many from my archdiocese took this matter into their own hands and, as a result, there was an exodus of clergy from our archdiocese.

Pope John XXIII wanted to let some fresh air into the stale institutional church, so, he cracked open a window. He let in more than was bargained for, so, his successors in quick order slammed shut that window. Despite the changes and upheaval within "Mother Church," the outcome was no different than rearranging the deck chairs aboard the Titanic. It was still sinking and perishing. The powers that be never did revisit the Council of Trent. That Council in the mid 1500's that lasted some 20 years.[1] The same Council that sealed the fate of the institutional Roman Church. It was that same Council that drove a stake through the heart of the true biblical Gospel when it declared that faith in Jesus Christ alone was just not enough for salvation. The Council of Trent declared Christ was not the complete, perfect Savior; that by living a perfect life and dying an atoning death upon the cross of Calvary, He did not accomplish all that was necessary for salvation. They anathematized anyone holding those "heretical" beliefs.[2] To be saved, they contended, one had to add one's good works, which is completely contrary to Holy Scripture. Mother Teresa summed up their views when she uttered those famous words, "Jesus did 95% of the work; I must do the other 5%." No, you are wrong, Mother Teresa, Jesus did 100% of the work. One cannot earn salvation; it is a gift. You do not buy a gift. Once again, I refer you to Ephesians 2:8-9. Because of man's pride, he wants to do something to earn that which cannot be earned.

So, despite all the fury, pomp, and circumstance, what did the Council known as Vatican II accomplish? For me personally, much was accomplished; I benefited greatly from it. It drove me to start questioning authority. I was not yet searching God's Word to see how it matched up with church teaching and practice. That would unfold later, in fact, after I left the Institution. I do recall a point in the mid 1960's when I stopped reciting the rosary. The council, to its credit, did put Mary in a more balanced role, one where she was less exalted. However, this would last but for a mere decade before the first Polish pope came into office. He reinstated her, and even elevated her beyond her previous high and exalted position. I witnessed this firsthand when visiting the pilgrimage site of Knock, in Ireland, where Mary supposedly appeared in 1879. How did Moses react when witnessing the Israelites worshipping that golden calf? Would he have good reason to act differently to the idolatry practiced there at Knock, parading and bowing down to a bigger than life statue of Mary in that auditorium as the rosary was being piped in?

---

1 It opened on December 13, 1545 and issued its decree on Indulgences on December 4, 1563.

2 The exact words of the Council are, "If anyone shall say that justifying faith is nothing else than confidence in the divine mercy which remits sins for Christ's sake, or that it is this confidence alone by which we are justified: let him be anathema [cursed]." Henry Denzinger, *The Sources of Catholic Dogma*, (B. Herder Book Co., 1957), Number 822, Canon 12

Personally, during the latter part of the 1960's and then into the 1970's, I was becoming more frustrated and disillusioned. For instance, how does one square this? The Vatican for ages proclaimed that eating meat on Fridays was a mortal sin that would damn one to hellfire for all eternity; but then, out of the blue, declare a counter declaration saying that this infraction was now no infraction at all. I ask, "How can this be?" Basically, there are only two sources of knowledge: God or man?

Henry as a Catholic Priest 1972

From where does the institutional Roman Church get its knowledge? God or man? If it came from God, it would square with His Word as contained in the Scriptures. Does it? It does not. Hence, it is arbitrary knowledge coming from man, from the world, and ultimately from the devil himself. Moses writes, *"Then the Lord saw that the wickedness of man was great on the earth, and that every intent of the thoughts of his heart was only evil continually."* (GENESIS 6:5) More and more, I was likening the hierarchy of the Roman Catholic Church to the Pharisees of Jesus' day.

Preparing to Leave the Priesthood

It was in the early 1970's that I was ready to pull the plug and leave. However, leaving is not so simple considering the ties I had with family, friends, and especially associates within the clergy. What a scandal it would be! Even though I was not the first, I would be bringing shame upon my older brother, a faithful and devoted functional priest serving as a chaplain in a large hospital. I did not have the intestinal fortitude at the time, so I stalled and hung around. Neither did I have the truth of the Biblical Gospel. I was lost myself. I was blind. I could not sing fully John Newton's hymn, "I once was lost, but now I'm found; once was blind, but now I see."

During my seminary days, I served as a cadet in the Canadian Air Force, spending three summers assisting chaplains. During the summer of 1961, I was posted to Germany, with the 3rd Wing. This became my escape hatch. I applied and was accepted into the Canadian Forces chaplaincy corps in 1975. My archbishop grudgingly gave his permission. During the next three years, being paid a Captain's salary, I was able to accumulate a small stash of cash to tide me over as I got established in the real world. I certainly could not count on any financial support from the institutions I was soon to leave: the institutional Roman Church or the Canadian military. They did not disappoint; I expected nothing, I got nothing.

The Breakaway

After being cloistered for years, it was with much trepidation that on July 1, 1978, Canada Day, I officially left the institution in which I had been an active player for some 22 years. Moreover, like Abraham, I journeyed to a foreign land. I came to Los Angeles, California to commence my new life.

I see the next season of my life as a time of awakening. At the time, my entire belief system was totally confused. What did I really believe? I was so disappointed and disillusioned by my past experiences. I now looked to Metaphysics, to Science of Mind, to Eastern Meditation, to make sense of all of it.

However, I had more than that to occupy my mind. I had to hustle to make my way, finding work wherever I could find it. I found myself with Farmer John's packing sausages; there was Forest Lawn, selling pre-need cemetery property. Eventually, I settled into telemarketing, selling over the phone everything from investment grade diamonds to oil and gas leases. I made friends along the way. One, in particular, Leo Villela, became a close friend and confidant. He and I collaborated on a number of ventures and it was he who introduced me to Dr. Walter Martin, the Bible Answer Man on radio. Dr. Martin was instrumental in bringing me eventually to acknowledge my sinfulness and my need for a Savior.

I came to see that all my good works were as filthy rags in the sight of God. Isaiah puts it this way, *"And all our righteous deeds are like a filthy garment."* (ISAIAH 64:6) That is the Old Testament. What about the New Testament? Is it as harsh? I found this truth expressed even more forcefully in the New, namely the Apostle Paul's inspired letter to the Romans. By the way, this book of the Bible became my favorite. It begins the explanatory section of the New Testament Scriptures. Paul explains what the coming of the Messiah means. Yes, He lived; He died. Yes, He rose again. But what does it all mean? In the Book of Romans, the Apostle, through the inspiration of the Holy Spirit, explains it all; namely, the condition of natural man: dead in sin, destined for hell—the bad news. Let us look at that. *"As it is written, there is NONE righteous, NO, NOT ONE: ... there is NONE that seeketh after God... They are ALL gone out of the way.... NONE that doeth good, NO, NOT ONE..."* (Romans 3:10-12) I would say Isaiah is mild compared to this. Paul continues, *"For ALL have sinned and fall short of the glory of God."* (Romans 3:23) Here I saw myself utterly condemned. Paul, however, does not leave us there. He now gives us the Good News: the Gospel. Romans 5:1 begins the good news. After all, without bad news, there can be no good news. Paul states, *"Therefore, having been justified (aorist tense in the Greek, meaning one time, completed act), by FAITH (not by baptism: not by any other rites of any church or by any works, no, by faith, by believing. Faith is an empty virtue; hence, it is not a work.) we have peace with God, through our Lord, Jesus Christ."* (Romans 5:1) Our faith is in Jesus Christ, our Savior, and in Him alone.

Paul reiterates this same truth when he writes, *"But, God demonstrates His love toward us, in that while we were sinners, Christ died for us."* (Romans 5:8) Again, *"For the wages of sin is death, but the free gift of God is eternal life in Christ Jesus, our Lord."* (Romans 6:23) I had read these words many times before but now I was reading them for the first time with spiritual eyes, opened by God's Holy Spirit.

Going to the Cross

Once I had acknowledged my sinful condition; i.e., the bad news, I was able to go to the foot of the cross and accept as a free gift the Good News, the Biblical Gospel of the perfect Savior, Jesus Christ. And so it was, by the grace of God, that in April of 1982, I knelt down by my bed in the little house I was renting in Downey, California, and received Christ the Messiah, as my personal Lord and Savior. It was on that occasion that I was BORN FROM ABOVE. Jesus talks to Nicodemus of this second birth in John 3. I must say, that day was the most glorious of my life. What a burden was lifted from my shoulders, a burden carried for years, dating back to childhood. After all those years of seminary training, of ministry, of striving, of penance, I was awakened to the simplicity of the Gospel. It was God's doing, from beginning to end. Unless the Lord opened my eyes, I would be forever in darkness.

For years, I had been deceived, misled, lied to, intentionally or not, makes little difference. "What a treasure I have found," was my thought.

260 ON THE WINGS OF GRACE ALONE

My natural desire was to say, "I must share this, especially with my family, all those old friends, all those "good" Catholics. Pardon me, *"There is none that doeth good, no, not one."* (ROMANS 3:12) I would over time find out that salvation is of the Lord. He calls; He elects whom He will.

Family Concerns

Who, in the Catholic faithful, and of right mind, would believe a traitor to the cause, one who abandoned the "true faith," the "one, true, Holy, Catholic, Apostolic Church?" After all, its lineage dated back to St. Peter, the first pope. Moreover, I was the "black sheep" destined for hell fire if I did not repent and return to the "Mother Church." My oldest brother reminded me of this on more than one occasion, but he was praying for me to return, of course. In fact, every year for Christmas, I received through the mail a card informing me, "You will be remembered in my Christmas Masses," signed, Father John. Yes, my family, in particular, wanted me back, to have their "prodigal" returned. When I flew back for my father's funeral in late January of 1984, this was clearly, although unspoken, the desire of all. "If you return, you will be welcomed back." I remember well how generous my youngest sister was on that occasion. That, I will not forget. Very apropos to my situation were the words of the Lord, *"Jesus said to them, 'A prophet is not without honor except in his own home-town and among his own relatives and in his own household.'"* (MARK 6:4)

How does one throw away a treasure, the treasure of eternal life? One wants to share it, not cast it away. What? Go back to error and falsehood? No way! Once in the light of the Biblical Gospel, my desire was to share it and not retreat into the darkness. However, over time, I had to resign myself to the truth that God is sovereign, He is in control over ALL things and the ALL includes salvation itself. It is He who elects. Romans 9 came to mind. The Apostle Paul there writes, *"....And not only this; but when Rebecca also had conceived by one, even by our father Isaac; (For the children being not yet born, neither having done any good or evil, that the purpose of God according to election might stand, not of works, but of him that calleth;) It was said unto her, 'The elder shall serve the younger. As it is written, Jacob have I loved, but Esau have I hated.'"* (ROMANS 9:10-13) Paul continues, *"What shall we say then? Is there unrighteousness with God? God forbid. For he saith to Moses, I will have mercy on whom I will have mercy, and I will have compassion on whom I will have compassion. So then it is not of him that willeth, nor of him that runneth, but of God that sheweth mercy."* (ROMANS 9:14-16) Paul further makes the point, *"Thou wilt say then unto me, Why doth he yet find fault? For who hath resisted his will? Nay but, O man, who art thou that repliest against God? Shall the thing formed say to him that formed it, Why hast thou made me thus? Hath not the potter power over the clay, of the same lump to make one vessel unto honour, and another unto dishonour?"* (ROMANS 9:19-21)

Romans chapter 9 is the most forceful text of Scripture to drive home this point, but, it is evident throughout God's Word. In John chapter 3, the Lord Jesus explains to Nicodemus that one cannot enter heaven unless he is born again; in other words, a spiritual birth—a birth from above. He proclaims, *"Marvel not that I said unto thee, Ye must be born again. The wind bloweth where it listeth, and thou hearest the sound thereof, but canst not tell whence it cometh, and whither it goeth: so is every one that is born of the Spirit.."* (JOHN 3:7-8)

When selecting His Apostles, was it not Jesus Christ who said, *"Ye have not chosen me, but I have chosen you"?* (JOHN 15:16) He selects whom He will to be His chosen, His elect. Whatever God decrees comes to pass as He has decreed it.

A corollary to God's sovereignty would be man's responsibility. Yes, the Bible teaches God's sovereignty, but it also teaches man's responsibility. Both are clearly taught in the Scriptures when we read, *"...Him, being delivered by the determinate counsel and foreknowledge of God, ye have taken, and by wicked hands have crucified and slain."* (ACTS 2:23) Even though Christ's death was sovereignly decreed and predetermined by God, He still holds those responsible for Jesus' death culpable and responsible. They are paying and will pay for their actions.

So, how can this be? Personally, I do not know. These two truths are a dilemma no man can fully fathom. The best answer I have found comes from the Prophet Isaiah. Through the prophet, God declares, *"For my thoughts are not your thoughts, neither are your ways my ways, saith the LORD."* (ISAIAH 55:8) Always remember, God is God and man is not. Our minds are like a thimble of water compared to the immeasurable mind of God, the difference between the finite and the infinite, actually no comprehensible comparison. The 1980's were precious to me. Not only did God open my eyes and bring me to a true Biblical faith but He also opened up work and business opportunities so that I became more financially stable. However, next to salvation that He freely provided, He gave me the next most precious gift of all, for it was in September of 1984 that I met my future wife, Edith. We were married in December of that same year. Over the years, she has been a faithful, loving mate, companion and friend, exuberant, joyful and exciting, a true inspiration to me in countless ways. Even more endearing is her love for God and His Word. Together, we have grown in that love. God was surely blessing me in so many ways. My heart is filled with gratitude towards Him in how He has blessed me. And, over these many years, my theology was sharpened and refined by reading, studying, and especially sitting under the preaching and teaching of such men as Chuck Swindoll, Michael Horton, Kim Riddlebarger, Bob Morey, and my present pastor, Philip De Courcy, with his practical, expository preaching at Kindred Community Church. That, along with Bible studies and Shepherding Groups, has brought me to this point as I write this in January 2013.

Reminiscing

As I reminisce, my thoughts and memories travel back over the years. I ask myself, what truths have impacted me most? First of all, as I read and meditate on God's Word, I admit the most basic truth forced upon me by the honest study of the Scriptures is the sovereignty of God. God's Word is infallible. I used to believe at one point in my life, when I was very gullible, that the Pope was infallible, but no longer. Only God is infallible as is His inspired Word; i.e., His Revelation, from Genesis to Revelation.

As I further reminisce, the next thought I have is the contribution made by the Reformers of the 16th century, particularly Martin Luther and John Calvin. They rescued the Gospel from the darkness of Roman thought and theology. Opposition to them was fierce. Many paid with their lives, martyrs every bit as much as those of the church of Apostolic times. If I had lived during the 1600's and did what I have done in my time, there is no doubt I would have been a candidate for beheading, burning at the stake, or a torture victim for the Inquisitors.

The Five Solas

The five "solas" of the Reformers are a benchmark for me. They expressed their beliefs so succinctly. Salvation for them was by grace alone, through faith alone, because of Christ alone, according to Scripture alone, to the glory of God alone. How very Biblical, a reflection of the Apostle Paul's words, *"For by grace are ye saved through faith; and that not of yourselves, it is the gift of God; not of works, lest any man should boast."* (EPHESIANS 2:8,9) It is also a reflection of the Book of Romans, which is Paul's treatise on salvation.

The Roman Church of the day could abide these five "solas" if the word, "alone" were to be eliminated. That one word was anathema to them and they declared it so at the Council of Trent. Yes, they said, salvation is by grace and faith—but not alone. You need works; you need the Roman Church's sacraments. Yes, it is by Christ—but not alone. He needs our help to save. He needs Mary and the saints. In other words, He is not a complete, perfect Savior. He did not pay the price in full. Yes, we believe in the Bible—but not alone. You also need our traditions. Yes, God should get the glory—but not all of it. We deserve some. Just like the angel of light, Lucifer himself, pride is systemic and shows its ugly head.

His Marvelous Light

Finally, the study of Scripture has brought me to a place where I admit to being a doctrines of grace person i.e. a Reformed Evangelical Christian, born from above. Truly I am new creation in Christ and one who believes God gets all the glory for who I am; and how He has led me, protected me, brought me out of darkness and into His marvelous light, the light of the Biblical Gospel. I can surely pray with David the words of the 23rd Psalm:

> *The Lord is my shepherd; I shall not want. He maketh me to lie down in green pastures: he leadeth me beside the still waters. He restoreth my soul: he leadeth me in the paths of righteousness for his name's sake. Yea, though I walk through the valley of the shadow of death, I will fear no evil: for thou art with me; thy rod and thy staff they comfort me. Thou preparest a table before me in the presence of mine enemies: thou anointest my head with oil; my cup runneth over. Surely goodness and mercy shall follow me all the days of my life: and I will dwell in the house of for ever."*

To God be the Glory forever and ever. Amen

—HENRY NOWAKOWSKI

If you have any questions or comments kindly email me at: bloomski1@aol.com

JOE FLAHIVE

A Great Sinner Coming to Know the Only Savior Jesus

As I share the most amazing event in my life, I would like to interject along the way truths I have found from verses in the Bible, which explain the utter despair of my early life, indeed anyone's life—apart from true faith in the Person of Jesus Christ and the amazing peace and joy that came from being made a "new creature" in Him. *"Therefore if any man be in Christ, he is a new creature: old things are passed away; behold, all things are become new."* (2 CORINTHIANS 5:17)

I feel it is most important, in fact essential, that anyone searching for absolute truth to determine the source he/she will utilize in that search. For me, that absolute truth was found in the Bible, the very Word of God, and nowhere else. We can learn from great preachers/teachers and church tradition, but everything must be tested and stand under the authority of Holy Scripture.

Additionally, I feel it is important to make a brief comment about the Catholic faith in which I was raised and turned away from when I was saved at the age of thirty-seven. I left the Catholic Church when I came to know Jesus as my personal Savior, not out of rebellion toward my upbringing, but because by God's grace, I had come to know the Truth—and as Jesus had promised that Truth had set me free. I had come to realize I could never earn forgiveness for my sins and eternal life through anything I could or would ever do—a doctrine which stands in total opposition to the Catholic Church's teaching that salvation must be "earned" through good works along with faith in Christ's death on the Cross. The Catholic religion had placed a burden on me that I could never, ever meet. Saving faith in Jesus' finished work on the Cross and that alone had set me free. *"Then said Jesus to those Jews which believed on him, 'If ye continue in my word, then are ye my disciples indeed; And ye shall know the truth, and the truth shall make you free.'"* (JOHN 8:31, 32)

The Early Years, Questions With Seemingly No Answers

I was raised in a strong Catholic family and attended Catholic schools up through my sophomore year in college. Looking back over those years, I believe it was in elementary school where I was most aware of spiritual things and the perceived need to strive to please God. Those first eight years of my education took place at our family parish where Irish nuns taught and ran the small school. I do not know if their Irish ancestry can be credited solely for their teaching style, but I do know we received a strong dose of discipline along with the academic studies. I distinctly remember them impressing on the students our sinfulness—particularly as it related to us boys. They seemed to be reading my mind when they spoke of "impure thoughts," among other things. I will always be thankful for God's providence in allowing me to be raised in this environment, for the one thing I did learn was to fear the Lord. *"The fear of the LORD is the beginning of wisdom: and the knowledge of the holy is understanding."* (PROVERBS 9:10)

Those years of being brought up and taught the Catholic faith were filled with questions my inquisitive mind kept asking. My friends and I did not speak of it much, for religion was not "cool" for one thing, and for another, one had the sense we were to just believe and not question what was taught. I do not ever remember being encouraged to raise questions about the faith, so I did not, but I held those questions inside. Considering the multitude of questions I had, three were dominate in my early years.

1. What Made the Priest So Special?

I was raised to respect all my elders but priests were placed on somewhat of a pedestal. They had that "special" power to turn an ordinary wheat host and regular wine into the actual body and blood of Jesus! As an altar boy, I watched them perform this mysterious act numerous times but wondered what really was going on. We were taught it was a "mystery" and so accepted it to a degree, but the question which lingered was, "Why would someone want to crucify Jesus over and over again?" And particularly at the whim of a man, even if he was a Catholic priest!" Did the priest get permission from God to crucify His Son every day of the week?

Catholic confession was another difficulty for me. I had to go a lot and, at least in my early years, entered the confessional with great sincerity and a true desire to find forgiveness. I was faithful at carrying out my penitence, but without fail, I never felt a relief from my burden of guilt. My mind would ask, "Did this priest really talk to God, and did he really have some 'special' power from the God of the Universe to grant me forgiveness?" If I was forgiven from making those treks to the confessional, it never felt like it, and I knew I would be back the following week to repeat the same process.

Joe in Jesuit High School

Trying to find a satisfactory answer to this looming question was difficult for me, as my dad, who had many close friends who were priests, had one priest in particular who visited our home frequently. I really liked this priest, as he was Irish and a lot of fun—but he drank a lot. Often, I could easily perceive he was quite intoxicated at family occasions. I was searching for someone who indeed was almost perfect, almost sinless; whom I could depend on to be the way to God—it was not to be my dad's friend. I felt sure no priest could measure up to what I felt I needed—a way to God.

"Jesus saith unto him, 'I am the way, the truth, and the life: no man cometh unto the Father, but by me.'" (JOHN 14:6)

Much later on in life my wife and I would see two close college friends' marriage broken up when the pastor of our local Catholic parish began having an affair with the wife. Their encounters took place in the church's residence hall. Once again, that something "special" about Catholic priests was brought to question.

The answer to that question which I arrived at only after coming to know the truth through God's Word, was there is nothing "special" about a Catholic priest, be he pope or local pastor. As with every human being, and me, Catholic priest are sinners destined for an eternity in hell unless they repent of their sins and turn to faith in Christ and Him alone for their salvation. *"As it is written, 'There is none righteous, no, not one.'"* (ROMANS 3:10)

In addition the Bible tells us there is only one intercessor between man and God. His name is Jesus. *"Wherefore he is able also to save them to the uttermost that come unto God by him, seeing he ever liveth to make intercession for them."* (HEBREWS 7:25)

2. If the Bible is God's Book, Why Did We Not Study It?

Throughout my Catholic education, and in our home, the Bible was spoken of as being from God to His people. Yet, we never read it in our family, never opened it at school (even through college) and treated it as some mysterious book not to be considered by the average person. The priests would read a few verses at Mass but even their sermons often wandered far from anything specific the Bible taught. This never made sense to me. It always seemed we should study the Bible, in addition to other religious material.

It would be years later before I posed the question to our parish priest. His answer was, "You wouldn't understand the Bible if you did study it; only priests have the education to rightly decipher what the Bible teaches." To me that was not a very satisfactory answer at all. My thought was, "If God wrote this book to His people, surely He would write it so His people (not priests alone) could understand it."

Catholic history tells us that up to the early sixteenth century the Church of Rome (Catholic Church) had kept the original transcripts of the Bible under lock and key—away from the ordinary man. The only translation they allowed was Latin, which was not a common language among the people. During the Reformation, which began in 1517 AD, godly men stood against the Church of Rome on many matters of apostasy, which the church carried out. One of the greatest outcomes of the Reformation was the translation of the Bible, God's very Word, into German, and then English, so that the common man had access to Truth as revealed by God Himself. This was the beginning of the Protestant Reformation, which turned the world upside down, and with the preaching of the Word, now in the hands of common men, people were set free. Outside of the beginning of the true church at Pentecost in 33 AD, I believe this was the most significant move of the Holy Spirit in the past two thousand years of human history.

> O how love I thy law! it is my meditation all the day.
> Thou through thy commandments hast made me wiser than mine enemies:
> For they are ever with me.
> I have more understanding than all my teachers: for thy testimonies are my meditation.
> I understand more than the ancients, because I keep thy precepts.
> I have refrained my feet from every evil way, that I might keep thy word.
> I have not departed from thy judgments: for thou hast taught me.
> How sweet are thy words unto my taste! yea, sweeter than honey to my mouth!
> Through thy precepts I get understanding: therefore I hate every false way.

(PSALM 119:97-104)

Twenty-seven years ago when by God's grace I came to believe in Jesus as my Redeemer, one of the first people I wanted to tell of the new joy I had found was our parish priest. I had served as a lay reader for years and felt I knew him well and anticipated he would join in my joy. However, he said I had joined a cult (small Bible based local church) and should renounce it immediately. Regarding the truth I had found in the Bible, he said I could not understand the Bible on my own and should leave the study of it to priests!

3. It Seemed God Changed His Mind Often about His Decrees!

I grew up in the Catholic Church when Catholics abstained from eating meat on Fridays under penalty of sin. The number of meatless "meat" patties I ate during my early years would be almost impossible to count. I took the church's command seriously only to find they dropped it years later for some reason. I was taught that church ordinances came directly from God Himself—so, why did He change?

In addition, there were a multitude of indulgences available by which we could earn merit before God and somehow gain His favor in various circumstances. One, I remember distinctly, had to do with the assurance of having a priest present when you were dying. God had impressed an awareness of eternity on my heart as a young man and that when I died I would stand before a holy and perfect God to be judged for my actions in this life. God's Word tells us He has placed this awareness in the heart of all His human creatures: *"He hath made every thing beautiful in his time: also he hath set the world in their heart, so that no man can find out the work that God maketh from the beginning to the end."* (ECCLESIASTES 3:11)

Because of this, I lived with a fear of death, feeling the need to at least have a priest present, should I die, to confess my sins. The particular indulgence I remember stated that if a person went to confession, attended Mass, and received communion on the first Friday of each month for nine consecutive months, they were assured a priest would be present as they died. I faithfully completed the requirements to only find out later in my life that that indulgence was no longer valid. None of this made sense. Surely the God I wanted to know and find acceptance from was not as flippant as these changing ordinances seemed to indicate. *"I know that, whatsoever God doeth, it shall be for ever: Nothing can be put to it, nor any thing taken from it: And God doeth it, that men should fear before him."* (ECCLESIASTES 3:14)

The Emptiness Nothing On Earth Could Fill

Despite my reasonably faithful adherence to the Catholic religion, I always had a sense of fear concerning God and felt quite sure I would be doomed to hell should I die.

While I was blessed to have above average abilities and found success in most things I became involved in there was emptiness in my heart that nothing seemed to fill. I married the "love of my life" at twenty-one and spent the next four years in the Navy during the Vietnam War. After the service, I entered the University of Texas, in Austin, where I earned an electrical engineering degree—with honors.

Upon graduation I started work at a major electronics company in Dallas. I felt sure this was what I needed to fill that emptiness: a wonderful family (we were expecting our second child), a very promising career making more money than I had ever imagined I could make, and our first home.

Two years passed and, from the outside, everyone probably thought I was doing great; our children were healthy and doing well, my career was advancing, and we had "money in the bank" for the first *Joe age 26 while serving in the Navy* time in our married lives. But that emp- *during the Vietnam War* tiness was still there. In a sense of desperation, I decided that I needed to get closer to God—for me that meant making a point to attend daily Mass during the week. There is a well-known saying attributed to a man named Augustine (often referred to as Saint Augustine) who served as the bishop of Hippo, Africa in the forth century; "Lord, You have created us for Yourself and our hearts are restless until they find rest in You."

The shepherd, David, writes of God's amazing involvement, not only in man's creation, but everyday of our lives: *"My substance was not hid from thee, when I was made in secret, and curiously wrought in the lowest parts of the earth. Thine eyes did see my substance, yet being unperfect; and in thy book all my members were written, which in continuance were fashioned, when as yet there was none of them. How precious also are thy thoughts unto me, O God! how great is the sum of them! If I should count them, they are more in number than the sand: when I awake, I am still with thee."* (PSALMS 139:15-18)

For the next two years, I faithfully attended Mass at least three to four times during the workweek—every week of the year. At the end of that exercise, I distinctly remember thinking; "I do not know God any better now than I did two years ago!"

Two Strangers Testify of God's Mercy and Grace

Near this time, I received a phone call at home one night from an old acquaintance. We had worked together for eight to nine months at a small engineering company in the Dallas area where he served as my technician. His background was quite different from mine—he made most of his spending money at pool halls during the nighttime hours. He met his wife at a bar, and while my wife and I really liked her, she, too, was very different from us. He knew I was a practicing Catholic from occasional conversations we had concerning religion.

That night he called to invite me to church—not a Catholic church but an Assembly of God church! That night, which I will never forget, my "pool-hustling," "bar-hopping" friend told me he had come to know Jesus and trusted Him as his Savior! From his voice, I was convinced he was sincere in what he was saying. To this day, I remember the feeling of fear that came from that conversation so long ago—here I had been really working to try and know the God in Whom I had always believed, and this friend, who seemed to have little interest in the things of God, claims he now knows God and the "key" is Jesus. My defenses rose up, and I quickly told my friend, "I am happy with my Catholic faith." I lied! That was the first time I remember thinking there must be a way to really know God other than the way I had been trying.

After being in Dallas for over four years, I moved our family to the country in central Texas. Once again, I was searching for something to fill—to satisfy—to ease that emptiness. I designed and built my own home—it was as perfect as I could make it.

I soon began work in Austin at an engineering firm and began steadily advancing. Our family was quite involved with the local Catholic Church where I served as a lay reader. The pursuit of knowing God—truly knowing Him—was still my fervent desire, but I did not know the "Way."

During the months while I was building our home, I received another phone call that has been forever etched in my memory. It was a cold and rainy night, with the wind howling and shaking the mobile home we temporarily lived in. The man on the phone introduced himself, but I could not place the name. He reminded me that he was the owner of a construction business I had used for remodeling our home in Dallas. That small project had ended with this man being less than totally honest when he billed us for the work. I had forgotten all about it, dismissing it as "business as usual."

The words that followed shook my very being. This man, a forgotten stranger in my life, was calling to ask for my forgiveness for his dishonesty regarding that remodeling job three years earlier! The reason for this remarkable change of heart: *he had come to know Jesus and forgiveness of his sins.* He was calling long distance to repent before me and ask for my forgiveness.

Once again I had this astounding experience of hearing of changed lives—men no different from myself—sinners one and all, who had been set free through a faith, undoubtedly a true faith—in Jesus.

Faith Comes by Hearing

Well, I was beginning to sense that Jesus had to be the "key" to knowing God. I had not found Him after almost thirty-seven years of being "religious," so I knew a new source of Truth had to be found. I was taught as a child that the Bible was God's Word, so I felt that must be the source that could lead me to the "Truth."

In the providence of God's grace, about this time, my wife had joined a Bible study with a group of ladies near our town. Soon, we heard of a couples' Bible Study at night, in town, and my wife and I decided to try it. It only took a few weeks of hearing the true gospel, as I had never heard it before, that I knew I had found that which I had sought for the first thirty-seven years of my life—God's truth.

The gentleman who taught the Bible Study was the pastor of a small evangelical congregation. He invited the members of the class to worship with his church on Sundays. At this point in my life, I had never even entered any church other than Catholic, but I knew the joy I was discovering was worth whatever discomfort my old flesh might have to endure.

The Most Important Step I Ever Took

On the second Sunday in May of 1980, my wife, our three children, and I went to the Evangelical church. We loved the hymns, the pastor's message, and sensed a joy we had not experienced before. During the service the pastor asked if anyone wanted to share their testimony of what Jesus meant

to them. I didn't respond to his offer that Sunday but when we arrived home I gathered our entire family and told them that I if the pastor makes a similar offer the next Sunday I would tell the congregation that I wanted Jesus more than anything in my life. The following Sunday the pastor did make a similar offer. I rose from the pew—everything in my flesh fought me that day— almost like I could not make my feet move to get out of that pew. But by God's grace, I stood before the small congregation. When the pastor asked what I wanted to share, I spoke words that seemed to come solely from my heart. I spoke of my love for Jesus and of my need for forgiveness for a sinful life. That day, by God's grace, I was made a new creature in Christ. Now I see that I had been saved by believing on Jesus Christ through faith alone, all by His grace alone, praise to His glorious name!

—Joe Flahive

If you wish to contact me I would gladly welcome your message.
My email address is: flahive.joe@gmail.com

JOHN M. TURACK
(Lt. Col., USAF Ret.)

Saved from the Train to Destruction

DURING THE TERRIBLE HOLOCAUST IN THE MIDDLE OF THE 20TH CENTURY, the Germans employed trains to carry Jews and their sympathizers to their physical destruction. A few were saved. From birth, we are all on a religious train bound for eternal destruction. It is the course of events set in motion by our father Adam in his garden rebellion, which we confirm with our own individual rebellion against our kind Creator. Some travel through life in austere train cars of humanism with no care or inkling of their destination or destiny. Others, like me, began life on the ornate, gold encrusted, scarlet draped, comfortable sleeping cars of Roman Catholicism, lulled into complacency with an expectation that our works and God's grace will land us in heaven some day. The only one who can deliver them, our one mediator the Lord Jesus Christ, rescues a few. (1 TIMOTHY 2;5) This is the story of my rescue from the "train to destruction" by the love of the sovereign God of the universe.

Leaving the Station

I was born in Norfolk, Virginia USA to a Navy family. My parents agreed to raise me Catholic although my mother was raised Baptist. When she married my father she became a nominal Catholic, only attending Mass at Baptisms, first Holy Communion, Confirmation and Marriage. The photo to the right was taken at the time of my confirmation in 1973. My father grew up Catholic, but had some problems with abuses by his church leadership in New York. He took my two older sisters,

my younger brother and me five miles to church faithfully until we were able to get there on our own or chose not to go. I attended catechism and confirmation classes and was part of a youth folk group that led singing at Saturday night services. The church was not the center of my life, but it was a very real part in satisfying my attraction to the things of God.

Church was our place for religion in our lives, which allowed us to "clean up" with confession and communion at the end of a week. We considered ourselves good Catholics, but did not do many of the things devoted Catholics did. We did not have pictures of Jesus or saints, candles, statues, holy water, or crucifixes in our home and none of us prayed the Rosary (nor were we encouraged at church to do so). We had small Bibles that we got at first Holy Communion, but we did not feel a need to read them since the priests told us about the history of God's actions in ancient times.

I had no concept of a personal relationship with a living Savior. Along those same lines, we never had priests or nuns over for dinner or just to visit. In his youth, my father was an altar boy and had priests drop by before dinner, give a blessing after dinner, and expect some "payment". Often payment was in the form of alcohol. He saw this as an abuse of position. He also did not like the waste of building and then air-conditioning our large cement Catholic Church and refused to give beyond the Catholic school tuition he paid for my brother. The church would not perform a marriage for his brother who married a Methodist, and it rejected my sister who was divorced. Though these offenses affected my father personally, I did not feel the personal sting of these issues, and I liked the discipline of the Catholic Church and the well-ordered services. That would continue as I attended the United States Air Force Academy at Colorado Springs to become an Air Force officer where I became active in the Catholic Chapel and Choir.

How Shall They Hear?

As I consider the events leading to my deliverance, I cannot help but think of my friend who lived one street over. I sometimes walked home with this daughter of the Baptist pastor in our neighborhood, but she never once in the twelve years I attended school with her told me I was destined for hell or, more positively, that I could personally know God's love. She never invited me to her church though I was sometimes curious about the differences among the denominations. I had a very close friend who is now a Presbyterian minister, but in all our years of school and Boy Scouts the subject of the only way to heaven never came up. My friends probably saw me as very confident in my religion, and comfortable with the traditions of the Catholic Church. But we must not assume Catholics will reject the effectual call of God if they are chosen from the foundation of the world to be redeemed by the blood of His Lamb, our Lord Jesus Christ. As the Scripture says, *"According as He hath chosen us in Him before the foundation of the world, that we should be holy and without blame before Him in love: having predestinated us unto the adoption of children by Jesus Christ to Himself, according to the good pleasure of His will, to the praise of the glory of His grace, wherein He hath made us accepted in the beloved."* (EPHESIANS 1:4-6)

We must not refuse when prompted by the Holy Spirit to speak to those without hope. In the book of Romans the Holy Spirit says, *"For whosoever shall call upon the name of the Lord shall be saved. How then shall they call on Him in whom they have not believed? And how shall they believe in Him of whom they have not heard? And how shall they hear without a preacher? And how shall they preach, except they be sent? As it is written, "How beautiful are the feet of them that preach the gospel of peace, and bring glad tidings of good things!"* (ROMANS 10:13-15)

I was at the Air Force Academy and had an acquaintance who shocked me one day. She said, "Our relationship can't get any closer than it is because you are a Catholic and I cannot be unequally yoked with you since I am a Christian." What a statement! I was not interested in her as more than a friend at that point, but with that statement she turned and walked out of my life. Scripture plainly says, *"Be ye not unequally yoked together with unbelievers: for what fellowship hath righteousness with unrighteousness? And what communion hath light with darkness?"* (1 CORINTHIANS 6:14)

We need more godly young people who will say, "God says this is wrong, so I'm not going to do this." I wondered once again if there was that big a difference between Catholicism and other denominations. I began reading my Bible more and found some troubling inconsistencies between it and the religion I practiced during the remainder of my four years at the Academy.

Years of Questioning

It started at confession at the Academy after I came back from a leave. I confessed the same contentions with my brother that I did at my home parish, but the priest at the Academy said, "That's not a big deal. That is just normal interactions with a brother." At home I was given penance, but at college I was told it was not to be considered sin. This troubled me because I realized sin is just subjective to the church, not truth-based.

As I continued to read my Catholic Bible, I approached the priest one day and asked what "Paraklete" meant. He seemed troubled and asked where I ran across that word. I told him that in my Bible study I saw that the Lord Jesus would be our paraklete with the Father when we sin. First John explains it clearer in the King James Version, *"My little children, these things write I unto you, that ye sin not. And if any man sin, we have an Advocate (parakletos in the Greek) with the Father, Jesus Christ the righteous: And He is the propitiation for our sins: and not for ours only, but also for the sins of the whole world."* (1 JOHN 2:1-2)

To this day I don't know whether he was more troubled that I was searching my Bible or that I found that we have one completely capable Intercessor who made atonement for our sins as our Expiator. Since Jesus Christ the righteous is our Advocate, why would we request intercession from any other? The book of Hebrews says Jesus saves us to the uttermost (completely) and ever lives to make intercession for us. (HEBREWS 7:25) We don't need to petition Mary or dead Catholic saints when we can go directly to the perfect Son of God who prays for us to His Father! As I alluded in the introduction, Paul wrote young pastor Timothy, *"For there is one God, and one mediator between God and men, the man Christ Jesus."* (1 TIMOTHY 2:5) Any other veneration or supplication is false worship and disrespects our Lord's sacrifice.

One More Sacrament

Though I began to be enlightened by God's Word, I stayed in the Catholic Church and married Chris Gwinn on the day of my graduation and commissioning as an Air Force officer. Ironically, Chris also grew up Baptist as did my mother, but was not saved until years after our marriage. The Chapel did not require that she convert to Catholicism, so we married in the Catholic chapel as the photos on the next page show.

We attended the nearest Catholic church when we got to our first Air Force assignment, but found liberal theology that sounded new age, so I was open to attend the Evangelical chapel near us. When I came home at night in Washington D.C., we would tune into Evangelical Christian ra-

dio and listen to sound Bible teachers who seemed to shine the light of the Scriptures as a living truth, not a document of history.

In fact, it was listening to these teachers that I first realized that Jesus was physically raised from the dead because God accepted Jesus' perfect sacrifice for our sins. Please read the teaching of Paul to the Ephesians; *"The eyes of your understanding being enlightened; that ye may know what is the hope of His calling, and what the riches of the glory of His inheritance in the saints, and what is the exceeding greatness of His power to us-ward who believe, according to the working of His mighty power, which He wrought in Christ, when He raised Him from the dead, and set Him at His own right hand in the heavenly places, far above all principality, and power, and might, and dominion, and every name that is named, not only in this world, but also in that which is to come: and hath put all things under His feet, and gave Him to be the head over all things to the church, which is His body, the fullness of Him that filleth all in all."* (EPHESIANS 1:18-23)

God accepted Jesus' sacrifice as full payment for our sins! We are forgiven completely and the book of Ephesians goes on to proclaim, *"For by grace are ye saved through faith; and that not of yourselves: it is the gift of God: not of works, lest any man should boast."* (EPHESIANS 2:8-9)

It was God's gift, His Son's work, and the Spirit's leading; so where was the place for works, traditions, supplications to saints, purgatory, and other trappings of Catholicism? If our works could save us, then God did not need to sacrifice the life of His only Son, but there was no other way. We do not need to wonder if we are good enough, because we know Jesus is without sin, and we are justified in Him!

Delivered from the Train to Destruction

It was as dramatic as any Special Forces rescue of a doomed man in the clutches of the enemy. I consider it nothing less than a miracle of God that six months after our marriage my unsaved wife spoke to me

the truth she heard in the Baptist church growing up and I heard the Holy Spirit convicting me of sin and calling me from the way of destruction. After listening to one of our regular radio preachers, Chris told me that Jesus died to pay for my sins and that I could have a personal relationship with Him. I responded without hesitation and I desired to follow my Savior and put all

my trust in His finished work on the cross. Some would say that at that point I accepted Christ, but Ephesians makes it clear that it is we who are accepted in the beloved. (EPHESIANS 1:6) He is God. Chris was saved several years later when God reached down and revealed to her real life in Him. We have nine children and sometimes have to explain "No we are no longer Catholic, but are open to the blessings our sovereign God will give us."

In my further study, I found a verse, which clearly proclaims that Jesus "by Himself" purged our sins, meaning that there is no need for a place called Purgatory to perfect us, because the work is done. (HEBREWS 1:3) The Bible says that by one offering Jesus perfected sanctified believers forever in the eyes of God. (HEBREWS 10:14) How many will spend eternity in hell thinking, "Just a little bit longer..."? Praise God! He finished the work of justification and keeps us through His work of sanctification!

I read the Apostle Peter's first epistle in which the Spirit tells us that our only "indulgence" paying for sin comes from the blood of Jesus, not silver and gold. (1 PETER 1:18-19) We don't need to be rich so we can buy forgiveness of our sins because Jesus paid it all! Jesus' was, is, and always will be sufficient to reconcile us to God. We serve Him out of gratitude and a desire to glorify God, not to win favor. Trusting Jesus plus anything proclaims that His sacrifice was insufficient.

Some pray to statues of Mary, name churches after her, pray to her while fingering beads, or consider her a co-redemtrix, but she considered herself co-redeemed with us. *"And Mary said, My soul doth magnify the Lord, And my spirit hath rejoiced in God my Saviour. For He hath regarded the low estate of His handmaiden: for, behold, from henceforth all generations shall call me blessed."* (LUKE 1:46-48)

Mary needed a Savior like all fallen humans; she was not born without sin. Additionally, Matthew tells us in his gospel that Mary had at least seven children, making claims that she was forever a virgin patently false. The people wondered, *"Is not this the carpenter's son? Is not His mother called Mary? And His brethren, James, and Joses, and Simon, and Judas? And His sisters, are they not all with us? Whence then hath this Man all these things?"* (MATTHEW 13:55-56) Mary was blessed among women, but only God is to be adored and worshipped! The book of Hebrews corrects those who would crucify afresh the Son of God and put Him to an open shame. (HEBREWS 6:6) The Catholic Mass purports to be a weekly sacrifice of our Savior and the crucifix leaves Him in perpetual shame on a graven image worn and displayed by many. The book of Hebrews further says that Jesus made one sacrifice for sins forever. (HEBREWS 10:12) Jesus sits in glory today at the right hand of the Father! (MATTHEW 26:64)

I could give additional examples from Scripture of truths that are contrary to what is practiced in the Catholic Church. Jesus Himself taught, when giving His model for prayer, that we should not pray with vain repe-

titions, and yet "The Lord's Prayer" is repeated over and over. (MATTHEW 6:7)
I attended a Catholic wedding of a nephew and stood behind a relative who
delighted in the fact that he had been out of the church for twenty years
but could without effort say the parts of the Mass along with the priest. It
was vain repetition that meant nothing to him.

What to do about Catholic Discontent

If you suspect the ornate Catholic train car you are on is headed to a
place of destruction, and you realize you want to get off, don't move to
the drab train car of humanism or some other false religion! I spoke to
my father who was dying of cancer. The nurses, doctors, and neighbors
all loved this giving, easy-going man. He knew he was literally in his last
days on earth. He asked me to speak at the funeral because he had rejected Catholicism but also did not want a preacher. He had arranged almost
everything: from the funeral plans, the care of his wife, even to the care of
his once beautiful lawn, he planned everything in detail. He had planned
even the suit of clothes he would wear at death, but he did not have a robe
of spotless white for the judgment following death. I make that conclusion because I challenged him that he had taken care of all the physical
details, but not the spiritual. I had witnessed to him often and asked if he
was ready to submit to God and trust Jesus for his salvation. He said he
could never submit to God and did not believe the Bible. He thought his
goodness would count for something and that the pains he had suffered
would reduce his time in the (fictional) Purgatory. He wanted me to keep
my message short and light during the funeral and to be sure to say the
"Lord's Prayer" and sing "Jesus Loves Me." In my drafted words, which
he approved, I said Jesus loves those who obey Him and we can only call
God our Father if we trust in the sacrifice of His Son, Jesus Christ. To
my knowledge he never did that because I was with my father to his dying
breath.

Dear friend, if you are awakened to the anti-biblical nature of Catholicism, do not just drop out as my close relative did and make light of the
fact that you can still recite the vain repetitions while absenting yourself
from any influence of God. Do not reject God and go to hell with a chip
on your shoulder about a false church and reject the true Savior. God calls
His own to Himself. (ROMANS 9:18-23) If He is calling you today, I encourage you to respond and submit to Him, for one day every knee shall bow

and every tongue will confess that Jesus Christ is Lord, *"For it is written, 'As I live, saith the Lord, every knee shall bow to Me, and every tongue shall confess to God.' So then every one of us shall give account of himself to God."* (ROMANS 14:11-12)

The account I give will be that I was made righteous by the atonement of the Lord Jesus Christ. My sinful heart was washed white by the precious blood of the spotless Lamb of God, and I was transformed into His image by the power of the Holy Spirit. (2 CORINTHIANS 3:18) What will you say? Where is your trust? Are you fitted for destruction or for life?

—JOHN TURACK

Barbara Ann Merz

Life from the Hand of My Father

I was born in 1953 in Brooklyn, New York, to Sicilian-American parents, who brought me to church about a month later to be baptized into the Roman Catholic "religion."

Raised a Catholic

As a young child on Long Island, New York, I constantly felt drawn toward anything related to God. I cherished looking through our large, ornate Douay-Rheims Bible that otherwise remained in its red box. My mother consistently warned me to be careful as I looked through it, indicating that this was a special book, and I solemnly promised that I would. Too young to read, I gazed at the portraits of Jesus.

Among my favorite books were two on the lives of the saints—one each for male and female saints—with portraits on the left-hand pages and biographical summaries on the right. A certain quality in their heavenward gazes especially impressed me; they obviously loved God. While my older Catholic relatives would pray to them, I hoped to one day be one of them. I recall aspiring to become a nun when I would grow up, presuming that this was how one would become a saint—my true "goal."

My mother, deeply religious, insisted that my sister and I attend church every Sunday and never missed Mass, even after cancer made it difficult for her to walk unassisted. When her aggressive disease rendered her unable to attend, Mom had our two aunts take us, while she stayed home and read her Missal.* I do not remember my father ever attending.

Since the Mass was in Latin, I got very little out of it. Despite desiring to know God, I found it a chore, much like school. I was about ten years old

---

* The Missal is the book that contains the prayers said by the priest at the altar as well as all that is officially read or sung in connection with the Mass.

when the Mass changed to English, but I still did not feel whatever it was that those picture-book saints appeared to be feeling.

Teenage Years Without God

Shortly after my mother died in 1966, so did my attendance at church. My father, not sharing my mother's religious zeal, no longer demanded a God-centered life of me or of my sister. After my father had remarried, family life became tumultuous. The first years of marriage are hard enough under the best conditions, and our family had death and step-relations to handle. Without God as my foundation, I felt hopeless and often cried myself to sleep.

By 1970, I was spiritually starving. Therefore, when one of my aunts, dabbling in the occult, asked me to accompany her to various paraphernalia shops, I was eager to go. I found it all fascinating, but I wanted something more. This only added to my despair.

Later that year, fond memories of my mother's Bible came to mind, which I had never actually read. Fortunately, although my father had rid himself of many things that could rekindle any memories of my mother, he did not dispose of that family Bible.

First Evangelized by John

At first, I tried to read the Bible like any other book—from beginning to end. Genesis was interesting and enlightening. Moving on to Exodus, I read this passage. *"Thou shalt not make unto thee any graven image, or any likeness of any thing that is in heaven above, or that is in the earth beneath, or that is in the water under the earth: Thou shalt not bow down thyself to them, nor serve them...."* (EXODUS 20:4,5) I shuddered to think that I had broken this commandment whenever I had knelt praying before a statue of a saint. Leviticus was cumbersome, and I entered Numbers, drowning in a sea of genealogies.

Remembering my original intention—to learn about the Lord Jesus—I closed the Bible in frustration. Where were stories about Jesus? It might sound odd that I was ignorant of the arrangement of the Bible, but Catholics of my childhood were not Bible-readers, nor were they encouraged to be. While the priest read excerpts at church, we never received much urging to read it ourselves. As I closed the Bible, I saw on the title page the words, "Words of Christ in Red." I began to flip pages, desperately scanning for those red words. Finally, I found them. Realizing that the second portion of the Bible, the New Testament, spoke of Jesus, and wanting so much to learn about Him, I began reading the Gospel of Matthew. Settling in to read, I hit another genealogical list, but continued through the book. I proceeded to Mark, a bit easier, if only because to me it read like Matthew, only shorter. The opening of Luke sounded so familiar, due to what I had heard from Christmas cards.

When I started reading John, Jesus was revealed to me. His words sounded so incredibly familiar, as if I was recalling the words of some long-lost relative from my distant past. Not only familiar, these words felt comforting and safe. I could almost feel Him comforting me and giving me assurance, confirming that God was very real. For this reason, I tell anyone who is reading the Bible for the first time to begin with John. Although I did not know it at the time, the Lord was drawing me through His Word.

Introduced to the True Church

I proceeded to the Book of Acts, in which I found stark differences between the early church and the Roman Catholic religion in which my family raised me. The more I read, the more I desired to be part of a church like that of the apostles.

Continuing through the epistles, I came across this warning. *"Now the Spirit speaketh expressly, that in the latter times some shall depart from the faith, giving heed to seducing spirits, and doctrines of devils; Speaking lies in hypocrisy; having their conscience seared with a hot iron; Forbidding to marry, and commanding to abstain from meats, which God hath created to be received with thanksgiving of them which believe and know the truth."* (1 TIMOTHY 4:1-3) Was the apostle Paul writing of celibacy and the "no-meat-on-Friday" rule? Could this be pointing to the very religion of which I was a part?

For the remainder of my senior year of high school, I often tried to explain to my contemporaries what I was feeling but could not. My Catholic background left me without the words to understand (no less explain) what I desired. Whenever I tried, the other girls looked at me as if I had just landed from another planet. I felt like a foreigner on earth.

When I stopped accompanying my aunt to those shops, explaining to her that I felt that God did not want me to have any part of it anymore, she became furious over my implication that it was evil. This began our history of repeated debates over crystals, Ouija boards, communicating with the dead, horoscopes, and many other issues.

"Real Life" Gets in the Way

I graduated high school in 1971, and, at my parents' urging I "got my head out of the clouds" and began thinking of more "serious" things. I bought a car, took driving lessons, got my license, and got a job.

Through this job, I met a young man who could really make me laugh. With home life filled with strife, it was a welcome change. Within a year, we decided to get married, and we did so in 1973. However, we were both too young and entered marriage much too lightly, and I was certainly not waiting upon the Lord to show me the way to deal with the tension. Essentially, I had taken matters into my own hands.

I became friendly with my husband's younger sister, Diane, who read the Bible a great deal, So did her boyfriend, Bob, who also wrote songs based on the Psalms. My husband thought his sister was "wacky", but she and I began to have many discussions in great depth on Scripture, which rekindled pleasant memories of reading God's Word. Early in 1974, Bob, Diane, and I returned to church together—Roman Catholic, which was all we knew. We never once heard the salvation message at church, and we wondered among ourselves what Jesus meant when He said, *"...Except a man be born again, he cannot see the kingdom of God."* (JOHN 3:3) However, although Scripture was indeed beginning to influence my thinking, I did not comprehend the true meaning of this verse and would not for many years to come.

During this time, many of our contemporaries were experimenting with psychotropic drugs to discover the "meaning" of life. Sadly, many of them discovered death instead. We perceived that what they wanted was to know the supernatural; what they needed was to know the Lord Jesus. Although God had not revealed His truth to me yet, He did allow me to know that the only truth for them was in God's Word. Bob, Diane, and I thought it might inspire some of the young people at church to read it if they could hear the testimonies of three young people who had. Therefore, in our naiveté, we presented our parish priest with the offer of his using us in whatever capacity he thought best to accomplish this. I will never forget his reply—something like this...

> You know, in our experience, we have found that, when people come to church they tend to not like religion being crammed down their throats. Therefore, we try to keep things light here—not alienate them.

This kind of thing might appear to be cramming religion down their throats and make them stop coming. Frankly, we cannot afford that.

We could not believe our ears! Was the priest saying that the physical lives of those young people, not to mention their souls, were not as important as his financial bottom line? As we gathered our wits in the parking lot, Diane suggested an alternative action. We could type up our experiences of God's reality as revealed through the reading of the Word. She would then make copies, which we would place on the seats of the church before Mass the next week. This would not cause anyone to feel pressured—the paper could just remain there if one did not want to read it. The following Sunday, we did exactly that, making sure to be there especially early.

Asked to Leave the Church

Evidently, the priest did not share our enthusiasm. After Mass, he met us at the door, and asked us to stay until everyone was gone. That did not take very long, as the congregation was generally quick to exit and pursue their other Sunday activities. After everyone left, he chided us for "disobeying" him, and then he asked that we pick up all the papers, leave "his" church, and "never return."

Because one's address determined one's parish and one could not really join another, we were now without a church to attend. Not only did we wonder where we would go, we were also somewhat concerned over what our families' reactions to this incident might be.

Diane and Bob soon found a church whose pastor taught long sermons out of the Bible. We began to fellowship there, and many things began to make sense. However, we still misunderstood the John 3:3 text; thinking it meant that we had to commit our lives to Jesus and "turn over a new leaf" as it were. Believing I had done so, I soon took part in full-immersion baptism before the entire congregation. I was not yet truly born again, despite what I may have thought. I presumed that I had chosen to follow Jesus, and the result of this error would soon become manifest in my life.

Leaning on my limited knowledge of Scripture, I was able to endure my unstable marriage, built on the selfish, immature desires of us both. However, I was doing so under my own power, and this effort was therefore doomed to fail.

Pride Comes Before a Fall

The remainder of this was so painful for me to recall that it almost made me reconsider writing this testimony. However, it will serve to underscore how much we need a Savior and how important hearing the true Gospel can be.

Suddenly, without apparent explanation, my marital pressures exceeded my "commitment" to the Lord. With those pressures taking priority, I felt as if He had abandoned me. The truth is that I had built my house on sand—I thought that "I" had chosen to follow the Lord Jesus—I was taking credit for my own salvation. Not realizing that dead souls cannot choose to follow the Lord Jesus, I held salvation in light esteem and not as the treasure that it is. My life was a lie; I had never truly been "born from above"; God's work does not fail. Consequently, I eventually found it easy to depart from any fellowship. Without accountability to anyone, I increasingly focused on my wants, my needs, and my self. Not long after that, my husband and I separated, and we divorced after only four and a half years of marriage.

The next twenty-four years were totally devoted to me. I imagined that I was so independently controlling my life, but my only success was in breaking every commandment. What else should I have expected? I was living in total rebellion against God. I was, in fact, my own god. I thought I had it all, but I had nothing.

In 1985, still in rebellion, I met my current husband. He was a serious, thinking man who held integrity high on his list of priorities. Since we held most of the same principles, and we both wanted to have children, we began a life together and planned to get married—eventually. I found his family friendly, intellectual, and well educated. However, because they apparently considered discussing "religion" to be rude and possibly offensive, I kept my beliefs to myself, continuing to deny the Lord in order to be accepted.

Home School Leads Me Home

In 1988, we were married; in 1989, I gave birth to our daughter; and in 1991, I gave birth to our son. In 1998, as my daughter was nearing the end of third grade and experiencing some problems in school, my husband and I became increasingly dissatisfied with the performance of our public school system. We made a decision to homeschool her.

In order to obtain information and support, I joined a local chapter of a statewide Christian homeschool organization. At the first meeting, held at a nearby church, I found that a pastor of the church and his wife were the chapter leaders. After the meeting, they asked me what church I attended. Embarrassed, I did not know what to say. I barely remember what I actually did say, although I think it was something about being between churches. I felt continued guilt whenever I was around the other moms in this group. Although they never once lectured me or made me feel inferior, and I knew they loved me, I also knew I was living a lie.

After the first year of homeschool ended, at the urging of one of these home school moms, I enrolled my two children in Vacation Bible School (VBS) hosted by that same church. During the closing program, I felt like an outsider despite mentally agreeing with virtually everything they professed. Concluding that faith is not merely intellectual assent, I added a bit of Bible study to our curriculum for the following school year. Having now withdrawn our son from public school, we added him to our home school.

After the second year of homeschool ended, I again enrolled them in VBS. My daughter had just completed fifth grade, and the church program allowed for the fifth-graders to receive instruction from the senior pastor and his wife. During the closing program, they approached me and told me how much they had enjoyed having her in their class. A huge lump formed in my throat; I knew I had to take some responsibility toward my children's Scriptural education, even if I was to continue in my own rebellion. I recalled a verse from Ezekiel, *"But if the watchman see the sword come, and blow not the trumpet, and the people be not warned; if the sword come, and take any person from among them, he is taken away in his iniquity; but his blood will I require at the watchman's hand."* (EZEKIEL 33:6) How could I leave my children exposed to the enemy? How could I not teach them about God?

Therefore, in our third year of homeschool, we started every school day with Bible study. We also enjoyed the luxury of impromptu discussions on the Bible during the school day and beyond. Sometime during that school year, as I continued in sharing Scripture with my children (exposing myself to His Word as well), the Lord began to draw me to Himself. Slowly at first, He increasingly filled me with a desire to read His Word.

One night, in March 2001, after everyone had gone to sleep, I sat up reading, and my eyes fell upon a long forgotten verse. *"These things I have spoken unto you, that in me ye might have peace. In the world ye shall have tribulation: but be of good cheer; I have overcome the world."* (JOHN 16:33)

I had spent twenty-four years ignoring the One Who truly loved me enough to die for me—and Whom I had professed as Lord besides—while living entirely for myself. The tears fell as I saw my life of hypocrisy. I also began to consider that perhaps the decision to homeschool was actually neither my husband's nor mine. Maybe this decision was part of God's purpose to bring me into His fold. I grieved over the fact that I had forgotten so much of what I used to know from Scripture and prayed that the Lord would give that to me again. In His goodness, He allowed me to have that. However, knowing Scripture is not the same thing as understanding His Word. Still not having a clear understanding of the gospel, I "decided" to "really commit my life to the Lord this time."

It sometimes seems to me as if Roman Catholic teachings resemble brainwashing; they seem to entrench human self-righteousness deeper than it already is. I was still deluded into thinking that I could commit myself to the Lord; I was still trying to be "good" under my own power. As soon as some personal trials came along, I again thought I could take matters into my own hands and "fix" things. Failing miserably, I progressed through guilt, self-hatred, and severe depression, which immobilized me for three months. I felt foolish to think I had ever considered myself a Christian. Thoroughly ashamed, I could no longer pray or read Scripture. Slipping into despair, I could not bear to think of Him. A concerned friend recommended a women's support group, which included a Bible study. One night, we came across this. *"For thus saith the high and lofty One that inhabiteth eternity, whose name is Holy; I dwell in the high and holy place, with him also that is of a contrite and humble spirit, to revive the spirit of the humble, and to revive the heart of the contrite ones."* (ISAIAH 57:15)

This verse perplexed me for days, even as I visited a therapist to obtain a prescription for anti-depressants. Sitting in my car, thinking of how miserably I had failed God, I heard in my mind, "That is all you can do, but it's not about what you do. It's about what I have done."

How I needed to hate my sin and to stop imagining any potential for good in me. How I needed to be confronted with the bad news before being able to hear the good news. Since God dwells with him of a contrite and humble spirit, my soul was not devoid of hope.

Except a Man Be Born Again...

This much is true. I "thought" I had come to that place of repentance before my baptism in 1974 but had not. Consequently, I had never really died to myself. I had thought I was born anew, but the Lord was yet drawing me. It was not until that summer in 2003 that God saved me by breaking me. There was no choice but to call upon His mercy.

For the first time, I had a hunger for His Word, in contrast to what was previously mere curiosity. God opened His Word to me, and the Lord Jesus appeared in a number of Old Testament passages—something I had never expected to find. However, the most profound revelations came to me from where I had started—John's account of the Gospel.

"Ye have not chosen me, but I have chosen you, and ordained you, that ye should go and bring forth fruit, and that your fruit should remain: that whatsoever ye shall ask of the Father in my name, he may give it you." (JOHN 15:16) The Lord Jesus had chosen me? I had not chosen Him? I found more. *"No man can come to me, except the Father which hath sent me draw him: and I will raise him up at the last day."* (JOHN 6:44) I could not have come to Jesus unless the Father had drawn me? In addition, *"...no man can come unto me, except it were given unto him of my Father."* (JOHN 6:65) If the Father had not given it to me, I would have not been able to come to Jesus? I recalled Lazarus in the tomb, unable to exit the tomb until Jesus spoke the words, and later found another passage. *"And you hath he quickened, who were dead in trespasses and sins; Wherein in time past ye walked according to the course of this world, according to the prince of the power of the air, the spirit that now worketh in the children of disobedience: Among whom also we all had our conversation [lifestyle] in times past in the lusts of our flesh, fulfilling the desires of the flesh and of the mind; and were by nature the children of wrath, even as others."* (EPHESIANS 2:1-3)

Finally, an often-repeated Scripture made sense, *"For by grace are ye saved through faith; and that not of yourselves: it is the gift of God: Not of works, lest any man should boast."* (EPHESIANS 2:8,9) Thinking that I had chosen to follow Jesus was, in itself, faith in a works salvation—one sure to fill me with pride and cause me to fall. *"Pride goeth before destruction, and an haughty spirit before a fall."* (PROVERBS 16:18)

The verse that I could not understand years earlier was clear, *"...Except a man be born again, he cannot see the kingdom of God."* (JOHN 3:3) Unless one is born from above, as a new creature, he cannot comprehend or even perceive the things of God's kingdom. This verse is not about what we do to get into heaven; it is about what God does to open our eyes. My salvation did not come from my family, religion, or something I "chose" at the age of twenty. I was *"...born, not of blood, nor of the will of the flesh, nor of the will of man, but of God."* (JOHN 1:13)

I have grieved over how my life—especially while professing that I was one of His—has mocked the holy name of the Lord Jesus Christ. Yet, I am unspeakably grateful to the Lord God for His grace in convicting me, leading me to repentance, forgiving me, and transforming my mind. The Scriptural truths expressed by the Apostle Paul have become my personal story, *"You hath he quickened, who were dead in trespasses and sins; but God, who is rich in mercy, for his great love wherewith he loved us, even when we were dead in sins, hath quickened us together with Christ, (by grace ye are saved). For we are his workmanship, created in Christ Jesus unto good works, which God hath before ordained that we should walk in them."* (EPHESIANS 2:1, 4-5, 10) Truly this is not my testimony; it is His. All glory to Lord God forever!

—BARBARA ANN MERZ

If you wish you can email me at: Bamerz@aol.com

Richard Bennett

(Formerly Father Peter Bennett)

The Rest of the Story: The Political Aspect of My Conversion

In my main testimony,* I explained how the Jesuits trained me in my early years in Belvedere College, Dublin, Ireland. Then I received eight years of theological instruction and preparation for the priesthood with the Dominicans, completing my education in 1964 at the Angelicum University in Rome. I spent twenty-one years as a Roman Catholic priest in Trinidad, West Indies, twenty years of which I served as parish priest. I had, therefore, the best of academic training in things Catholic, plus twenty-one years of being a parish priest applying Catholic teachings to everyday life. After a serious accident in 1972, in which I nearly lost my life, I began to seriously study the Bible. After fourteen years of contrasting Catholicism to biblical truth, I was convicted by the Gospel message. In 1986, I saw that justification is not being inwardly just as Rome taught, but being accepted in Christ. The apostle Paul wrote, *"To the praise of the glory of his grace, wherein he hath made us accepted in the beloved."* (Ephesians 1:6) I was then saved by God's grace alone, and formally left the Catholic Church and its priesthood.

Near Death Encounters

In that account of my testimony, I told of the incident in my life where I nearly died, being also unconscious for three days. That was not my only "near encounter" with death. Another traumatic incident happened while I was involved in contending for Liberation Theology. I believe this political side of my testimony must be written, because it reveals the Roman Catholic mindset to replace the Gospel with socialist concerns. Liberation

---

* The testimony *From Tradition to Truth: A Priest's Story* is on his website at: www.bereanbeacon.org/ It is also available from Chapel Library, 2603 W. Wright St, Pensacola, FL 32505 (850-438-6666)

Theology is just one example of many movements in the United States and across the world that attempts to bring in an active socialist agenda that is based on a Roman Catholic philosophy. It affects the Congress of the United States and parliaments throughout the world. In a word, it is the politics of guilt and pity, presented in a quasi-Christian fashion. We have seen it at work in America as present-day Americans (especially white Americans) are made to feel guilty for actions committed by their forefathers more than one hundred and fifty years ago. They are made to feel guilty about slavery of the African and guilty for the killing and displacement of the American Indian. It does not matter that many whites living here today had no relatives living in America during those times. It also does not matter that during those times only a few Americans were engaged in either pursuit. The vast majority of Americans were quietly living their lives trying to make ends meet just as they are trying to do today.

Liberation Theology has been very active in some African nations, the most notable being Zimbabwe, where the ruling Zimbabwe National Unity Party issued an official document calling for "Revolutionary Theology." Therefore, in this account of my life as a priest, I give some details of my political socialistic involvement.

Defending the Poor

In the first parish to which I was assigned, in Southeast Trinidad, called Mayaro, I saw working women gathering coconuts for a few dollars a day. Some of them explained to me that their working condition was worse than that of their forefathers under slavery. They said that they did not have enough money to provide food for themselves and their children. I was reading at the time the quite famous book by Jose Miranda, "Marx and the Bible," outlining the great sins of the rich against the poor. I took this as just one of many examples of the oppression of the poor, and I decided that I would do something for the cause of the poor.

I began preaching on the cause of the poor and underprivileged. I moralized in sermons to estate owners, and the wealthy merchants from the principle cities of Port of Spain and San Fernando, who came to their holiday homes on the beach in Mayaro for the weekends. I used such passages in my preaching as, *"...is not this the fast that I have chosen? to loose the bands of wickedness, to undo the heavy burdens, and to let the oppressed go free, and that ye break every yoke?"* (ISAIAH 58:6, 7) I proclaimed that if they were to be truly Christian they must pay fair wages and thus let the oppressed go free. I announced that the poor had a right to a fair share of the community goods. I quoted Scripture passages such as the end of Matthew chapter 25, saying that at the last day men will be judged on how they have treated the poor and the needy. I preached to sound the alarm that we needed to do something to lift the oppression from off the poor peoples' backs. The majority of my congregation was, in fact, the working classes and they quite liked what I said. Estate owners and merchants did not; invitation to dinners no longer came my way. Most, however, continued to attend as there was just one Catholic church in the area, and they were obliged, under pain of mortal sin, to attend.

Putting Substance to My Sermons

My conviction is what I preached, and then I saw that I had to apply what I preached. I took a case against the local doctor for cruelty to a child. The doctor would not treat the child at the local hospital where the government paid for all visits, unless the mother of the child paid an additional bribe. The mother came and told me of the cruelty done to her child, and I prepared to take judicial action against the doctor. At the same time, I was asked to pay a bribe myself to get plans approved for a building in one of the smaller villages. I also threatened a judicial action against the minister in charge of that section of government.

Personal Attacks

It was while considering these two judicial processes, that I was attacked in my parish house. Just after sunset one evening, three men came to the back door, one carrying a machete, the other a revolver, the third a knife. I did not realize until later that a fourth man had come through the front door, which was not locked at the time. They looked intent on killing me. I lectured them on my holiness as a Catholic priest, and how the wrath of God would be on them as a curse for the rest of their lives if they put one finger on me! I told them that they could have all the money in the safe, and they could take whatever they liked in the house. However, I told them that if they put one hand on me, that the blight of God would be on them, and that their lives would be eaten up with disasters. The men were for the most part Indian, and maybe Hindus. They listened to me as I continued to preach on the wrath, fury, and rage of God that would be on them, and they contented themselves with what money they could find in the house. After tying my hands and feet to my bed, they departed.

Liberation Theology

That incident did not end my desire to see the poor liberated; rather, I got even more determined. I reported the incident to the local *Express Newspaper* and it carried the headline, *"LET'S STOP THIS 'BOBOL,' SAYS ROBBED PRIEST."**

The "Black Power" movement in Trinidad worked hand in hand with Liberation Theology, just as with the Sandinistas in Nicaragua. What happened then continues to happen in nations like Zimbabwe. I consulted with one of the leaders of the "Black Power" movement and gave the movement all the support I could muster in my preaching at Mass. The Black Power coup d'état did not succeed in Trinidad; in curfews imposed after the aborted revolution, much hatred and strife broke out. In Mayaro, some of the homes of the white estate owners were burned down. I feared for my own life as gangs of black youth threw poles of burning pitch, called "flambos," into white peoples' homes at night. I prayed to God that the black youth would remember which side of the conflict I was on. I was in Mayaro for more than six years, the last two and a half being the most dramatic. Nothing much came out of all my work and turmoil. Even an automotive trade school that I had started in the small village of Mafeking had to close down because of a lack of interest by those that I was trying to assist. I was emotionally drained when, in 1971, I left for an extended vacation to Ireland.

The whole idea of winning people through revolution, instead of the Gospel, is part and parcel of Liberation Theology. It had major successes in Nicaragua and San Salvador. In Brazil, there were an estimated 80,000 Basic Christian Community (BCC) cells advocating the principles of Liberation Theology. This type of theology attracts many people. When I was involved as a priest, we invited people into our Basic Christian Community Groups, telling them that we would work together to do whatever was needed to bring equality into that community. With some of us priests in Trinidad, the rule was that we would not speak about anything regarding

* Bobol: A local term for corruption, the article told of my efforts to free the poor from destitution and oppression. See the newspaper clipping at end, scanned from the newspaper at that time.

religion for two years, i.e., until we had people involved in social projects. Afterwards, of course, when we did speak about religion, it was about the Catholic religion and how a person could be received into the Catholic Church.

As I was becoming disillusioned with the Liberation Theology movement in the early 80's, I had the opportunity to visit the island of Grenada, which is quite close to Trinidad. It was there that Maurice Bishop had succeeded in a revolution with the aid of Castro and other communist powers. I saw with my own eyes the oppression of the very poor people that were supposed to have been liberated. I saw the huge jail where people who opposed the movement were confined and tortured. Even on street corners, young military personnel harassed people in show of their power; rifle butts and curse words were what the populace had to endure. On my return to Trinidad, I renounced Liberation Theology because I thought it did not work. Now I see that it brings people into servitude and under Catholicism—and away from the Gospel. I see that the very principles of liberation are false, and liberation that is discovered in the Gospel of Christ Jesus is kept from the poor.

Christ Jesus—the Redeemer and Liberator

In Liberation Theology, Christ is made to look as if He were a revolutionary. He is presented as one who liberates from existing political and social structures. People are told that the Lord wishes them to be free from slavery and that they would come into a state in which they are free to exercise their God-given rights. Those who hold to Liberation Theology say that Christ completely committed Himself to the destruction of poverty, and that it is His will that we should have a classless society. They show Christ as a hero in the struggle against oppression, to free the victims of the Bourgeoisie.

When we study the historical, biblical accounts of Christ, we find a very different picture. Christ Jesus said *"...render therefore unto Caesar the things which are Caesar's; and unto God the things that are God's."* (MATTHEW 22:21) Christ Jesus strongly rebuked violence and proclaimed peace and forgiveness. *"...Love your enemies, do good to them which hate you, bless them that curse you, and pray for them which despitefully use you."* (LUKE 6:27, 28) Moreover, Christ Jesus taught good, wise stewardship and investment. (MATTHEW 25:14-28) The Lord Jesus spoke of the eternal, unchangeable God and His unalterable Word. He did not advocate a mobile, fluctuating theology as Gutierrez's, but a theology that is consistent with the mind of God, expressed in His written Word. Christ Jesus mixed freely with, and gave His message to, every social class, including government workers. Most of all, Christ Jesus spoke of "spiritual hunger." *"Blessed are the poor in spirit: for theirs is the kingdom of heaven."* (MATTHEW 5:3) Jesus gave His life freely for the atonement of sin. Sin, for Christ Jesus and His written Word, is an offense against God. Sin that brings all evil and catastrophe upon man is personal sin, and that must be repented of. Jesus clearly taught that one must repent and believe the Gospel. He did not differentiate between those who were oppressed, or who had suffered, from all other types of people—all must repent and believe. Jesus' message to us is *"...except ye repent, ye shall all likewise perish."* (LUKE 13:5) His message is to repent of our personal sinfulness, to repent of looking to any theology or church for salvation, and to look to Him alone.

Subjection to Higher Authority

Jesus Christ's purpose and intent were and are to save His people from their sin. He did indeed speak of "being made free"; the means, however, is the truth, as He the Lord stated, *"if ye continue in my word, then are ye my disciples indeed; and ye shall know the truth, and the truth shall make you free."* (JOHN 8:32) When the Jews of His day did not understand His words, He explained to them, *"Whosoever committeth sin is the servant of sin. And the servant abideth not in the house for ever: but the Son abideth ever. If the Son therefore shall make you free, ye shall be free indeed."* (JOHN 8:34-36) Jesus also spoke strongly against tradition that contradicted and made void the biblical truth of the Word. This is exactly what Liberation Theology and political socialistic policies of the Vatican do. The New Testament teaches that the believer must obey legitimate governing authorities. *"Let every soul be subject unto the higher powers. For there is no power but of God: the powers that be are ordained of God. Whosoever therefore resisteth the power, resisteth the ordinance of God: and they that resist shall receive to themselves damnation."* (ROMANS 13:1, 2) *"Submit yourselves to every ordinance of man for the Lord's sake: whether it be to the king, as supreme;* or unto governors, as unto them that are sent by him for the punishment of evildoers, and for the praise of them that do well."* (I PETER 2:13, 14)

---

* Supreme only as it relates to human authority, God is the ultimate supreme authority.

Social Fruits from the Gospel

The failure of Liberation Theology is admitted even among those who persist in trying to implement its fantasies, as the following description states,

> *The revolutionary fervor of the 1980s has not abolished the grueling*
> *poverty that some now call an economic holocaust for the poor in*
> *Nicaragua, Honduras, El Salvador, Guatemala and, more recently,*
> *Costa Rica. So this new generation of Latin American theologians is*
> *'rereading the Bible,' searching for words to describe what Christians*
> *have traditionally called the 'new creation'═a transformation that*
> *ultimately alters the political and economic spheres, though it does not*
> *begin there. Realizing that political and economic power is too easily*
> *corrupted and that it too readily ignores the needs of the poor, these*
> *new liberationists look first for a pastoral response to the suffering all*
> *around them.**

It is quite interesting when we see where the true Gospel has gone forth throughout the world, there has been a freedom from sin, and there has followed better social conditions. It is most interesting that after the Reformation there came the whole economical structure of the western world whereby we have finance, credit, bank accounts, title deeds to land and property, etc. These things came about by an understanding of imputation; that is, things being credited to someone. Because men were freed from sin against God, due to genuine salvation, they were also set free to live better social and political lives. By the Gospel, man is made free before God, and free also to serve God, and to live a better quality of human life.

The Founding Fathers of the United States were for the most part Christian, and the very principles behind the Declaration of Independence and the Constitution are principles that show the depravity of man. Because they recognized the depravity of man, they saw the necessity to separate the judicial, legislative, and executive powers. These divisions have meant, for the most part, a stable form of political and social life for the United States. Even though many of the founding principles are no longer predominant in a post-modern United States, there is still a solid base because of the biblical understanding of the Founding Fathers.

---

* http://www.villagelife.org/church/archives/pres_latinamerican.html 11/3/2014

A correct understanding of the Bible is to see man as a sinner, utterly destitute in sin. To see his personal need of salvation before God, and then as he trusts on Christ and Christ alone, he knows the true freedom in peace that comes with salvation, and thus he becomes a responsible citizen. This is the "Good News," and Liberation Theology and other political socialistic policies are a curse because they subordinate the Gospel and biblical evangelism to a secular ideology.

It is important that we see how Christ Jesus explained our human nature. He said, *"…that which comes out of the man, that defiles the man. For from within, out of the heart of men, proceed evil thoughts, adulteries, fornications, murders, thefts, covetousness, wickedness, deceit, lasciviousness, an evil eye, blasphemy, pride, foolishness: all these evil things come from within, and defile the man."* (MARK 7:20-23) Both Old and New Testaments tell us that we are spiritually dead to God. Adam's sin brought spiritual as well as physical death. (GENESIS 2:17) Ezekiel states, *"The soul that sins, it shall die,"* (EZEKIEL 18:20) and the Apostle Paul says, *"The wages of sin is death."* (ROMANS 6:23) We are not simply "wounded" as Catholics, we are spiritually dead. Then the Apostles Peter and John tell us, *"ye were not redeemed with corruptible things, as silver and gold, from your vain conversation received by tradition from our fathers; but with the precious blood of Christ, as of a lamb without blemish and without spot."* (1 PETER 1:18, 19) *"And he is the propitiation for our sins; and not for ours only, but also for the sins of the whole world."* (1 JOHN 2:2)

Jesus Sets the Captive Free

Christ Jesus, in the Gospel, has purchased freedom for all true believers. He alone has authority and power to make them free. His cross and resurrection made satisfaction for their guilt as they trust solely on His absolute deed of pardon. In their place, Christ Jesus has answered all demands of the All Holy God against sin; in Him, they are acquitted and vindicated. As an act of God's grace they are not only forgiven but *"…are built up a spiritual house, an holy priesthood, to offer up spiritual sacrifices, acceptable to God by Jesus Christ."* (ISAIAH 53:5-6) Then the Son of God, with right and power, as heir of all things, has liberated those who are His own from their slavery to sin.

If you then would have a bond with God that is real, rightful, and enduring, you must be justified by the Son and adopted into the family of

Almighty God. The light and liberty of the Gospel is transforming. In the words of the Apostle *"…we all, with open face beholding as in a glass the glory of the Lord, are changed into the same image from glory to glory, even as by the Spirit of the Lord."* (2 CORINTHIANS 3:18) Where there is true faith and love of the Lord, there is in the midst of all things a joy unspeakable and full of glory. God is the only All Holy One. His holiness is the distinguishing factor in all His essential characteristics. This is the reason why we need to be in right standing before the one and only All Holy God on the terms He prescribes. By grace turn to God in faith alone for the salvation that He alone gives, by the conviction of the Holy Spirit, based on Christ's death and resurrection for His own, and believe on Him alone.

In the Old Testament the prophet Isaiah declared: *"But he was wounded for our transgressions, he was bruised for our iniquities: the chastisement of our peace was upon him; and with his stripes we are healed. All we like sheep have gone astray; we have turned every one to his own way; and the Lord hath laid on him the iniquity of us all."* (ISAIAH 53:5,6) The Apostles Peter and John tell us, *"ye were not redeemed with corruptible things, as silver and gold, from your vain conversation received by tradition from our fathers; but with the precious blood of Christ, as of a lamb without blemish and without spot." "And he is the propitiation for our sins; and not for ours only, but also for the sins of the whole world."* (I PETER 1:18-19, I JOHN 2:2) The Bible clearly states that salvation was Christ's work and His alone: *". . .by himself purged our sins, sat down on the right hand of the Majesty on high"* (HEBREWS 1:3) Romans 3:26 says that God is *"just, and the justifier of him which believeth in Jesus."* One is saved by God's work. Salvation is God's majestic, finished work. Woven through the other twenty-nine testimonies of this book is the same scarlet thread of God's sovereign grace. Before him, each person is dead in sin. One is saved by grace alone, through faith alone. *"To the praise of the glory of his grace, wherein he hath made us accepted in the beloved."* (EPHESIANS 1:6)

—RICHARD BENNETT

If you wish to contact me please do so by email at:
richardmbennett@yahoo.com
Thank you

"I am proud of Trinidad but am disgusted by what I see the man in the street going through"

LET'S STOP THIS 'BOBOL' SAYS ROBBED PRIEST

By JEROME TANG-LEE

A ROMAN CATHOLIC priest wants the lid blown off on crime in Trinidad — especially crime in top places.

He is Father Peter Bennett, 32, parish priest of the nation's top seaside resort — Mayaro.

Within the past week, Fr. Bennett has come face to face with various aspects of crime — from "bobol" to robbery.

Last Wednesday, he alleges, a civil servant in a Port-of-Spain government office asked him for a "quiet" $250 so that plans for a church hall which Fr.Bennett intends building could be passed.

The safe ... and inside the fridge is the telephone.

Earlier, one of his congregation told him that she had been approached by a hospital doctor for $100 so that her son could be admitted to hospital for an operation.

And on Friday Fr.Bennett was tied, gagged and robbed of $200 in collection money at his Mayaro presbytery. Before his attackers left they told him: "Remember to pray for us, father."

But the Irish-born priest believes that prayers are not enough to stop the growing crime wave. He wants a full-scale investigation in particular into what he calls "the easy deal" type of offences.

He said yesterday: "I have been restless about the whole thing for a long time. I am proud of Trinidad but I am disgusted by what I see the man in the street go through.

"I have had countless experiences of people coming to me and relating how they have to pay to get jobs, hospital beds and just about anything.

"It is all too prevalent and what is worse it seems to be condoned by people in authority."

He added: " As much as I wish to see the three men who raided my house brought to justice, we must awake to see the ever even greater crimes that are happening around us."

He asked: "Which is worse $200 at gun point or 'you might never get your plans pass without a quiet $250?'

"If I were given to conspiracy theories I would believe that there is an effort to cover many types of crime in Trinidad."

Since the robbery, Fr. Bennett, who came to Trinidad in 1964 and became Mayaro's parish priest two years ago, has been living a sort of restricted life in the presbytery.

For he has been told by police not to disturb anything in the house so that clues would not be lost. He was told that a fingerprint expert would visit the scene.

But up to yesterday the expert had not arrived.

Said Fr. Bennett: "It's all very silly, I surely can't move around without touching something. The telephone is still in the fridge where the robbers put it after cutting the telephone wires."

Speaking of the robbery he said he was in the dining room around 7 p.m. when the men came in armed with a gun and cutlass and forced him to open an iron safe.

He said: "They tied me up three times. On two occasions they had to untie me so that I could open the safe for them. They had the gun at my head. After they took the money they tied me to my bed and put a towel in my mouth."

The robbery showed up the shortcomings of the Mayaro station — just one mile away.

NO TRANSPORTATION

Phoning from a nearby hotel, Fr. Bennett said he had to make three calls over a half hour period before the police came.

Reason: The police station at Mayaro has no transportation. Whenever something breaks lawmen pin their hopes on a lift. And they have been doing so for the last 11 months.

The station has a driver and he has been collecting pay all this time - even though he doesn't drive.

A spokesman at the station which looks after law and order for an area with about 50,000 people said yesterday: "Time and again we have made requests for transport. No one seems to hear our plea. We are forgotten. If something serious breaks I don't know what will happen."

9 781599 253497